CW00751329

The Genesis Book

The Genesis Book

The Story of the
People and Projects
That Inspired Bitcoin

Aaron van Wirdum

Bitcoin Magazine Books
Nashville, TN

The Genesis Book by Aaron van Wirdum

© 2024 by Aaron van Wirdum; Creative Commons License 2.0
https://www.creativecommons.org/licenses/by-nc-nd/2.0/legalcode

ISBN 979-8-9876364-6-6 (First Single Edition Paperback)

ISBN 979-8-9876364-7-3 (Limited Edition of 20 Paperbacks)

ISBN 979-8-9891326-2-1 (General Trade Release Paperback)

ISBN 979-8-9876364-9-7 (eBook)

Published by Bitcoin Magazine Books
An imprint of BTC Media, LLC
438 Houston St. #257 Nashville TN 37203

Address all queries to contact@btcmedia.org

Interior design by MediaNeighbours.com

I don't believe that we shall ever have a good money again before we take the thing out of the hands of government.

Since we can't take them violently out of the hands of government, all we can do is, by some sly roundabout way, introduce something they can't stop.

- Friedrich Hayek (1984)

Contents

Introduction

E-GOLD WAS BOOMING. By 2005, over a million accounts had been created on Douglas Jackson's innovative online payment system, which together were responsible for almost $2 billion worth of transactions per year. The fully backed digital tokens that e-gold customers used to make all these transactions, represented 3.8 metric tons of gold, stored away in vaults across the world. As one of the first successfully operating implementations of electronic money, e-gold had in less than ten years grown to be the go-to digital currency on the internet.

But Jackson was in for a rude awakening.

Just before the year's end, in December 2005, the US Secret Service raided Jackson's company as well as his home in Melbourne, Florida. Books and records were taken from his office, while federal agents confiscated anything that appeared even mildly interesting to them: besides legal documents and business contracts, this included his wife's address book, their kids' passports, and the credit cards laying around on the nightstand. At that same time, at an AT&T facility in Orlando some 70 miles northwest, e-gold's servers were taken offline, and all transaction records were seized.

The Secret Service, assisted by the IRS and the FBI, believed that the payment processor had become a hotbed for criminals, who could create e-gold accounts with little more than an email address—essentially anonymously. In a time when credit card fraud on the web was running rampant, Jackson's payment system would have worked like a magnet for scammers. Worse, law enforcement officials alleged that child pornographers were making use of e-gold's relative anonymity, and perhaps terrorists did as well.

Jackson was indicted and charged with money laundering and running an unlicensed money transmitter.[1]

Digital Gold

Jackson never intended for e-gold to be abused for illicit purposes. Nor did he believe it was, on any serious scale. In fact, he contended that e-gold had a better fraud detection system than any other payment processor out there, and was always more than willing to cooperate with law enforcement. e-gold was also a founding member of the National Center for Missing & Exploited Children's Financial Coalition Against Child Pornography, and Jackson maintained that the data collected through this coalition indicated that e-gold practically wasn't used for such purposes at all.

Rather, as a successful and independently wealthy oncologist and veteran of the US Army Medical Corps, Jackson had in the 1990s taken an interest in monetary policy and its effects on the economy. He had found that modern currencies—dollars, pounds, yen—were no longer backed by anything, and could therefore essentially be created out of thin air with the press of a button. As he dove into the topic, he eventually became convinced that this was distorting the economy in very bad ways.

Jackson had therefore intended to offer an alternative.

During his studies into currencies, Jackson adopted a newfound appreciation for the "classic money"—gold. He found that humans had valued the shiny yellow metal since at least predynastic Egyptian times, and for good reason: the natural element was unaffected by the whims of men.

Yet, predynastic Egypt was long gone, and even Jackson had to admit that the precious metal wasn't particularly practical for day-to-day transactions. With the new millennium nearing, Jackson realized that people weren't going to return to paying with gold coins. In fact, even copper coins and paper bills would probably seem old-fashioned before long.

No, the future of money had to be digital.

With that foresight, Jackson (quite literally) saw a golden opportunity. He teamed up with attorney Barry Downey, and in 1996 founded Gold &

Silver Reserve Inc., to be headed by Jackson. The startup would operate a payment system for the twenty-first century, but based on that classic money. They would provide an electronic equivalent to gold: *e-gold*.

The basic idea was straightforward. Gold & Silver Reserve Inc. rented vaults, and these vaults were stuffed with gold, the actual physical metal. For each piece of gold in these vaults, the company issued a digital "token"—essentially a number in a database. These tokens represented a claim on the gold. If someone held tokens representing the equivalent of ten grams of gold, ten actual grams of gold in one of the vaults was legally theirs.

The main innovation was that Gold & Silver Reserve Inc. also maintained a server that hosted a publicly accessible accounting system for the tokens. People from all over the world could log in to the server and create a personal account, allowing them to send and receive tokens to and from any other account. For each transaction, Gold & Silver Reserve Inc. updated the account balances accordingly.

This meant that, thanks to the power of the internet, e-gold users could essentially pay one another over vast distances, instantly, at minimal cost. On the borderless *information superhighway*, anyone with access to an internet connection could pay anyone else, with no restrictions on national borders or bank regulations.

Jackson created e-gold, he liked to say, as an institution to advance the material welfare of mankind by opening up access to global markets:

"e-gold is a payment system that, unlike any other, allows people from any region or economic background to operate globally: a migrant worker can send value back home easily and a merchant can accept payment from someone in a third-world country who may be without access to a charge card or bank account."[2]

In addition, Jackson put forth that e-gold provided the option to use a type of money immune to debasement. And thanks to its digital form, e-gold was actually much more accessible for many people than real gold.

In the long run, e-gold even had the potential to become the backbone of an entirely new financial system, Jackson optimistically suggested.

"How to discover a banking system which will not be the cause of cata-strophic disturbances, which is least likely itself to introduce oscillations, and most likely to make the correct adjustment . . . is the most acute unsettled economic problem of our day," he at one point quoted from Economist Vera Smith's book *The Rationale of Central Banking and the Free Banking Alternative.*

To add: "A system and currency like e-gold, particularly after emergence and integration into the financial mainstream as a reserve asset used as a medium of settlement, can definitively solve this problem."[3]

Legal Issues

e-gold had by the early 2000s started growing rapidly, while Jackson con-tinued to improve his service. He made more types of precious metals available, while also adding new spending features, like automated monthly payments, and mobile phone access through the then-new WAP protocol.[4]

But there was also something Jackson hadn't done: he hadn't registered his company as a money transmitter. Consequently, he also wasn't applying all the types of Know-Your-Customer (KYC) and Anti-Money Launder-ing (AML) checks that a money transmitter is supposed to. He didn't know he had to.

This wasn't due to nonchalance. Operating a money transmitter without a money transmitter license (for every state that requires one) had only been made a federal crime with the PATRIOT Act, passed in response to the September 11 terrorist attacks in 2001—several years after e-gold's launch. Even more to the point, it was not clear that Jackson's business would be considered a money transmitter at all: the e-gold system didn't transmit dollars or other national currencies, for which such rules typically applied.

Nevertheless, Jackson had tried to get more clarity on the issue. Gold & Silver Reserve Inc. had, itself, proposed to the relevant government agencies that e-gold could be classified as a currency for regulatory pur-poses, which would then also allow the company to register as a currency exchange. But in response, the US Treasury had reaffirmed that defini-tions of currency excluded e-gold.

In addition, Jackson had voluntarily initiated a Bank Secrecy Act compliance examination with an agency of the Treasury, just to find out how they thought his company should be regulated.[5]

He was waiting for an answer when the raids took place.

The legal proceedings that followed inflicted major wounds on the e-gold business. Bank accounts were frozen and company funds were confiscated. The legal battle that ensued between Jackson and the US government lasted throughout the next two years, draining resources: legal costs would eventually add up to seven figures. And insofar Jackson's company could continue operating at all, it now also had to do so under a cloud of suspicion.

Meanwhile, the US government issued seizure warrants to have fifty-eight large e-gold accounts closed on suspicion of money laundering; targets of the action were independent e-gold exchanges, some of which were based abroad. Leveraging the 1961 Racketeering Act—a tool for law enforcement originally installed to fight organized crime—1,000 kilograms of gold backing these accounts (about a quarter of e-gold's total supply) was confiscated and liquidated.

When an initial verdict finally came in 2008, the judge determined that e-gold was in fact a money transmitter under the law, thereby rejecting Jackson's motion to dismiss the case. Now faced with the possibility of significant jail time and huge fines, Jackson agreed to a plea deal.[6]

In one of the few bright spots in the entire saga, the judge did show some leniency in her final sentencing, stating that "[. . .] the intent was not there to engage in illegal conduct."[7] Still, Jackson was sentenced to thirty-six months of supervised release ("home arrest"), of which six were enforced through an ankle bracelet. He also had to perform 300 hours of community service, and pay a $200 fine. His company, meanwhile, was fined for $600,000, while two of his employees—cofounder Barry Downey and Douglas's brother Reid Jackson—were each sentenced to thirty-six months probation, 300 hours of community service, a $2,500 fine, and a $100 assessment.

And of course, e-gold had to acquire a money transmitter license. The only problem? As a convicted felon, Jackson was no longer eligible to apply for such a license—something he hadn't immediately realized when he agreed to the plea deal. Just when he thought he could finally leave the legal battle behind for good and try to save his businesses in whatever way it could still be saved, Jackson learned that it couldn't happen under his leadership.

In the end, e-gold never reopened at all.

Jackson had created e-gold to advance the material welfare of mankind by offering an alternative to conventional, unbacked currencies like the US dollar. Locked up in his own home, down over a million dollars in legal fees, and with his company shut down, he had learned the hard way that offering such an alternative was not so easy.

Satoshi Nakamoto

The fate of Douglas Jackson and e-gold served as a vivid warning to anyone with aspirations of offering an alternative form of money. Governments— and the US government in particular—could decide to crack down hard, potentially inflicting severe personal and financial damages. For most, this probably wasn't worth the risk.

Yet, it would not deter an unknown person or group known only as "Satoshi Nakamoto." Around the same time that Jackson was spending his days at home with a bracelet around his ankle, Nakamoto was preparing the release of an electronic cash scheme of his own.

The design of Nakamoto's digital currency system was very different from e-gold, however. And although not much is known about Satoshi Nakamoto's background or motives, it is clear that this mysterious entity—the name is almost certainly a pseudonym—purposefully designed his own system explicitly to avoid it befalling a similar fate as e-gold.

This design probably wasn't the result of a spontaneous hunch, either. For years, even well before Jackson launched e-gold, a small but dedicated group of technologists had been trying to create a digital form of cash: they shared ideas, developed technologies, and designed various proposals, over time inching closer to a working solution. But they never quite succeeded.

Until Nakamoto finally made the pieces of the puzzle fit.

This book traces back the ideas and technologies that (probably) helped guide Satoshi Nakamoto in the creation of this electronic cash system.

In Part I, the book explores the diverse origins of some of these foundational ideas and technologies that came to form the basis of electronic cash, ranging from heterodox views on monetary economics to a rebellious revolution in cryptography, and from the emergence of hacker culture in the 1960s and '70s to techno-utopian visions of space colonization, molecular nanotechnology, and eternal life.

Part II tells the story of the Cypherpunks, a group of cryptographers, hackers, and privacy activists who throughout the 1990s developed and distributed privacy tools for the internet, and were trying to create an electronic form of cash. This part of the book also hones in on some of the specific attempts to develop such electronic cash systems.

Finally, Part III of the book explains how Satoshi Nakamoto designed and developed his electronic cash system, what inspired this design, and how it compares to other forms of (digital) money.

Together, they form the story of the monetary reformers, computer scientists, privacy activists, futurists, entrepreneurs, and other pioneers who, all in their own way, contributed to the emergence of the world's first successful peer-to-peer electronic cash system: *Bitcoin*.

PART I

FOUNDATIONS

Chapter 1:
Spontaneous Order

FRIEDRICH AUGUST VON HAYEK wanted to become a biology professor like his father, but the First World War changed everything.[8] Born in 1899, and raised in what would later turn out to be the late years of the Austro-Hungarian Empire, he was called to fight on the Italian front after turning eighteen. He spent the final stage of the conflict as a spotter in airplanes.

When he returned home after the war ended in 1918, Hayek (the aristocratic prefix "von" was dropped after the collapse of the dual monarchy) found his hometown Vienna in complete devastation. With the war lost, the economy destroyed, and the empire falling apart, morale in the city was broken.

Making matters even worse, the new Austrian government was spending so much to pay for the country's postwar expenses that it sent the value of its national currency into a nosedive. While the krone had already lost well over 90 percent of its purchasing power throughout the war, it would really spin out of control in the postwar years. Where a US dollar traded for about nine kronen in 1917, the same dollar could by 1923 buy over 70,000 of the Austrian currency units. The nation's money was effectively destroyed.[9]

Having been confronted up close with the atrocities of the Great War, which cost almost eighteen million men and women their lives, Hayek decided his time and energy was best spent trying to prevent a repeat of such dramatic conflicts in the future. He became determined to find better ways of organizing society.

A keen learner from an educated family—both of his grandfathers were academics as well—Hayek enrolled at the University of Vienna, the oldest university in the German-speaking world and among the most renowned academic institutes in all of Europe. Motivated by his newfound sense of mission, Hayek decided to study political science and law, while taking philosophy, psychology, and economics classes on the side.

He didn't immediately enroll in all economics classes, however; one economics professor at the university in particular seemed to be a bit too deep in free-market thinking for the mildly socialist-leaning student. It was only when that same economics professor hired Hayek to staff a temporary government office in the city that he finally decided to give his teachings a chance as well.[10]

The professor's name was Ludwig von Mises, who, Hayek soon learned, was a leading economist within a relatively new school of economic thought.[11]

Austrian Economics

The First World War had been the violent climax of an era with a strong sense of nationalism, the ideology that holds that collectives of people with a common descent, history, culture, or language—*nations*—should self-organize as states, and act in the interest of these states.

Nationalism had throughout the nineteenth century also permeated the field of economic science. Whereas *classical economics*, with its strong emphasis on free markets as advocated by pioneering economists like David Hume, Adam Smith, and David Ricardo, had been dominant in the late eighteenth century, European universities throughout the 1800s started to adopt the methods of the *historical school* of economics. Its most influential practitioners advocated for state interventions in the economy, like labor legislation, protective tariffs, and progressive taxation.[12]

The methodology of the historical school of economics (the body of methods used to study the economy) excluded general economic theories, and maintained that the "rules" by which economies operate differ across cultures and time. Instead of constructing models or theorems, historical economists compiled massive amounts of historical data to be used for empirical analysis.

But University of Vienna Professor Carl Menger had by the 1870s rejected this approach. He believed that humans, and human interactions, were too complex to be able to deduce valuable scientific insights from empirical data alone. An innumerable amount of factors influence a typical person's thoughts and actions, he reasoned—never mind the number of factors that influence a whole society. No empirical dataset could be large enough to encompass all these factors, Menger believed. Any conclusion drawn from such a dataset would necessarily be inconclusive, at best.

Instead, Menger argued that economists should try to understand and explain economic phenomena using deductive reasoning. By starting from first principles, steps of logic could lead to irrefutable insights that would expand the scientific understanding of economic processes, *a priori*. (The Latin phrase *a priori* refers to knowledge that is independent from experience, like mathematics, contrasting *a posteriori* knowledge which depends on empirical evidence, as is more typical in most fields of science.)

Menger had brought this approach into practice for the first time in his 1871 book *Grundsätze der Volkswirtschaftslehre* ("Principles of Economics"). In it, he outlined the theory of marginal utility, which explains that the price of goods and services in part depends on how much added satisfaction is derived from having more of them.[13]

This represented a fundamental shift in perspective. Until then, economists (both from the classical and from the historical school) had always assumed that the value of a product was derived from its cost of production. A pair of shoes is valuable, they'd say, because producing it comes at a cost—most notably the cost of labor, leather, and equipment. The reason that the leather and equipment comes at a cost is in turn because producing the leather and equipment requires labor (and perhaps other costs) as well. This was called the labor theory of value.

Through the theory of marginal utility, Menger had instead argued that value is actually subjective: individuals value products and services if these products or services fulfill a personal want or need. A pair of shoes doesn't derive its value from the cost to produce it, but rather, a pair of shoes is valuable because *people value wearing shoes.*

This means that the value of any particular product can vary from person to person. Someone who owns no shoes at all will probably value a new pair more than someone who already owns several. Similarly, the *same* person can value the same product differently at different times. After the shoeless person in the previous example has acquired a pair, he probably wouldn't value a second, identical pair of shoes as much as he valued the first.[14]

With this *subjective theory of value,* Menger put the individual back at the heart of the economy. He posited that it wasn't nations or other collectives, but people and their subjective preferences that were ultimately responsible for all economic decisions. Rather than taking the state as a starting point for analysis, Menger therefore believed that the study of economics had to begin by understanding what moves the smallest parts of any economic system. Indeed, individuals.

Offering what is perhaps best understood as a rebirth of classical economics centered around subjective individual experience, Menger's approach gained support from several of his colleagues at the University of Vienna. And by the 1880s Menger had, through the publication of his second book,[15] sparked a philosophical debate about the methodology of economic science across German-speaking universities.

During this sometimes adversarial *Methodenstreit* ("battle of methods"), German economists—who by and large subscribed to the historical school—began referring to Menger's approach somewhat pejoratively as the "Austrian school of economics." Although originally intended as a sneer (Germans at the time associated the predicate "Austrian" with Austria's defeat in the Austro-Prussian War of 1866), the name stuck. Economists that adopted Menger's methodology were since then referred to as Austrian economists—even when they weren't from Austria themselves.[16]

The antagonistic spirit of the Methodenstreit in the late nineteenth century culminated in a de facto ban of Austrian economics from German universities, which would remain in place for decades. It largely prevented Menger's ideas from spreading through the newly unified nation-state.

Instead, nationalism remained dominant, while another, homegrown, collectivist ideology was starting to spread through German universities with little substantive opposition as well: *socialism* was on the rise.

Economic Calculation

Originally spearheaded by German author and social commentator Karl Marx, socialists believed that the economic history of the world was best understood as a class struggle between those who own capital (goods that can be used as a means of production, like factories and their machinery) and the working class—those who only have their labor to sell. Marx had predicted that this struggle would continue to work out in favor of the capital-owning class (the *capitalists*), as they'd accumulate more and more capital and enjoy ever-growing profits—until the working class (the proletariat) would inevitably revolt.

The eventual solution to the economic disparity, according to Marx, was socialism, an economic system where the means of production are brought under common ownership, and their gains distributed throughout society. This would initially have to be managed under supervision of the state, to gradually be replaced by an anarchist form of self-government.

Although Marx's ideas only seemed to gain in popularity after his death in 1883, socialism had its fair share of critics as well. One common objection was that people would have no incentive to work in a socialist system, since they'd receive a fixed share of all produced goods anyways, while at the same time the goods they'd help produce themselves would be distributed across the rest of society. A second objection concerned the risk that socialist leaders would turn against their own population, claiming many of the goods produced under state supervision for themselves instead of distributing them fairly.

It hadn't stopped the rise of socialist doctrine in the Russian Empire, however. In 1917, in the midst of the First World War, revolutionaries organized through workers' councils known as "Soviets" overthrew the sitting government, and established the Soviet Union as a communist state.

It was about three years after these events when Mises, the professor who'd hired Hayek for his government office, offered a groundbreaking new critique of socialism.[17] Importantly, this critique would hold up *even* if people were motivated to work, and *even* if socialist leaders remained committed to a fair distribution of the economic gains. Instead, Mises argued that the more fundamental problem of socialism was the lack of a direct feedback mechanism to inform producers whether value was being added to society at all.

Let's take a car factory to illustrate this argument. In a free market, a factory that produces cars and turns a profit clearly adds value to society: people are willing to pay more for cars than the factory needs to pay for the resources—steel, machines, labor—to produce them. Profit indicates that the factory output is valued more than the input.

Conversely, a car factory that operates at a loss clearly *isn't* adding value to society, as people value the input more than the output. This factory would eventually have to shut down, and the resources it was using can be bought up (or in the case of labor, hired) by more profitable businesses instead, and put to better use. (The Austrian-born economist Joseph Schumpeter would later call this "creative destruction.")

A state-run car factory in a socialist society, however, would produce cars by decree of a central planner. And if the cars are produced by decree, there is no feedback mechanism from society in the form of profit or loss. The car factory might be wasting resources to make cars that people don't value, or don't value as much as other products that could have been made with those same resources.

Without a free market, there can be no *economic calculation*, rendering impossible the core task of any economic system: the efficient allocation of scarce resources throughout society.[18]

"Without economic calculation there can be no economy," Mises concluded. "Hence, in a socialist state wherein the pursuit of economic calculation is impossible, there can be—in our sense of the term—no economy whatsoever."[19]

Prices

Mises, and his concept of economic calculation specifically, would have a major influence on Hayek. At the University of Vienna, he transformed into an eager student of the Austrian school of economics, studying the works of Menger as well as other "first-generation" Austrians like Eugen von Böhm-Bawerk. He also became a regular at private discussion seminars that Mises organized twice a month in his government office, where a small group of scholars met to discuss economic theory as well as philosophy, or whatever other topics Mises and his guests considered interesting in that particular week.

Mises would even personally set Hayek up for an academic career in the field of economics. In 1927, after graduating from the University of Vienna, Hayek was appointed as director of Mises's newly formed Austrian Institute for Business Cycle Research. It offered the young economist the perfect environment to expand on his former professor's theory of economic calculation.

Hayek would in particular focus on the function and effect of *prices*. Prices, he went on to explain in the following years, are the market's decentralized and socially scalable means of communication.[20] Although established as a simple function of supply and demand for goods and services in an economy, Hayek described how prices actually embed a wide array of relevant information that individuals require to make economic decisions.

Let's take Mises's car factory as a (simplified) example again. As mentioned, this factory requires resources like steel, machines, and labor to produce cars—but we'll just focus on steel for now. And let's say that this particular factory operator buys his steel from a steel producer located in a nearby city. This steel producer, in turn, gets iron ore from a mine halfway across the country. Meanwhile, in the opposite direction of the supply chain, a local car dealership buys the cars from the factory, in turn selling them to customers.

Everyone in this supply chain has the information they need to run their own business, and they communicate this to everyone else through prices.

The car dealer has a good idea of how to sell cars, for example; he knows how much demand there is for new cars, and he knows what he needs in order to sell them—perhaps a showroom in a favorable location and some wax to make the cars look nice and shiny. The prices that customers are willing to pay for cars, and the price he needs to pay for a showroom and wax, will therefore determine the price he himself is willing to pay the car factory for new cars.

The steel producer, meanwhile, knows what he needs to pay for ore, how much his furnace to turn the ore into steel cost him, and what he needs to spend on salaries. As long as his customers, like the car factory, are paying a higher price for his steel than it costs him to produce it, he'll produce steel.

While everyone in the supply chain depends on each other, no one needs to know *exactly* how anyone else does their job. The cost of a showroom might affect how much the car dealership is willing to pay the factory for a new car, but the factory operator doesn't actually need to concern himself with the real estate market for showrooms. Nor does the factory operator need to concern himself with the scarcity of ore. That information is embedded in the prices that the car dealer is offering for new cars, and the steel producer is asking for new steel.

By extension, if anything changes in the economy, prices can facilitate the reallocation of resources.

If the iron ore mine for example has to partly close down because of a fire, ore will be in shorter supply, and overall demand for the remaining ore will bid up the price of iron. The steel producer would then in turn have to increase the price of his steel to remain profitable. This increased steel price essentially communicates to the car factory the relevant information he needs to make economic decisions accordingly. (The car factory could in response, for example, decide to buy steel from a different producer that gets its ore from a different mine.)

Similarly, if consumer demand for kitchen equipment rises, the kitchen equipment factory would want to buy more steel, driving the price of steel up as it outbids the car factory. The steel producer would shift the allocation of steel from the car factory to the kitchen equipment factory, not because he knows anything about (the demand for) cars or kitchen equipment, but simply because the price system informed him that that would be more profitable. (In the longer term, the steel producer would also be incentivized to produce more steel.)

Relevant information is communicated throughout the economy using the price system, Hayek explained, which allows markets to efficiently allocate resources across society to where they are valued most.

"Fundamentally, in a system in which the knowledge of the relevant facts is dispersed among many people, prices can act to coordinate the separate actions of different people in the same way as subjective values help the individual to coordinate the parts of his plan," the Austrian wrote: "a marvel."[21]

And importantly, all of this is possible without central planning. The free market, Hayek argued, is best understood as a bottom-up form of self-organization: a *spontaneous order*.

Interest Rates

Where Mises had shaped Hayek's understanding of spontaneous order across *space*—the allocation of resources from one point in society to another—the works of von Böhm-Bawerk helped shape Hayek's understanding of spontaneous order across *time*.

Von Böhm-Bawerk had in the 1890s introduced a new concept in the field of economics, which became a cornerstone of the Austrian school: *time preference*. People, von Böhm-Bawerk argued, typically prefer to get goods and services sooner rather than later. How strongly they prefer this varies from individual to individual, however; everyone has a different—and subjective—time preference.

These time preferences, von Böhm-Bawerk had argued, are reflected on the market in the form of interest rates.

Let's say, for example, that both Mary and James would like a new car. Both of them would prefer to have a new car today, rather than next year.

But Mary, whose car just broke down and who has to drive to work every day, values a new car today significantly more than a new car next year. James, meanwhile, still has a reasonably good car and works from home, so he isn't really in that much of a hurry to get a new one. Mary has a higher time preference than James.

Now let's say that a new car would cost $20,000, but Mary is broke, while James has $20,000 in savings. At face value, this would suggest that James will buy a new car before Mary: James can afford it today, while Mary still has to save money in order to be able to afford a new car.

But there is another option. James could lend Mary $20,000.

Whether this is a good deal for both of them can easily be discovered through interest rates. Let's say that since Mary has a high time preference, she would basically value a car today 10 percent more than a car next year; that is, she'd be willing to pay $22,000 for a $20,000 car if she can have it today instead of a year from now. She is therefore willing to pay 10 percent interest on a $20,000 loan. James, who has a low time preference, would value a new car today only 1 percent more than a car next year, a difference of just $200.

James could therefore decide to delay his purchase, and instead lend $20,000 to Mary, to be repaid the money plus an additional $2,000 interest in one year from now. This would allow Mary to buy the car today, while the extra $2,000 for James easily offsets the $200 "cost" of delaying his purchase. Both would benefit; interest rates allowed them to allocate resources between them across time, to best match their individual time preferences.

While this is of course a very simplified example, credit markets do something like this at scale. Money lenders and borrowers settle on an interest rate where supply and demand for money meet, based on aggregate time preferences. As such, interest rates are essentially prices as well; they are the price of money.

And like all prices, the price of money communicates relevant information. Hayek believed that the average interest rate reveals something about the economy as a whole. If interest rates are high, it indicates that many people have high time preferences, and are not very willing to lend money;

they prefer to purchase goods and services sooner rather than later. Conversely, if interest rates are low, it suggests that many people have relatively low time preferences, and are more willing to delay their purchases if that means they can earn some interest in the meantime.

Hayek, therefore, believed interest rates informed producers about the stage of production they should allocate resources to. Low interest rates signal to producers that they should take advantage of this "cheap money" and improve their production processes for the long term by investing in higher-order goods, like a new furnace to produce steel, which can later be used in the production of cars (or kitchen equipment). Conversely, high interest rates make borrowing money expensive, which incentivizes producers to use the resources already at their disposal and focus on completing late-stage production, the last part of the process where the final consumption goods like cars are made and displayed in showrooms for people to buy.

The nice thing about this, Hayek recognized, is that people's time preferences neatly correspond with the economy's production capacity. If time preferences are low, people invest their money (or in most cases, they'd "save" it in a bank account and the bank invests it for them), and producers are incentivized to invest in their long-term production processes. So when time preferences increase in the future, people can spend their money and the interest they earn on the fruits of all this increased productivity.

Interest rates, Hayek explained, facilitate spontaneous order across time!

That is, of course, *if* interest rates do in fact accurately reflect time preferences. However, Hayek found that in practice, this often wasn't allowed to be the case.

The Federal Reserve

A few years earlier, even before his student had graduated from the University of Vienna, Mises had helped Hayek land another temporary job as research assistant at New York University.

When the young Austrian in 1923 arrived in the United States, the *Roaring Twenties* were in full swing. The American economy was booming, and people were happy to borrow money to buy Ford's mass-produced cars, new technological wonders like washing machines, or real estate in the suburbs of major cities. Or they would use the money to invest it in stocks: the Dow Jones stock market index breached all-time highs year after year.

Hayek's research would focus on the economic role of one institution in particular: the relatively new central banking system of the United States, called the Federal Reserve. The "Fed," as this central banking system is often referred to, had been instituted in 1913 to bring trust and stability to the American banking system.

An anchor for trust and stability was considered necessary, because commercial banks ran on *fractional reserves*: they had less actual money in their vaults than depositors had attributed to them in their bank accounts—with the balance lent out to borrowers and earning some interest for banks and their depositors. But it could also cause economic instability: if too many depositors lost trust in a bank and opted to withdraw their money at the same time, the bank could be short of funds, leaving them unable to honor all withdrawal requests.

In the scenario of such a *bank run*, the Federal Reserve could now step in to act as a *lender of last resort* by issuing a loan to the troubled bank. It would supply the bank with sufficient liquidity (cash) to weather the storm, so there'd be no reason for depositors to worry.

But the Fed's role as lender of last resort found an early critic in the young researcher who had come all the way from Austria to study its effect on the American economy.

Hayek believed that the guarantees offered by the new institution misaligned economic incentives. He worried that favorable economic prospects could induce commercial banks to extend loans more freely than before, which essentially increased the money supply: more bank loans means more money spent into the economy.[22] This "new money" would drive overall prices up—*inflation*—thereby boosting business profits across the board, in turn further confirming the favorable economic outlook. Commercial banks' ability to essentially issue new money through loans could trigger a feedback loop of exuberant credit creation.

The music would stop when this credit creation inevitably slowed down, however. When the amount of new money spent into the economy decreases, overall prices would fall—*deflation*—and businesses would be confronted with their overly optimistic assessment of economic prospects: they wouldn't be able to sell their products for as much money as they had anticipated. Some businesses would have to scale down, and unemployment would rise, slowing the economy down even more as people would have less money to spend. Other businesses would go bankrupt, rendering them unable to repay their loans, which would in turn make commercial banks hard-pressed to honor all deposit claims. They'd have to stop issuing new loans, only further slowing down the economy, resulting in more layoffs and loan defaults, and so on.

Economists would later refer to such a dynamic as a *deflationary debt spiral*. It were these same kinds of dynamics that had been the cause of some of the banking crises that motivated the establishment of the Federal Reserve in the first place.[23]

However, there was no reason to assume that the establishment of a lender of last resort would limit this perverse dynamic, Hayek argued. Rather, it could actually magnify it.

At least in the old system, he pointed out, commercial banks had a good reason to be careful not to issue too many loans:

"In the absence of any central bank, the strongest restraint on individual banks against extending excessive credit in the rising phase of economic activity is the need to maintain sufficient liquidity to face the demand of a period of tight money from their own resources."[24]

The establishment of a lender of last resort could indeed prevent bank runs and panic. But in doing so, Hayek reasoned, it also removed the incentive for banks to impose some restraint on themselves when issuing loans in the first place.

"It must therefore inevitably tend to generate a steady increase in the volume of credit being utilized and thereby render the recurrence of recessions even more unavoidable," Hayek concluded.[25]

Such a misalignment of economic incentives, where certain economic actors—in this case, banks—are rewarded for taking more risks but do not bear the full cost of these risks, is called *moral hazard* in economics; Hayek believed that the Federal Reserve introduced moral hazard into the economy.

And Hayek thought this wasn't even the most important way in which the Federal Reserve incentivized unsustainable, credit-induced, economic bubbles . . .

The Austrian Business Cycle

Reading the 1923 annual report of the Federal Reserve would determine the trajectory of Hayek's career as an economist for decades to come.

In the document, the American central bank explained how it used its control of the quantity of money to ensure stabilization of economic activity. More specifically, the American monetary authority explained how it leveraged interest rates as a policy instrument: a very new concept at the time, put forward by what was itself a very new institution.[26]

The idea was fairly simple. By injecting currency into the banking system (typically by buying government bonds), the Fed could supply commercial banks with more reserves and thus make them more willing—and able—to issue loans at lower and lower interest rates, which would incentivize businesses and people to borrow. Alternatively, by extracting reserves from the banking system (by selling government bonds), banks could be discouraged from issuing loans, thus increasing interest rates, and putting the brakes on economic activity.

By carefully managing interest rates, the Federal Reserve believed it could smoothen out the business cycle. If the Fed could slightly decrease interest rates during recessions, and increase them a little bit during upswings, they would offer the market a little boost when it's in a slump and slow it down a bit when it's getting ahead of itself.

That policy found a major critic in Hayek.

The Austrian believed that the Federal Reserve was sending false signals to the market by keeping interest rates artificially low. Cheap money was being used to invest in businesses, who used this capital to allocate more resources to their production processes. However, Hayek warned, there was no deferred consumption on the other end of the equation to match the future increase in production. Interest rates weren't low because many people had low time preferences and were saving their money for future expenses; interest rates were low because the Fed made them so.

When interest rates would eventually rise and the creation of new credit would slow down, businesses would have to complete late-stage production—only to find that there was no real demand to match it. With no one to buy their goods, or at least not at the prices they had anticipated, businesses would have to lay off workers and possibly default on their loans, setting in motion a deflationary debt spiral.

When Hayek had arrived in the United States, the economy was booming, as both consumption and investment soared, but he came to realize that this could not last. The manipulation of interest rates was disturbing the emergence of spontaneous order across time. Instead of smoothing out the upswing and downturn of the business cycle, Hayek was concerned that the Federal Reserve was actually fueling it.

And indeed, when the Fed finally increased interest rates by the end of the decade, investments dried up while there was no increase in consumption to compensate for it. The Roaring Twenties ended with a bang in 1929 when the American stock market came crashing down. In the following years, the Dow Jones stock index lost almost 90 percent of its value, tens of thousands of businesses went bankrupt, unemployment soared, and—despite the Federal Reserve's mandate to act as a lender of last resort—thousands of banks failed, too.

However painful, Hayek believed that the best course of action at that time was to let the deflationary debt spiral run its course. Where artificially low interest had ushered in a fake economic boom, the bust would recalibrate the economy to more sustainable levels; as unprofitable businesses went belly-up, profitable businesses could start scooping up their resources (including their employees) and put them to better use. It would probably take a while, but would eventually result in a more healthy economy.

In the midst of the astute economic crisis that later came to be known as the Great Depression, Hayek's proposed solution was not very popular, however. Most people believed that *something had to be done.*

The Rivalry

And something could be done, proposed a Cambridge academic by the name of John Maynard Keynes. The British economist would during the Great Depression quickly make a name for himself by offering an unconventional, but desperately longed-for solution to get the economy back on its feet. In stark contrast to the painful solution that Hayek had to offer, Keynes spread the type of message that many people eagerly wanted to hear.[27]

Ignoring Hayek's analysis of what caused the depression, Keynes posited that the slump was the unfortunate result of a simple downturn in aggregate demand. He argued that the economy was grinding to a halt because people were spending less money than before, essentially for psychological reasons, or what he described as "animal spirits." In order to get out of the depression, spending had to resume.

In what would become the foundation of yet another new school of economic thought—*Keynesianism*—the British economist argued that if the general public wouldn't spend money, the government had to do it instead. It could invest in public infrastructure works, for example, even if that meant it'd have to borrow money to do so. Borrowing should be cheap, anyways, Keynes argued; the central bank would have to cut interest rates.

By spending money on public infrastructure works, the government would create jobs, ensuring that people have paychecks to spend, and money could start flowing through the economy again. Then, when people get back to spending on their own, the government should cut spending. Keynes proposed that policymakers adopt a *countercyclical* approach to government expenditures.

One particular policy maker was very much up for the task. Franklin D. Roosevelt, who in 1932 won the first US presidential election since the stock market crash, had run his campaign on a promise to use his presidential mandate to proactively end the depression. And as he assumed office, Keynes's ideas supplied the economic framework to back his policy (albeit to some extent *after* this policy was announced[28]). Through a series of government programs dubbed "the New Deal," FDR quickly started spending billions of dollars on roads, airports, bridges, dams, and more.

Hayek, however, was not at all convinced by Keynes's ideas. Since he believed that the economic bust was merely correcting the unsustainable boom that preceded it, he believed that government spending only prolonged an ultimately unsustainable situation even more.

On top of that, a perhaps even more important objection to Keynes's countercyclical approach was not even really about economics at all. This objection was of a political nature: Hayek did not believe that politicians could be trusted to decide when an economy is in an economic upswing or in a downturn. Instead, they would be tempted to borrow and spend money into the economy whenever there is popular demand to do so . . . which could well be all of the time.

"There will always be sections of the country or population groups that consider themselves sufficiently hard-pressed to be entitled to support," Hayek wrote. "Can a rational counter-cyclical policy under these circumstances be devised if it is entrusted to political bodies?"[29]

For Hayek the answer was a resounding "no."

It ignited what is often considered to have been one of the greatest intellectual clashes of the twentieth century. Throughout the 1930s, Hayek—by then a professor at the London School of Economics—and Keynes—still at King's College, Cambridge—regularly debated their differences in public as well as in private correspondence; their respective universities in the southeast of England serving as the battlefield for the two up-and-coming titan economists and their contrasting schools of thought.

And it was, in important ways, a sharp contrast. Whereas Keynes believed that the economy operates under different rules when analyzed on a national scale (the macro level), Hayek maintained that everything ultimately emerges from individuals and their subjective choices (the micro domain). Where Keynes liked to focus on price averages and aggregates, Hayek was more interested in price differences. And while Keynes argued that governments should play an active role in managing the economy, Hayek maintained that the free market was best left to its own devices.

If Hayek represented bottom-up spontaneous order, he had found his contemporary intellectual rival in Keynes and his top-down interventionism.

Chapter 2:
Free and Open Source Software

RICHARD STALLMAN HAD been fascinated with computers ever since he, as a young boy in the early 1960s, borrowed programming manuals from his summer camp counselors. There hadn't been a computer in sight—back then these machines would easily cost over $100,000 each—but he wasn't going to let that little detail spoil his fun. He spent the trip writing out entire programs on paper.

It would take a few more years until the young New Yorker first got acquainted with the real deal. In 1970, fresh out of high school, the now seventeen-year-old Stallman landed a summer job at the IBM Scientific Center in Manhattan, where he was tasked with writing a numerical analysis program. He finished the project within just a few weeks, which allowed him to spend the rest of his summer at the research facility designing a text editor and a programming language processor just for the fun of it.

After that summer, Stallman enrolled to study physics at Harvard. He could carry on programming in the university's fairly new computer center, but after a while he also began scouting for other hosted computers at different universities and computing facilities in Cambridge. He learned that a particularly powerful machine was hosted at MIT's Artificial Intelligence Lab (AI Lab), a research center founded by two pioneers in the field of AI—John McCarthy and Marvin Minsky—and financed by the US Department of Defense on a no-strings-attached basis.

The Harvard student decided that he wanted to study the MIT computer's documentation, to gather more information about the machine, and to understand how it differed from what they had at Harvard. But on visiting the AI Lab, Stallman learned that they didn't have any such documentation.

Instead, they gave him a job.

It was indicative of the rather anarchic culture at the AI Lab. The people running the research center didn't care much for experience or qualifications; what they truly valued was skill and potential. It was obvious that this Harvard whiz kid who visited the lab just to study their computer's documentation would be a great fit.[30]

Hacker Culture[31]

This anarchic culture at the AI Lab had first emerged about a decade earlier.

It started when Lincoln Lab, a military research and development center for advanced technology affiliated with MIT, around 1960 ushered in a small revolution by gifting the university the TX-0, an early fully transistorized computer. Whereas prior computers at the university had always required a dedicated operator, this machine was, for the first time, accessible to students.

The machine, which filled a room and weighed a ton, had quickly drawn the fascination of a particular group of students: the tinkering techies from the university's model train club. Having never actually cared too much for the model trains themselves—they mostly just enjoyed designing the electrical system of wires, switches, and repurposed telecom equipment that controlled their direction and speed—they realized that a much more interesting game had arrived in town.

The young men—they were initially all men—were determined to master the mighty TX-0 from the first moment it arrived on campus. And indeed, before long, they discovered how to access and edit the source code of the different programs embedded in the machine. Shortly after that, they figured out how to write completely new programs themselves.

Soon enough, they spent entire nights coalescing around the TX-0, when they'd have the machine all to themselves. United by their shared passion, the boys challenged each other to make the computer perform increasingly difficult tasks. Bragging rights were earned by solving the challenges with especially eloquent code, while particularly nifty solutions were in their internal lingo called "hacks"; the boys proudly identified themselves as "hackers."

As the boys progressively improved their programming skills in a bond of camaraderie, they increasingly adopted the computer as a way of life. Nothing was more important to them than hacking, and nothing was more fun. Leveraging the potential of these powerful machines gave them a tremendous feeling of empowerment.

With it grew a sense of responsibility.

The hackers instinctively knew that computers were going to have a lasting impact on the world, and over time they developed a philosophical and ethical framework around programming and technology to go along with that. It would come to form the basis of a distinct subculture, centered around technology, and characterized by experimentation and innovation. Even as the group of hackers evolved—new students arrived at MIT, while older students left—hacker culture remained.

As an integral aspect of this culture, hackers liked to take matters into their own hands: they wanted to modify whatever they thought could be improved, and fix what was broken. Asking for permission was considered a waste of time; a good idea was something to execute on, and potential restrictions would have to be ignored. Bureaucracy was the hacker's natural enemy.

If restrictions proved to be a challenge, well, hackers liked challenges, and they especially liked overcoming challenges . . . preferably with a little elegance and style. Hackers believed computers could be used to create beauty: code could have aesthetic value, and hackers admired well-written programs and original solutions.

And perhaps most important of all, they shared.

Hackers believed it benefited everyone when code and files were freely accessible, and they were proud when people used the programs they wrote. They believed they had an ethical duty to share their code, and to facilitate access to information for others. There were no passwords, no restrictions, and no "personal" documents.

The hackers would eventually develop a special operating system to serve that purpose, the *Incompatible Time-sharing System* (ITS) (a play on the *Compatible Time-Sharing System* that had preceded it), which allowed them to code collaboratively. If someone logged in and found that one of his compatriots had been developing a new text editor or strategy game, they could simply pull up the file and immediately contribute to the project themselves. Or, if two hackers were using the computer at the same time, they could debug and improve the code simultaneously.

This was the free and collaborative culture that Stallman found at MIT's AI Lab.

Anarchism

Indeed, the AI Lab's computer itself was free to use, by anyone, without restrictions. Employees as well as visitors of the lab could use the machine at any time they wanted, and access or even edit any program or file that was on it. The machine operated as a shared resource, available to all.

This did open the door to potential complications. Anyone who used an ITS computer could, for example, delete any file, even if they hadn't created it. Similarly, if someone crashed the machine, it disrupted every active user's process.

But in practice, such incidents were rare. Destroying someone else's work had no place in hacker culture, and while crashing the computer would be an annoyance for other users, it also gave them an opportunity to collaborate in debugging the code and finding a fix for whatever caused the crash.

This had been very different at the computer environments at the IBM Scientific Center and Harvard that Stallman had become accustomed to. Those machines were designed around security features that required some people to have more powers than others: certain programs were only accessible to selected users, like system administrators or some professors. The "elite"—those with privileged accounts—could unilaterally decide what others could and could not do on the machines, which meant that regular users had to frequently ask for help or permission.

Stallman's new colleagues at the AI Lab were disgusted by these policies. In their view, these administrators had essentially set up police states in their respective computer environments, claiming for themselves the authority to control other users.

Now that he experienced their free alternative, Stallman resoundingly agreed with them. While the AI Lab was proving that their form of anarchy could facilitate a fruitful working environment, he became convinced that these restrictive and controlled systems essentially represented a digital form of fascism.[32]

"Users of our system were free men, asked to behave responsibly. Instead of an elite of power, we had an elite of knowledge, composed of whoever was motivated to learn," Stallman later wrote. "Since nobody could dominate others on our machine, the lab ran as an anarchy. The visible success of this converted me to anarchism. To most people, 'anarchy' means 'wasteful, destructive disorder', but to an anarchist like me it means voluntary organization as needed, with emphasis on goals, not rules and no insistence on uniformity for uniformity's sake."[33]

Although Stallman was not exactly an anarchist in the fullest sense of the word—he still believed that the state carried out many important functions (including funding the AI Lab)—he thought the anarchist model could work in other computing environments, too. Indeed, it was around this same time that hacker culture first started spreading outside of MIT, most notably to Stanford University, which got its own AI Lab. By the early 1970s, the hacker community established a new base in the San Francisco Bay Area.

And Stallman believed that hacker culture would be viable beyond the academic domain as well. With the AI Lab as a successful showcase, perhaps the free and collaborative ethos could become a model for the nascent computer revolution.

Trouble in Paradise

But it turned out that propagating hacker culture wouldn't be so easy.

Still working at the lab almost ten years later, Stallman noticed that hacker culture was in fact starting to be pushed out of its original home. People in and around the AI Lab were increasingly embracing passwords and—worse—copyright licenses. Meanwhile, MIT administrators wanted computer users to fill out forms before they could operate the machines, a practice that Stallman actively resisted.[34]

And yet, these were minor issues compared to what was about to come.

In 1979, Richard Greenblatt, one of the lab's most respected hackers, and Russell Noftsker, a former lab administrator, wanted to take one of the AI Lab's most prominent projects to market. They were to found a startup to sell special computers designed for LISP, the programming language for AI that had been in development at the research institute.

But it soon became clear that Greenblatt and Noftsker had very different ideas for the startup. Greenblatt wanted to stay close in spirit to the AI Lab and its anarchist culture, which meant steering clear from investors and avoiding breaches of the hacker ethos as much as possible. Noftsker considered Greenblatt's approach unrealistic, however. He envisioned a more traditional company, which would protect its products with software licenses and copyright.

Greenblatt and Noftsker failed to reach a compromise, and decided to split up. Each of them would run their own company instead: Greenblatt's LISP Machine Incorporated (LMI) and Noftsker's Symbolics became competitors.

Initially, LMI and Symbolics did share the code they produced at the AI Lab, and by extension, with each other. However, by early 1982, Symbolics broke with that three-way arrangement. Noftsker decided that the AI Lab could use Symbolics's modified version of the LISP software, but LMI could no longer have it. It presented an ultimatum that forced every hacker at the lab to choose a side.

Although Greenblatt, who'd done a lot of the work to realize the LISP project, possessed the brains and the knowledge, he had sparse resources. Symbolics's business plan, meanwhile, had allowed Noftsker to secure investor funds. He proceeded to put these funds to work by hiring several of the AI Lab's best hackers. And, to ensure that the newly recruited hackers would work for his startup exclusively, he banned all Symbolics employees from contributing to the AI Lab.

In one fell swoop, many of the lab's top programmers were gone, and they took their work with them.

The AI Lab was effectively bought out. MIT's oasis of free collaboration had finally clashed head-on with merciless corporate interests, as the hackers' little utopia was stripped from its most valuable resources, leaving behind little more than a hollowed-out remnant of the research center that had during a brief golden era served as a showcase for effective anarchism.

For Stallman, it represented the end of the lab.

As the heartbroken hacker summarized in a letter shortly after:

"The people remaining at the lab were the professors, students, and nonhacker researchers, who did not know how to maintain the system, or the hardware, or want to know. Machines began to break and never be fixed; sometimes they just got thrown out. Needed changes in software could not be made. The nonhackers reacted to this by tuning to commercial systems, bringing with them fascism and license agreements. I used to wander through the lab, through the rooms so empty at night where they used to be full and think, 'Oh my poor AI lab! You are dying and I can't save you.' Everyone expected that if more hackers were trained, Symbolics would hire them away, so it didn't even seem worth trying . . . the whole culture was wiped out . . ."[35]

Stallman had at one point dreamed of a future inspired by the free and collaborative hacker culture, but he now believed that he was witnessing its dying breaths instead.

"I'm the last survivor of a dead culture," Stallman bemoaned with a sense of drama. "And I don't really belong in the world anymore. And in some ways I feel I ought to be dead."[36]

Free Software

Yet, Stallman was not quite ready to give up.

Mostly blaming Noftsker for the demise of the AI Lab, the hacker initially committed to reimplementing all of Symbolics's software upgrades. He kept up with their documentation of new features, then wrote code that offered the same features, basically single-handedly redoing the work of the startup's six developers. He shared this code with LMI, offering Greenblatt's startup a fighting chance against Symbolics, and kept this up long enough for Greenblatt to hire new programmers and get his company back in shape.[37]

Then, Stallman decided it was time for a fresh start. He had convinced himself that hacker culture could still change the world, but concluded that a new plan was needed: "an ambitious project that strikes at the root of the way that the commercial, hostile way of life is maintained."[38]

Specifically, Stallman wanted to reverse the general trend towards *proprietary software*, software restricted by licenses and copyright, which was by the 1980s becoming increasingly widespread. In line with the hacker ethos, Stallman believed that a computer program offered the maximum benefit if people could help improve it. And as computers had made copying information virtually free, preventing software from being shared "sabotages humanity as a whole," the hacker argued.[39]

Even worse, proprietary software typically cannot be inspected. If people do not have access to the human-readable source code of the software they run on their computers, they can't be sure what their own machine is actually doing. A program may be malicious, and for example restrict, censor, spy on, or otherwise abuse its user.[40]

Stallman believed that running proprietary software essentially meant surrendering control to whoever developed it.[41]

"If the users don't control the program, the program controls the users," he reasoned. "With proprietary software, there is always some entity, the 'owner' of the program, that controls the program—and through it, exercises power over its users."[42]

Stallman instead wanted computers to be tools of empowerment and freedom. He believed that users should at all times be in control of their own machines.

To help realize this, he developed a philosophy that required any computer program to offer four essential freedoms:[43]

- *The freedom to run the program as you wish, for any purpose (freedom 0).*[44]

- *The freedom to study how the program works, and change it so it does your computing as you wish (freedom 1). Access to the source code is a precondition for this.*

- *The freedom to redistribute copies so you can help others (freedom 2).*

- *The freedom to distribute copies of your modified versions to others (freedom 3). By doing this you can give the whole community a chance to benefit from your changes. Access to the source code is a precondition for this.*

Or in short, users (roughly) needed to have "the freedom to run, copy, distribute, study, change and improve the software."[45] This requires that the human readable source code of a program is published, and that it isn't subject to restrictive copyright licenses. Stallman would classify software that offered all four essential freedoms as *free software*. (With "free" as in "freedom," the hacker liked to emphasize—not as in "free beer.")

GNU

To really fulfill the promise of free software, Stallman understood that each program on a computer needed to offer the prerequisite freedoms. This included—first and foremost—the operating system. A text editor adhering to the four freedoms cannot secretly spy on its user, but if the operating system the text editor runs on isn't free software as well, there's no telling if the operating system is spying instead.

This is why Stallman in 1983 announced his incredibly ambitious project to offer an alternative to the popular Unix operating system. Where Unix was proprietary software, Stallman's operating system consisted entirely of free software. Fittingly, he named the project GNU: GNU's Not Unix! (Indeed, a recursive acronym.)[46]

Embodying the hacker ethos, GNU represented a rejection of proprietary software altogether.

"I have found many other programmers who are excited about GNU and want to help," Stallman wrote in the GNU Manifesto that he released after the announcement, in which he outlined the purpose and state of the project. "Many programmers are unhappy about the commercialization of system software. It may enable them to make more money, but it requires them to feel in conflict with other programmers in general rather than feel as comrades. [. . .] GNU serves as an example to inspire and a banner to rally others to join us in sharing."[47]

Indeed, more than just a piece of software, GNU marked the founding of a new social movement: the free software movement.

To support the movement, Stallman in 1985 also founded the nonprofit Free Software Foundation. The foundation would advocate for free software, and raise money to fund free software projects. Additionally, the Free Software Foundation led the introduction of special free software licenses under the new "copyleft" umbrella, designed to encourage free software.

This included, most notably, the GNU General Public License: a license that grants the right to distribute and modify source code as long as this is done under equally free conditions. In other words, other free software developers could integrate free software released under this license in their own project in any way they'd please, but proprietary software developers could not.

With the GNU project underway and the new licenses in play, free software was about to become a force to be reckoned with.

The Cathedral and the Bazaar

Free software projects were traditionally carried out by small pockets of developers working from dedicated tech hubs, like MIT's AI Lab. But as he started working on GNU, Stallman invited other developers to help develop his project as well. Leveraging the nascent internet, hackers could even contribute code from all around the world.

Even though Stallman typically did not offer contributors any financial compensation for their work, many developers were willing to help make GNU a reality regardless. Maybe some of them hoped to earn respect or status from their programmer peers by contributing, as had always been a factor within the hacker community. Others may have contributed because they wanted to use GNU themselves. Yet others may have found the challenge inherently interesting enough to be a part of it. And, perhaps, some just wanted to make the world a better place, and saw this project as a means to that end.

Whatever their reasons were, they were contributing. What's more, their contributions were valuable. These volunteer programmers were, somewhat remarkably, producing high-quality code, which allowed Stallman to complete many of the separate parts of the GNU operating system a few years later—a momentous feat.

It was at this point that Finnish software engineer Linus Torvalds gladly used the freedom offered by the GNU General Public License. Taking much of Stallman's GNU code but adding his own kernel (a program at the core of a computer's operating system), in 1992 Torvalds released *Linux*.[48] It represented the first fully functional operating system consisting entirely of free software.

But Torvalds's main innovation arguably wasn't the Linux kernel itself. It was how he produced it. Over the years, the software engineer developed a process explicitly designed to collaborate over the internet.

As explored in depth by Linux contributor Eric S. Raymond in his 1997 essay "The Cathedral & The Bazaar" and (later) book with the same name, the biggest adjustment Torvalds made pertained to the project's approach to security.

Until then, free software developers had considered bugs and other vulnerabilities to be great risks that should be taken care of by dedicated experts who meticulously reviewed their software, including—perhaps most importantly—the code they received from outside contributors. They would only release the code once they were confident it was safe to use. Raymond dubbed this top-down approach the "cathedral" model.

Torvalds instead adopted what Raymond referred to as the "bazaar" model. This model used a more flexible process to integrate contributions, which also allowed developers to more directly upload their changes into different versions of the software. Other contributors could then download this software, test it, and potentially adopt the changes into their own versions.

This could lead to versions of the software with more bugs than the software of their cathedral counterparts. However, with the development process happening out in the open, other contributors also tended to more quickly catch these mistakes, and fix them. If needed, the fix was immediately included in a new release; under the bazaar model, software updates happen faster and more frequently.

"Given a large enough beta-tester and co-developer base, almost every problem will be characterized quickly and the fix obvious to someone," Raymond wrote in his essay, summing up one of the key lessons he'd learned over the years. "Or, less formally, 'Given enough eyeballs, all bugs are shallow.'"[49]

He dubbed the adage *Linus's Law*.

Interestingly, Raymond believed that this development model could offer benefits even to businesses and people that did not share Stallman's concerns about proprietary software, but just wanted high-quality code at low cost. He suspected, however, that many of them (businesses, in particular) were hesitant to use free software exactly because they were put off by the ideological narrative around it. To de-emphasize Stallman's original motivations and focus more on the pragmatic benefits, Raymond therefore in the late 1990s led the effort to rebrand free software as "open source software."

Stallman himself was not on board with the rebrand, however. For him, freedom was the point, and speaking of "open source" diluted that message.

Today, the terms "free software" and "open source software" in almost all cases refer to the same practical concept, but the difference in terminology continues to represent the philosophical rift. The term "free and open source software" (FOSS) is used to explicitly include both sides of the schism.[50]

Common Understanding

The bazaar model can produce high-quality code. But quality isn't a given. As per Linus's Law, high-quality code requires there to be enough "eyeballs," that is, contributors.

FOSS projects usually don't have the resources to offer financial rewards to potential contributors, while real-world power relationships are easily ignored in the context of free and open source development, and, as Raymond also pointed out in his essay, coercion was of course out of scope entirely on "the anarchist's paradise we call the Internet."[51] Attracting contributors has therefore turned out to be a crucial skill for free and open software developers.

Drawing from nineteenth-century Russian anarchist Pyotr Alexeyevich Kropotkin, Raymond explained that project leaders had to learn to recruit and energize effective communities of interest based on the principle of common understanding. To get developers to contribute, a project's lead needs to figure out how contributing to the project benefits these developers. Incentives would have to align around some shared goal, Raymond proposed, a "severe effort of many converging wills."[52]

What this actually means is that no one is really in charge of bazaar-style FOSS projects. A project's leader cannot steer the project in an unpopular direction without losing the developers he so crucially needs. Under the bazaar model, software is in a very real way controlled by its body of contributors, each with their own personal reason to be involved.

When these incentives do align, and such a body of contributors is willing to work towards a common goal, the results can be incredible. Even though no one is ever really in charge, these large-scale collaborations between strangers with widely diverging levels of knowledge and skill, have managed to produce highly complex programs, the Linux kernel only being one example of many.

In this way, free and open source software development resembles that other form of large-scale leaderless collaboration: free markets. Like free markets, FOSS projects consist only of voluntary interactions, they utilize the knowledge distributed across participants, and perhaps most interesting of all, they can outperform top-down forms of organization.

Like free markets, free and open software projects could form a spontaneous order.

Raymond:

"The Linux world behaves in many respects like a free market or an ecology, a collection of selfish agents attempting to maximize utility which in the process produces a self-correcting spontaneous order more elaborate and efficient than any amount of central planning could have achieved."[53]

Chapter 3:
Neutral Money

FRIEDRICH HAYEK HAD in the 1930s explained the free market in terms of spontaneous order. He'd argued that individuals acting in their best self-interest could efficiently allocate resources throughout society using the price system: *a marvel*.

It was only natural, then, that Hayek was keenly interested in the stuff that goods and services are priced *in*—money.

Interestingly, money appears to contradict a cornerstone of Austrian economics. The school of thought is built on the assumption that value is subjective: people subjectively value products and services if these products and services fulfill a personal want or need. People value shoes because they can wear them, they value apples because they can eat them, and they value cars because they can drive them. But for most people money doesn't appear to fulfill any want or need at all. They don't wear money, or eat it, or drive it.

Money, in this sense, seems rather worthless. Yet, money is broadly accepted as payment in trade.

The apparent contradiction had in the early twentieth century been addressed by Hayek's mentor at the University of Vienna, Ludwig von Mises.[54] Mises's explanation, called the *regression theorem*, accepts that people don't actually want money. They want what money can buy. They want purchasing power.

Mises reasoned that the expected purchasing power of money is derived from past performance. If $10 could buy lunch at a restaurant yesterday, people will assume that it'll buy them lunch tomorrow as well. And the reason that $10 could buy them lunch yesterday, is that the restaurant owner knew it could buy him ten loafs of bread at the bakery the day before, and therefore probably also the day after. The baker in turn accepted $10 in exchange for his bread because that could buy him a pound of flour from the local miller the day before that . . . and so on.

But this of course still leaves an important part of the contradiction unresolved: when did people *first* start accepting money and, especially, why? If we go backwards in time—regress—far enough, someone must have been the first to start accepting money, without having any past performance to rely on to estimate future expectations of purchasing power.

Mises resolved this question by adopting Carl Menger's theory that money originally emerged from barter.

From Barter to Money

In a barter economy—an economy without money—people trade goods and services directly. If the shoemaker has a pair of shoes but prefers a loaf of bread, and the baker has a loaf of bread but prefers a pair of shoes, they would trade their products with each other, leaving both of them (subjectively) better off than before.

Such a barter economy, however, suffers from a problem known as the "double coincidence of wants." A trade can only happen if two people want the exact product that the other has to offer. The shoemaker can only trade shoes for a loaf of bread if the baker happens to need a new pair . . . but this probably isn't very often.

More specialized craftsmen have an even harder time getting what they want in a barter economy, because fewer people need their product. A watchmaker can almost never trade a watch for a loaf of bread or a pair of shoes, because bakers and shoemakers don't need a new watch all that often.

But the opposite is true as well: some products should be relatively easy to trade. Let's take salt as an example, and let's assume many people in this economy need salt on a fairly regular basis—to spice up a meal perhaps, or to conserve food. In the lexicon of Menger and the Austrian school, salt is more *saleable* (or "marketable") than a watch.

And salt has other benefits, too. It is quite durable; salt doesn't spoil. It is fairly portable; salt can be carried around in a bag. It is divisible; salt is trivially divided into smaller portions, and smaller portions are just as easily combined into a larger batch. Furthermore, salt is easy to identify, and it is reasonably fungible, meaning different portions are interchangeable; salt is salt. And last but not least, depending on where (and when) you are, salt can also be scarce; it might be hard to get more of it.

Menger therefore figured that, when given the option, the watchmaker would be wise to accept a batch of salt in exchange for a watch. Even if he doesn't have a need for salt himself, the baker certainly does, so the watchmaker can then trade the salt with the baker and finally get himself that loaf of bread.

And it wouldn't only be wise for the watchmaker to accept salt in exchange; it would be wise for the shoemaker, too. The baker would probably accept salt in trade more often than he'd accept a pair of shoes. This in turn gives the watchmaker even more options with the salt he'd receive in trade; he can spend it at the baker as well as the shoemaker.

As more people in this barter economy would start accepting salt in trade in the expectation that others will accept it in trade as well, this would set off a self-reinforcing cycle. For each additional person that accepts salt in trade, salt becomes more attractive to accept in trade for everyone else as well. Salt would emerge as a common *medium of exchange*.

Although some people in this economy wouldn't need salt themselves, nor have anything to spend it on right away, they'd learn to trust that it will come in handy eventually. They would therefore start stockpiling salt for future use. With that, salt also becomes a *store of value*.

And eventually, the people in this economy would start to measure the value of products and services in salt. A watch might cost a kilo of salt, a pair of shoes a pound, and a loaf of bread an ounce. Salt would be used to set prices, making it a *unit of account*.

As it would acquire these three properties—medium of exchange, store of value, and unit of account—salt would become money.

This would in turn also increase the demand for salt. Salt, in this economy, was initially valued for its inherent properties alone—its ability to spice up a meal or conserve food.[55] But as soon as it gets adopted as money, many people would be eager to get more salt, since this would allow them to buy any other product. The process of *monetization* would add a *monetary* premium to the value of salt.

This monetary premium explains why people are willing to accept money—in this example, salt—in exchange for goods and services that in and of themselves fulfill more wants or needs, overcoming the apparent contradiction introduced by the subjective theory of value.

Salt really has been used as money in the past. A few thousand years ago, soldiers of the Roman Empire were paid in salt; the modern word "salary" stems from the Latin word *salarium*, which means "salt money." Similarly, when the Italian explorer Marco Polo traveled to China in the thirteenth century, he found that locals paid each other with a type of pancakes made out of salt. And certain Ethiopian tribes even used salt as money as recently as the twentieth century.

Nevertheless, over the course of thousands of years, various civilizations from around the world found that there was another good that was even better suited as money. By the time Mises published his regression theorem, most of the world had settled on using gold.[56]

Gold

The properties of gold make it quite suitable as money. Gold is incredibly durable: it doesn't rot, rust, or spoil. It is fairly portable; gold coins can easily be carried around. It is divisible; with the right tools, gold can be melted into smaller chunks, and these smaller portions can be melted back together into larger bars. Gold's properties also make it relatively easy to recognize, while it is perfectly fungible as well. And perhaps most importantly, extracting gold from the crust of the Earth is a difficult and

expensive process, and getting more difficult over time as the most easily accessible gold mines are depleted, ensuring some level of scarcity. As
a bonus, the yellowish shiny metal is by many considered to be pretty.

Yet, in more recent centuries, gold was almost never actually used as currency in transactions at all; people generally used banknotes instead. These
banknotes could be redeemed for gold, which was initially held securely
in reserve by the note-issuing banks. Bank customers found it more convenient to use the notes as medium of exchange while the gold remained
locked up in bank vaults.

It meant that most of the gold held in the banks' reserves was never
claimed at all. This spurred banks to issue and lend out more banknotes
than they could actually account for with gold in their vaults; widespread
use of paper currency had ushered in the age of fractional reserve banking.
Over time, this had evolved into a complex system of credit, correspon-
dent banks, and clearing houses, tightly interwoven with stock markets
and the greater financial system.

And, ultimately, all of this came to fall under the supervision of central
banks like the Federal Reserve. These central banks had ended up managing their countries' gold reserves against which they issued national
currencies—paper notes that could be redeemed for a fixed amount of
gold. Actual gold was really only used for international trade; at the start
of the twentieth century, the world was on a gold standard.

But the First World War had effectively ended the *classical gold standard*.
Most governments abolished the convertibility of their currencies, allowing
them to more freely finance their war efforts.[57] Instead of representing gold,
the unbacked national currencies were simply considered to be money by
government decree, a form of money called "fiat currency." (The Latin
word "fiat" means "let it be done," and is typically associated with government decrees.)

In the first years after the war had ended, the fiat currencies freely floated
in value against one another. This meant that if someone from, say, the
United States wanted to buy (import) a product from England, they would
need to first exchange some of their dollars for pounds. If this happened

on a large enough scale, the added demand for pounds would in turn drive up the exchange rate against the dollar (it would cost more dollars to buy the same amount of pounds).

A strong pound would therefore make importing products and services from England more expensive for Americans, thereby putting a break on England's exports. Meanwhile, a weak dollar would make importing products and services from the US more attractive for Brits, potentially resulting in increased demand for American ware, in turn resulting in more demand for dollars. Currency value fluctuations would therefore in a way stabilize the trade balance between the two countries.

This was presumed to be a temporary situation, however; most countries intended to return to a gold standard. Still, influential economists of the time argued that this new gold standard should operate a bit differently than the classical gold standard. Since most of the gold that backed national currencies was never redeemed, central banks could actually issue more currency than they could account for with gold. (In the US, the Fed was allowed to do this as long as they remained within the *gold coverage ratio*: the ratio of gold in reserve versus dollars issued had to be at least 40 percent.)

This flexibility offered an opportunity to introduce a new type of monetary policy: central banks could inject and extract money from the banking system to manipulate interest rates in order to stabilize the value of money.

It was this policy that Hayek had so fiercely critiqued.

The Stabilizers

The earliest proponent for this new type of monetary policy had been Irving Fisher, a leading economist in the early twentieth century. Fisher was among the very first economists to be concerned about deflation, or more precisely, the deflationary debt spiral. He believed that only stable prices could prevent "the evils of monetary instability."[58]

The prices of specific goods and services do of course change sometimes, Fisher knew, since supply and demand for different products and services fluctuate over time for all kinds of reasons. It's the general, average price level that he believed should remain stable over time. To determine the stability of a currency's purchasing power, Fisher therefore needed some way to establish average prices. And he knew exactly where to look.

In prior research, the economist had offered empirical evidence to support the quantity theory of money. That theory states that the general price level of goods and services is proportional to the amount of money in circulation. To prove this, Fisher used indices, where each index consisted of a range of goods and services and their average price at a specific point in time. Comparing the indices across different time periods offered insights in the development of the general price level.

Fisher figured that similar indices could be used to create a stable form of money, where a dollar should buy the same share of an index across time. Such an index would include a sample of all products that the average consumer buys: a *consumer price index* (CPI). One year a dollar might buy more potatoes and less carrots, while the next year it might buy more carrots and less potatoes, but the average purchasing power of a dollar as measured using the CPI should remain roughly the same.

Fisher argued that the Federal Reserve could target stabilization of the dollar by manipulating interest rates, and had in 1920 founded the Stable Money Association to realize this policy change. The group of economists, politicians, and business leaders would push for a stabilization policy through congressional inquiries known as the "stabilization hearings," while also making their case at international conferences and other venues where monetary policy was a topic of discussion. It helped Fisher's ideas spread to the highest ranks of the Federal Reserve System, and beyond.

The Stable Money Association soon also found itself an ally in Hayek's contemporary rival, John Maynard Keynes. But Keynes went even further than Fisher and the Stable Money Association. He proposed that the gold standard should be abandoned altogether. In his 1923 treatise *A Tract on Monetary Reform*, the King's College economist argued that the precious metal wasn't well suited to guarantee stable prices, because it was itself subject to market sentiments.

While this could indeed be mitigated in part if central banks adopted a more flexible approach to achieve currency stability, Keynes argued that the gold coverage ratio would in the end fundamentally limit central banks' room for maneuver—and would in practice be ignored whenever that was considered necessary:

"In truth, the gold standard is already a barbarous relic. [. . .] All of us, from the Governor of the Bank of England downwards, are now primarily interested in preserving the stability of business, prices, and employment, and are not likely, when the choice is forced on us, deliberately to sacrifice these to the outworn dogma."[59]

If, instead, money was set free from the constraints of gold altogether, monetary policy could be as flexible as monetary authorities needed it to be.

Rejecting Stable Money

Hayek had rejected central banks' use of interest rates as a tool, as he believed that this only served to amplify the business cycle. But he also rejected the goal of stabilizing prices itself. Hayek rejected the stabilizers.

Prices, Hayek had explained, embed a wide range of information. Because of this, it's possible that the prices of otherwise identical goods vary in different locations. A crate of bananas might for example be cheaper in Colombia, where bananas are grown, compared to Iceland, to where the bananas would first need to be transported. The cost of transportation (and therefore, the cost of fuel and more) would be embedded in the price of the bananas in Iceland.

Hayek therefore reasoned that, technically, a crate of bananas in Columbia and a crate of bananas in Iceland should be regarded as two different products in an economic sense. The interspatial price system—different prices in different locations—allowed for efficient allocation of resources across space.

And the economist argued that something similar was true for otherwise identical products in different times; in the same way that the interspatial price system allows for efficient allocation of resources across space, the intertemporal price system allows for efficient allocation of resources across time.

Hayek:

"Strictly speaking, goods which are technically equivalent but available only at different points in time ought to be considered different goods in an economic sense, just as can be said of goods which are technically the same located at different places."[60]

Free markets foster innovation, and most products tend to become cheaper to produce because of it. Producing a crate of bananas, to stick with that example, becomes more affordable over time as banana farmers benefit from improved technology to manage their plantation. It follows, then, that a crate of bananas in ten years from now should be cheaper than a crate of bananas today; the differences in production cost would be embedded in the respective prices.

Hayek therefore did not believe that stabilizing prices based on indices was desirable at all. If prices are kept artificially stable, it would disturb the intertemporal price system, and ultimately disturb the allocation of resources across time.

Let's say, for example, that a banana farmer expects the price of bananas (like all other consumer products, on average) to remain stable into the future, while he also knows that his cost of producing bananas will drop. This would incentivize him to invest in production for the future at the expense of production today: he'll later be able to grow the same amount of bananas for less total cost, while he'll be able to sell each crate of bananas for the same price as today, thus increasing his overall profits.

If all producers in the economy think the same way—if they all follow the same incentives and invest in production for the future at the expense of production today—it would result in a shortage of total economic output in the short term and an oversupply in the long term.

Hayek wrote:

"If, during such a general expansion of output, the expectation is held with certainty that the prices of products will not fall but will remain stable or even rise, hence that at the point more distant in time the same or even a higher price can be obtained for the product produced at lesser cost, the outcome must be that production for the later period, in which supply is already at a relatively adequate level, will be further expanded at the cost of that for the earlier period, in which supply is relatively less adequate."[61]

For spontaneous order to emerge across time, prices had to be allowed to fall.

Hayek therefore concluded:

"Acceptance of the necessity for an intertemporal price system is not merely incompatible with, it is diametrically opposed to the prevailing notion that constant prices over time are a precondition for an undisturbed economy."[62]

Of course, the Austrian did acknowledge that a fall in prices could in some cases negatively affect the economy as well; he warned against the manipulation of interest rates exactly because it would eventually lead to deflation. However, Hayek argued that deflation is only a problem if the fall in prices is, in fact, caused by a decrease in the money supply. Businesses would in that case indeed earn less than anticipated which, as Fisher had also pointed out, could set in motion a deflationary debt spiral.

Hayek pointed out that if the fall in prices wasn't caused by a shrinking money supply and instead resulted from cheaper production processes over time, this problem shouldn't exist:

"[. . .] a fall in the price level due to continuous improvements occurring in all branches of production does not have the same troublesome consequences as a deflation. Theory has hitherto scarcely progressed beyond this distinction between the effects of changes in the price level originating on the one hand from the 'goods side' and on the other from the 'money side'."[63]

The Gold Exchange Standard

The Stable Money Association had, during the period shortly after the First World War, been quick to assert its influence. Just one year after its founding, the group successfully argued their case at the 1922 Genoa Economic and Financial Conference, where representatives of 34 major industrialized countries had gathered to resolve the major economic and political issues facing postwar Europe.

The representatives at the conference agreed to adopt a *gold exchange standard*. National currencies would maintain a fixed exchange rate against gold, but central banks were granted relative flexibility to pursue a monetary policy that targeted price stability through the manipulation of interest rates.

These price stabilization policies had to be managed per country: the stabilizers proposed that a currency's purchasing power should remain stable within its own national economy. But this meant that if the aggregate price levels in different countries began to vary, the value of their national currencies could fluctuate against one another, potentially affecting international trade.

The stabilizers acknowledged this, but thought it was worth the trade-off.

"[. . .] when stability of the internal price level and stability of the external exchanges are incompatible, the former is generally preferable" Keynes wrote, and "when the dilemma is acute, the preservation of the former at the expense of the latter is, fortunately perhaps, the line of least resistance."[64]

The stabilizers also believed that international trade could still happen relatively smoothly under a gold exchange standard, if central banks would adhere to what Keynes had called the *rules of the game*. In a nutshell, countries with a trade surplus (that export more than they import) and, therefore, an inflow of gold, were supposed to lower interest rates, thereby stimulating more borrowing, resulting in more currency in circulation, and higher prices overall. Countries with a trade deficit were expected to increase interest rates for the opposite effect.

The increased price level in countries with a trade surplus should make products from that country less attractive for export, which should help decrease the size of the trade surplus. Meanwhile, lower prices in the countries with trade deficits should make products from these countries more attractive for export, which should help decrease their trade deficit. Much like under a floating fiat currency system, the change in aggregate prices between countries should help bring the trade balance between them into equilibrium.

Hayek, too, acknowledged that such a trade equilibrium could be maintained under the gold exchange standard, as it could under the fiat currency standard. But he didn't agree that that was a good thing. . .

Monetary Nationalism

In 1937, Hayek tackled both the gold exchange standard and the floating fiat currency system in a series of lectures titled *Monetary Nationalism and International Stability*. The lectures offered a broad rejection of international currency arrangements as championed by the stabilizers, arrangements which Hayek had dubbed *monetary nationalism*.

Hayek pointed out that under both the gold exchange standard as well as a floating currency system, those businesses and individuals that benefit from an increase of exports (or, vice versa those that suffered from a decrease) are not necessarily the same businesses or individuals that are responsible for the increase (or decrease) of cross-border trade.

"Considering the methods available to the banking system to bring about an expansion or contraction [of credit], there is no reason to assume that they can take the money to be extinguished exactly from those persons where it would in the course of time be released if there were no banking system, or that they will place the additional money in the hands of those who would absorb the money if it came to the country by direct transfer from abroad," Hayek wrote.[65]

Specifically, the change in interest rates under the gold exchange standard probably wouldn't reflect what the free market interest rate otherwise would have been. This creates winners and losers; debtors benefit from lower interest rates, while creditors suffer. However, there is no reason to assume that the merchant who increases his exports is a debtor. He might just as well be a creditor, in which case he'd be harmed indirectly by his own increase in international sales.

Rather than just affecting the two trading parties who do business across borders, international trade under the gold exchange standard essentially caused a redistribution of resources through the credit markets, Hayek pointed out:

"There are on the contrary strong grounds for believing that the burden of the change will fall entirely, or to an extent which is in no way justified by the underlying change in the real situation, on investment activity in both countries."[66]

Similarly, under a floating fiat currency system resources are distributed beyond the parties that are directly involved with the increase (or decrease) of exports as well, Hayek explained.

To see why, let's say there's a shift in demand from the car industry in the US to the car industry in England. This means that Americans need to exchange dollars for pounds in order to purchase a new car, which affects the relative values of the dollar and the pound. As a consequence, *all* products from the United States become cheaper from the perspective of England, while all products from England become more expensive from the perspective of the United States. All exporters in the United States would, as a result, enjoy more sales—at the expense of businesses in England.

While the initial shift in demand in this example only happens between the two car industries, Brits would also be incentivized to buy American food, clothes, or electronics. Not because these products are actually better or cheaper to produce, but purely due to the mechanics of the floating fiat currency system.

Monetary nationalism, in either form, disturbed spontaneous order across borders, Hayek concluded.

Neutral Money

Hayek rejected stabilization policies, and he rejected monetary nationalism. Instead, he advocated for a homogenous, borderless type of money with a fixed supply. Or what he called *neutral money*.

Hayek dismissed out of hand the stabilizers' presumption that monetary stability should be measured at the national level. If money can move from one country to another as easily as it can move between regions within the same country, he argued, an overall price increase within a country would simply reflect an increase in demand for goods and services from that country, and it would accurately signal to the market that resources are best allocated to that country so it can produce more goods and services.

A homogenous money would function straightforwardly in international trade: the payment would affect the sender and the receiver and no one else, no matter in which countries they reside. A borderless currency would therefore best enable the interspatial price system, the Austrian reasoned, allowing people to compare prices across different locations.

Money with a fixed supply, meanwhile, would best enable the intertemporal price system, allowing people to accurately compare prices across different points in time:

"It would be possible to conceive of a structure of money prices at successive points in time being established which corresponds to the intertemporal equilibrium system only if the monetary system was one in which any change in the quantity of money was excluded," Hayek wrote.[67]

Perhaps most importantly, if the supply of money was fixed, changes in the cost of production across time would be clearly reflected in corresponding changes in prices. Barring other factors, if the cost to produce goods would fall over time, so would prices. A gradual drop in prices— deflation—was the natural outcome of any healthy economy, Hayek believed.

Yet, Hayek did reckon there was one very real problem with such a homogenous fixed supply currency. He did not think it could be done.

For one, even if such a currency could be created, people could still choose to use credit and other substitutes instead of actual money, which constitutes a de facto increase of the money supply.

"Obviously [fixing the quantity of the means of exchange once and for all] is out of the question, given the ever-present possibility of using a surrogate money in place of real money," the Austrian was sad to conclude. "The quantity of that surrogate could not be rigidly tied to that of the real money, and its creation would have precisely the same effect as that of any other expansion of the money supply."[68]

But even more importantly, Hayek did not think that a homogenous, fixed-supply currency could be adopted in the first place, because he did not believe there was any international authority that would be trusted to issue such a currency. Something as important as a global monetary standard should offer the strongest guarantee that it will continue to be universally acceptable and accessible, but no known institution could provide this guarantee, Hayek thought:

"[. . .] as long as there are separate sovereign States there will always loom large among these eventualities the danger of war, or of the breakdown of the international monetary arrangements for some other reason."[69]

Neutral money was impossible because, on a very fundamental level, nations could not trust each other.

Currency Wars

Indeed, this very lack of trust had by the late 1930s also contributed to the breakdown of the gold exchange standard.

For his own critique of the gold exchange standard, Hayek assumed a best-case scenario, where participating countries adhered to the rules of the game, which prescribed when and how central banks should adjust their interest rates. But it was already evident that even this best-case scenario had not played out in reality, as several of the participating nations instead engaged in a series of competitive devaluations, in what is sometimes referred to as a "currency war."

When a national currency is devalued, goods and services are relatively cheap from the perspective of other countries. Currency devaluations can therefore help boost exports, and thereby benefit the national economy, at least temporarily. But there is a flip side. When international demand shifts to the country that devalued its currency, it also means that demand shifts *away* from other countries. Their economies tend to suffer as a result.

The fastest way for these other countries to regain their competitiveness is to devalue their own currencies as well, which should restore trade balances to their original state. But all money, across all these economies, would as a consequence be worth less than before, which, most obviously, hurts savers, creditors, and people with a fixed income. If everyone engages in a currency war, no one wins.

Yet, this did not stop countries from doing exactly that. Even before the introduction of the gold exchange standard, Germany had started this series of devaluations rather spectacularly in 1921 by hyperinflating its currency in order to make reparation payments for the war, with Hayek's home country of Austria following shortly behind. France was next, though (as one of the victors of the First World War) not to the same extreme extent; it devalued the franc right before adopting the new gold standard in 1925. In response, England suspended gold convertibility in 1931, just a few years into the new international monetary arrangement, in order to devalue the pound.

As one of the few countries that had upheld (a limited form of) gold convertibility during the war, the United States was initially hesitant to partake in any currency devaluations. A troy ounce of gold was worth exactly $20.67, and the Federal Reserve was by the early 1930s still required to respect the gold coverage ratio of 40 percent.

But this coverage ratio started to represent a limiting factor as President Franklin Roosevelt was applying Keynesian methods in his attempt to spend the American economy out of its economic depression. He eventually decided to remove the obstacles he found in his way in an unprecedented manner.

Through Executive Order 6102, signed into effect with warm endorsements from Keynes,[70] FDR in 1933 outright banned "the hoarding of gold coin, gold bullion, and gold certificates within the continental United States."[71] All US citizens were ordered to exchange any gold they had for dollars at their local Federal Reserve member bank for the fixed rate of $20.67. Noncompliance was punishable by a $10,000 penalty and up to ten years imprisonment.

A few months later, Roosevelt devalued the dollar to $35 per troy ounce, in effect increasing the Federal Reserve's gold reserve ratio by roughly 69 percent overnight. It represented another nail in the coffin of the gold exchange standard.

Then it was Europe's turn again, starting with the French who in 1936 devalued their currency for a second time. And when more countries started following England's lead to drop gold completely in order to devalue their currencies in the years that followed, the gold exchange standard was abandoned completely barely a decade after it was installed.[72]

The series of currency devaluations, combined with a deep economic depression, was taking its toll—especially in the countries that had in 1918 lost the war. Destroyed savings, widespread unemployment, and a lack of prospects in large parts of Europe represented a source of uncertainty, despair and, ultimately, anger.

It provided a fertile feeding ground for a new and particularly violent, nationalist, racist, and authoritarian collectivist ideology. Fascism was taking hold across the continent.

Chapter 4:
Cryptography[73]

WHITFIELD DIFFIE ALWAYS had a thing for codes. Ever since his fifth-grade teacher introduced him to a technique called the *substitution cipher*—a basic starting point in the mathematical branch of cryptography—he'd been intrigued by this secret-keeping method. That such text-scrambling algorithms were at the time, in the 1950s, the domain of the Army, special agents, and spies only added to the mystique.

Young Whitfield was soon poring over any cryptography book that his father—a university professor—could find at the City College Library of New York. He studied standard works like Helen Forché Gaines's 1939 book *Cryptoanalysis,* which detailed various schemes to convert messages into unreadable *ciphertext*, ideally so that only the intended recipient could decipher them.

With the very basic *Caesar cipher* (supposedly used by Julias Caesar), messages can for example be turned into ciphertext by substituting every letter with a different letter. The encryption key "+1," say, replaces each letter by the next letter in the alphabet—"a" becomes "b," "b" becomes "c," and so on. The word "Secret" turns into "Tfdsfu." To decipher the scrambled text, then, the same encryption key is used, but in reverse; each letter is replaced by the previous letter in the alphabet; "Tfdsfu" turns back into "Secret."

This +1 encryption key isn't very strong, of course. An adversary determined to decrypt the resulting ciphertext—a *cryptanalyst*—would probably guess it on their first try. And even if they wouldn't guess it, a number of patterns in an encrypted text can help specialized codebreakers figure out which substitute letters likely correspond with which original letters. Especially in longer texts, the frequency of specific letters and the length of words, for example, offer clues.

Modern encryption keys therefore used far more advanced techniques, and for example applied some parts of a text to encrypt other parts. Encryption—and breaking encryption—was by the mid-twentieth century key to military operations, and executed by dedicated specialists who had advanced the field to the point where ciphertexts could appear entirely random. Without patterns to analyze, even the best cryptanalysts in the world were unable to break these codes.

Still, the basic idea remained mostly unchanged. Like in the Caesar cipher, the secret keys were always *symmetric*: the decryption key was the same as the encryption key, just used in reverse. To communicate securely, people first needed to share a key.

Sharing a key over an insecure communications channel was not an option, however. If eavesdroppers intercepted the key, they could decrypt all subsequent messages encrypted with that key, defeating the point of encrypting the messages in the first place. The keys were therefore typically shared in person. Both parties had to first meet up in a physical location before they could exchange encrypted messages.

This of course wasn't always easy, or even possible. Long distances or extreme circumstances like war could complicate the process significantly. But, as Diffie learned during his early studies, cryptographers believed there was no other way; exchanging keys in person was how it had to be done.

MIT

About a decade after he first learned about the substitution cipher, Whitfield Diffie studied mathematics at MIT, when the first computers arrived on campus. Now in his early twenties and a self-described peacenik, Diffie considered himself more of a pure mathematician than a computer scientist, but he decided to learn how to program in order to develop a more practical skill set.

It would work out well for him. After graduating from the technical university in 1965, Diffie accepted a job at Mitre, a defense contractor that had, a few years prior, spun out of MIT's Lincoln Laboratory. The job helped him get out of the Vietnam draft, while the work itself was unrelated to the war as well. Diffie would help develop the computer algebra system Macsyma.

Nor did Diffie even have to show up to the Mitre office. Instead, he could work from MIT's AI Lab, where he immersed himself in the newly emerging hacker culture and its free and collaborative philosophy.

Yet, Diffie in some ways deviated from the typical hacker ethos. He did not think that unrestricted freedom was desirable in all computing environments, and believed that software should in certain contexts offer privacy too. As people, companies, and governments were to increasingly migrate their activities to the digital domain, he recognized that it would become important to protect sensitive data—think personal health records, company finances, or military secrets.

Diffie set out to build a virtual "safe." Just like a physical safe, its digital equivalent had to be easy to enter by the legitimate owner of the data, but restrict access to anyone else. He believed that this was the type of problem strong encryption could solve.

Although the hacker hadn't really maintained his childhood passion— he was under the impression that all relevant avenues in the domain of cryptography had already been explored—his superior at the AI Lab, mathematician Roland Silver, helped him get back up to speed. And as Diffie learned how much progress had been made in the field of *crypto* since he studied it as a kid, his intrigue was once again sparked.

But Diffie now also learned that the real cutting edge of cryptography probably remained hidden behind closed doors. The National Security Agency (NSA)—the American intelligence agency which at the time operated in secret; it officially did not exist—had for years been scooping up many of the country's best cryptographers. It seemed likely that any truly groundbreaking research, and the superior cryptographic techniques that resulted from it, was kept classified.

The idea that the NSA could be withholding important knowledge from the public did not sit well with Diffie at all.

Stanford

When hacker culture first started spreading beyond MIT's university campus, it found an early home away from home in the San Francisco Bay Area, at Stanford University. And so would Diffie. When he in 1969 approached the draft cutoff age of twenty-four, the MIT graduate left Mitre to work for Stanford's AI Lab instead. Here, he found new challenges to fit his rejuvenated interest in cryptography.

The first of these challenges was inspired by John McCarthy. The cofounder of MIT's AI lab and original designer of the LISP programming language had gone on to found Stanford's AI Lab, and headed the research facility when Diffie first arrived. McCarthy had by then developed an interest in the prospects of digital commerce, which in turn led Diffie to envision the automated office, where software is used to digitally create, collect, store, edit, and relay work-related documents. And this made him consider the problem of *authentication*.

In the physical world, documents are typically authenticated using personal, written signatures. People sign a letter to prove that it was really them who wrote it, or they add their signature to a contract to make it legally binding. But as more documents would become digital, Diffie figured, people would need the digital equivalent of a signature to prove that it was really them who signed off on the content of these documents.

Creating such a form of digital authentication wasn't so easy, however; Diffie and McCarthy spent many hours at the research institute thinking about potential solutions. The central problem was that even some type of uniquely individual data—for example a long, personal number—would be trivial to copy. Anyone could take such a digital signature from one contract, and add it to any other contract. This would make them useless.

Another challenge was introduced by the Defense Department's Advanced Research Projects Agency (ARPA), which had in 1972 begun linking major research institutions across the country through a network of computers: ARPAnet. As part of this project, the director of Information Processing Techniques at ARPA, Larry Roberts, was looking for ways to keep messages over the network private. Having been denied any help from the NSA—the secret government agency refused to work on such a public project—he hoped that one of his principal investigators might have an idea.

When McCarthy—one of these principal investigators—discussed the issue with the hackers at Stanford's AI Lab, Diffie recognized the importance of the problem. If communication would in the future increasingly happen electronically—and a start had now been made—sharing encryption keys in person would likely become infeasible, rendering private conversations impossible. Diffie worried that unless people had access to tools that let them secure their communication anyone's activity could potentially be monitored at any time. A chilling outlook.

As he tried to come up with solutions for these challenges, Diffie's renewed interest in cryptography slowly became an obsession. He was further spurred on by reading *The Codebreakers,* a 1967 book by David Kahn that comprehensively chronicled the entire history of cryptography and was partly based on intel from two NSA defectors who had fled to the Soviet Union; he became more and more determined to uncover whatever cryptographic techniques and insights were still being suppressed by intelligence agencies.

Yet, this wasn't the only reason why the AI Lab hacker ultimately decided to go *all in.*

Touring America

When Diffie in the summer of 1973 visited an old friend, the Brooklyn-based animal trainer Mary Fischer, he didn't expect to fall in love. But when he did, his plans changed drastically. Instead of returning to the West Coast, he decided to quit his job at Stanford's AI Lab to spend time with his new girlfriend on the road. The two set out to tour the country in an old Datsun 510.

Incidentally, this also gave Diffie the time and opportunity to really commit himself to discovering superior cryptographic techniques. Living off his savings, he took Fischer with him on a quest for clues. He visited *The Codebreakers* author David Kahn in Great Neck on Long Island, scoured libraries for reference works, and set up appointments with cryptography experts in academia and private enterprise throughout the US.

Diffie was hoping to eventually develop a *logically formal theory*, a mathematical system to serve as a foundation for cryptography. To do this, he believed he had to start from the basics.

The simplest cryptographic phenomenon he could find was the *one-way function*: an equation where the solution is easy to calculate in one direction, but much harder to calculate in reverse.

A very basic type of one-way function—a *polynomial*—should be familiar to anyone who studied algebra in high school, and could for example look like $x^2 - 5x + 8$. If the input x in this example is 16, it's relatively easy to calculate that the equation would produce the output 184. However, when given only the output of 184, the equation can't be used in reverse as easily to calculate that the original input (x) was 16. A one-way function is the mathematical equivalent of a one-way street.

Furthermore, Diffie learned about the concept of a *trapdoor*, which, it was speculated, could be a part of some types of one-way functions. A trapdoor was essentially a secret piece of information—typically another equation—that would make the reverse calculation easy as well. If the equation in the example above contained a trapdoor, the output 184 could be used to calculate the input 16 as easily as it originally was to produce 184 from 16. If a one-way function is a one-way street, the trapdoor function would be a secret tunnel in the opposite direction.

These concepts fascinated Diffie. One-way functions and trapdoors intuitively seemed like something that could be of great use in the field of cryptography—though he didn't know exactly how.

Through a mutual acquaintance, Diffie's hunch eventually led him to Martin Hellman, a thirty-year-old assistant professor at Stanford. Hellman shared both Diffie's interest in cryptography and his ideological disposition that this technology should be much more widely available: he had just turned down a job offer from the NSA because he wanted his work to benefit the public. And Hellman, too, had been contemplating how one-way functions could be more broadly applied in the field of cryptography.

When Diffie and Hellman first met in 1974 and discussed the idea at the latter's Stanford office, they didn't immediately find the solution they were looking for. But in each other they found someone else who was interested in the same problem. From then on, the two of them would combine their brainpower by bouncing ideas off each other and sharing new insights.

When Diffie after more than a year of traveling decided to settle down in the Bay Area, he and Hellman became good friends and, soon enough, colleagues: Hellman hired Diffie as a part-time researcher at the university.

Public Key Cryptography

It was on a regular afternoon, while housesitting for his former employer John McCarthy, that it finally hit Diffie.

Two keys.

The solution was to use *two* keys.

Cryptographers had traditionally considered it obvious that encryption keys needed to be secret since they also served as decryption keys. But ignoring this "self-evident truth," Diffie came up with the idea of *key pairs*. Instead of just one secret key, everyone would have two keys: a private key that should indeed remain secret, and a public key that could be freely shared.

Diffie reckoned that the keys should be mathematically linked, where the public key would essentially be derived from the private key through some kind of one-way function. His vision was that a sender—let's call her "Alice," as cryptographers like to do—would encrypt a message with her private key, after which the intended recipient, "Bob," could decrypt it with her public key.

If Bob could indeed decrypt the message with Alice's public key, it would prove that the message had been encrypted with Alice's private key specifically. In effect, therefore, this would enable a form of authentication: the encrypted version of a message would serve as Alice's digital signature.

Such digital signatures would in fact be even more powerful than written signatures, because a cryptographic signature would only be valid in combination with the precise piece of data that was signed. If a digital contract is altered after it is signed, the cryptographic signature would no longer match. In a way, both the signature *and* the data itself would be impossible to forge.

What's more, Diffie figured that the inverse could work as well. Alice could encrypt a message to Bob with *Bob's* public key, after which Bob— and only Bob—would be able to decrypt it with his private key. *Public key cryptography* promised to offer both digital authentication as well as secure communication!

When Hellman had the concept explained to him that evening, he agreed that Diffie potentially came up with something significant—even if the idea only existed in draft stage, and the exact math still had to be worked out. In the following weeks, the duo laid out some early mathematical groundwork to make the idea more tangible.

It led to Diffie and Hellman's first coauthored paper. "Multiuser Cryptographic Techniques," was published in the spring of 1976, to be presented at the National Computer Conference in New York shortly after. In it, the duo acknowledged that big questions remained unanswered at that time; they didn't yet know how encryption or decryption would exactly work— nor how a public key would be derived from a private key.

"At present we have neither a proof that public key systems exist," Diffie and Hellman admitted in their paper, "nor a demonstration system."[74]

Still, they announced that they were working on something big; they put the idea of public key cryptography out there.

Ralph Merkle

The paper had barely been published when Hellman received a letter from a graduate student at the University of California, Berkeley.

The student had written a paper of his own, his letter explained. However: "The people with whom I try and discuss it either fail completely to understand what's going on, or regard any attempt at solution as impossible," he wrote, his frustration dripping from the page. Concluding: "The possibility arises of doing joint work, and I would be interested in this possibility."[75]

Signed: Ralph C. Merkle.

Although about seven or eight years younger than Diffie and Hellman, Merkle's story was not so different from theirs. He'd always been good with numbers, consistently topped every math class, and he'd taken a keen interest in computers since starting university.

He was introduced to the field of cryptography during a class on computer security in his last term as an undergrad. But as the lecturer went over the Caesar cipher and other forms of symmetric encryption, he had immediately realized that the required in-person key exchange made the approach very limited. Merkle believed that in a world where more and more communication would go digital, a better solution was desperately needed.

Rather than traversing the country in a quest for answers, however, Merkle had limited his search for a solution to his own creative mind. And he eventually came up with a scheme that could, at least to an extent, do the trick.

This is how it would work.

First, Alice would create a great many cryptographic puzzles, perhaps millions or even more. The solution to each puzzle would consist of a unique number and an equally unique secret key. Alice herself would already know the solution to each puzzle; she'd know which numbers are matched with which secret keys. But each individual puzzle could also be solved by anyone else, with a little bit of computing power.

Alice would then send all the puzzles to Bob. Bob would in turn randomly pick one puzzle, and solve it with a bit of computing power to find the unique number and the corresponding secret key. He would then send the number (but not the corresponding secret key) back to Alice.

Based on the unique number returned by Bob, Alice would immediately know which secret key Bob found along with it. This secret key would then be the encryption key they'd share. Like any other symmetric encryption key, it would be used to encrypt and decrypt messages between them.

An eavesdropper, meanwhile, could have seen all the puzzles that Alice sent to Bob, and he could also have seen which unique number Bob sent back to Alice, but he still wouldn't know the corresponding secret key.

To figure that out, the eavesdropper would actually have to randomly start solving all the puzzles (*brute force*) to try and find that one unique number that Bob sent back, which would then also reveal the secret key Alice and Bob settled on. This would be a computationally expensive process, however. Depending on the amount of puzzles that were initially created (and the difficulty to solve each puzzle), it could require a lot of processing power and take a long time.

Alice and Bob would therefore have an asymmetric advantage against the eavesdropper. They hardly needed to perform any computations at all to agree on a secret key, while the eavesdropper would have to perform many computations before he'd be able to listen in to their conversation.

This solution did, however, require that Alice and Bob share quite a bit of data in the form of puzzles. And the security of this solution would scale linearly with the total number of puzzles. To make the scheme ten times harder to crack, they would have to share ten times as many puzzles; to make the scheme a hundred times harder to crack, they'd have to share a hundred times as many puzzles, and so on. In practice, regular users' data resource limitations suggest that a well-funded attacker with a super-computer could in many cases decrypt messages within a matter of days.

Nonetheless, Merkle had conceived a solution that allowed two people to communicate fairly privately without the need to meet in person before-hand. Even if not perfect, he believed that this key-exchange technique was certainly novel, and potentially useful.

But Merkle hadn't been able to convince anyone else. His idea received little praise at Berkeley, while his paper was rejected by *Communications of the ACM*, the prestigious journal of the Association for Computing Machinery (ACM). Sending secret keys over an insecure network was considered unacceptable by reviewers. Besides, they had pointed out, no prior literature had established key-exchange as an important problem in the first place.

Unable to convey its potential to anyone around him, the disappointed student was about to give up on his idea altogether—until he got his hands on a preprint of Diffie and Hellman's paper. Merkle was quick to recognize that the duo was trying to solve a similar problem. It represented a form of vindication that he desperately needed, and he decided to reach out.

Unlike Merkle's Berkely professor and the journal reviewers, Diffie and Hellman admired the ingenuity of the proposal. Whereas Diffie's idea revolved around key pairs, Merkle's approach cleverly allowed Alice and Bob to settle on a shared key in such a way that only they could (easily) calculate what this key is. Although Diffie and Hellman ultimately concluded that the scheme was not robust enough for what they were trying to achieve, the puzzle scheme did invite them to look at the problem from a new angle.

Hellman decided to take Merkle on as a summer intern, where he helped the Berkeley student redraft his paper into a version that would eventually be accepted by the ACM journal. Moreover, having proved himself to be a creative and clever thinker, Merkle was also looped into further conversations about public key cryptography.

Now, three minds were thinking about the problem.

The Breakthrough

It was Hellman who finally made the pieces click.

Although his solution didn't tick all the boxes he and Diffie were aiming for—there was no digital authentication—Hellman came up with a scheme that would let two parties communicate privately, without the need to share an encryption key in person beforehand. Similar to Merkle's puzzle scheme, the idea behind the *Diffie-Hellman key exchange* (as this solution would come to be known) is that Alice and Bob can settle on a *shared secret*: essentially, a symmetric encryption key that only they know.

To generate this shared secret, Alice and Bob would use key pairs, the idea first suggested by Diffie. Their private keys would essentially just be very big random numbers—so big that not even the fastest supercomputers would be able to guess them in a million years. Each public key, then, could be derived from a private key through a one-way function. Calculating the public key from the private key would be easy, while calculating the private key from the public key would basically be impossible.

To produce the shared secret, then, both Alice and Bob would each multiply their own *private* key with the other person's *public* key. This should give both of them the same result: the shared secret.

This works because, in both cases, the shared secret is essentially a combination of both private keys put through a one-way function *once*. When Alice multiplies her private key with Bob's public key, the one-way function is already "embedded" in Bob's public key, and the opposite is true when Bob multiplies his private key with Alice's public key. Although Alice and Bob perform the math in a different "order," the outcome has to be the same.

(As a simplified analogy, this is similar to how the outcomes of 2 × (3 × 5) and 3 × (2 × 5) are both 30. In this analogy, 2 is Alice's private key, 3 is Bob's private key, × 5 is the one-way function, and 30 is the shared secret.)

Meanwhile, no one else would be able to generate Alice and Bob's shared secret. After all, if the two *public* keys are multiplied, the result is essentially a combination of both private keys, but put through a one-way function *twice*—one time too many. (Continuing the analogy, this would compare to (2 × 5) × (3 × 5), which would result in 150 instead of 30.)

Generating the shared secret, therefore, requires access to either Alice's or Bob's private key. As long as they'd keep these a secret, the two of them could enjoy mathematically guaranteed private communication.

Defying an entire body of knowledge, the Diffie-Hellman key exchange could realize something that was long thought impossible. With that, the technique had the potential to dramatically transform the entire field of cryptography, and the two unconventional cryptographers were well aware of this fact when they submitted their second paper, "New Directions in Cryptography," to *IEEE Transactions on Information Theory*—a prestigious scientific journal published by a professional association for electrical engineering.

"We stand today on the brink of a revolution in cryptography," Diffie and Hellmann announced in the paper, published in the journal's November 1976 edition. Foreseeing that their breakthrough would mark the beginning of a major upheaval, they continued: "theoretical developments in information theory and computer science show promise of providing provably secure cryptosystems, changing this ancient art into a science."[76]

Indeed, it soon became evident that Diffie and Hellman had opened the floodgates. A new generation of cryptographers was about to introduce a cascade of innovation into the world of crypto.

RSA

Among the first to be inspired by Diffie and Hellman's paper were three young mathematicians from MIT. United in their love for numbers and their urge to solve difficult problems, Ron Rivest, an assistant professor at the university, Adi Shamir, a visiting professor, and Leonard Adleman, a computer scientist at the same institute, set out to design a one-way function specifically for public key cryptography.

They succeeded a few months later, in 1977.

RSA, as their algorithm was called (each letter representing one of its inventors), leveraged centuries-old mathematical insights in prime factorization—multiplying of prime numbers—to create a one-way function with an embedded trapdoor. By wrapping calculations around a maximum number, two subsequent, but different multiplications would always return the original input. In effect, the first multiplication would encrypt the data, while the second would decrypt it.

As a simplified analogy, it's like doing math on a clock. Since a clock only counts to twelve, ten plus five results in three. Three plus seven, in turn, brings us back to ten. In this analogy, ten is the original data, adding five represents the act of encrypting, the initial result of three is the encrypted data, and adding seven again represents the trapdoor function, and the act of decrypting.

RSA brought encrypting and decrypting messages in line with Diffie's original idea. If Alice wanted to send Bob an encrypted message, she could simply encrypt the message using Bob's public key. Bob could then decrypt the message just with his private key. Bob no longer required Alice's public key, nor did either of them need a shared secret.

Perhaps even more importantly, the algorithm worked in reverse just as well. Two subsequent multiplications always return the original number, regardless which of the two multiplications is done first. Continuing the clock analogy where ten plus five plus seven got us back to ten, the reverse—ten plus seven plus five—gets us back to ten just the same.

In practice, this meant that a private key could be used to encrypt data, which the corresponding public key could then decrypt. With that, RSA enabled a cryptographic signature scheme: Alice can encrypt a message, which Bob (or anyone else) can decrypt using her public key, proving that the message was really encrypted with Alice's private key.

Where the Diffie-Hellman key exchange had enabled private communication, RSA for the first time also facilitated a form of digital authentication.

And last but not least, RSA security scaled (roughly) exponentially. Adding just a few digits to the original prime numbers used in this scheme would make it magnitudes more difficult to later find out which prime numbers were used—and therefore, magnitudes more difficult to break the encryption. With public keys so small that even casual computer users could easily share them, security was mathematically guaranteed for millions of years.

With RSA, Diffie's vision for public key cryptography had truly arrived.

David Chaum

Another young cryptographer inspired by Diffie and Hellman's breakthrough was David Chaum.

Growing up in the suburbs of Los Angeles in the 1960s and early 1970s, Chaum had developed an innate interest in security technology already as a teenager. This started with hardware, like door locks, burglar alarms, and physical safes, which by the time he was a young adult culminated in the design of a new type of lock. Chaum even came close to selling his design to a major manufacturer.

But his interest had by then also started expanding into the relatively new field of information technology. Hopping between universities—he attended the University of California, Los Angeles even before graduating high school, switched to the University of Sonora in Mexico to be close to his girlfriend at the time, and finally graduated from the University of California, San Diego—Chaum studied computer science and math, and by the late 1970s learned about cryptography and the recent breakthroughs in that field.

Chaum naturally recognized the potential of public key cryptography because he, too, had seen glimpses of the future. He foresaw that computers would become increasingly common, to the point where every household would have one installed in their home. And as ARPAnet was slowly starting to transform into the (more generally accessible) early internet, he expected electronic communication to transform the world.

But like Diffie before him, Chaum also recognized that this transformation could lead to a rather dystopian future. He understood that if messages, documents, or files are sent over the internet, all this data would be at risk of being monitored, intercepted, and exploited by tyrants on a scale never seen before. Because people's behavior changes when they think that might be watched, mass surveillance would create a prison of the mind, breed conformity, and ultimately destroy basic liberties, Chaum worried.

"Cyberspace doesn't have all the physical constraints," Chaum later explained to a reporter from technology magazine *Wired*. "There are no walls. . . . it's a different, scary, weird place, and with identification it's a panopticon nightmare. Right? Everything you do could be known to anyone else, could be recorded forever. It's antithetical to the basic principle underlying the mechanisms of democracy."[77]

But he recognized there was now an alternative; another potential future. Chaum realized that the brand new developments in cryptography could be turned into tools for protection. Society was at a crossroads, and innovations like public key cryptography offered hope for a world where people were empowered to control their own data.

In part because he knew Ralph Merkle had attended Berkeley (but unaware that Merkle's initial puzzle scheme hadn't been received particularly well there), Chaum chose the Bay Area university to pursue a PhD. Here, he witnessed from up close how the field of cryptography was by the turn of the decade evolving from a niche interest exclusive to small university departments and academic journals into a small revolution in the field of computing, pushed forward by a dedicated and growing community of like-minded mathematicians.

This resulted in the first-ever *Crypto* conference in 1981, hosted at the University of California, Santa Barbara. The field's greatest innovators—Diffie, Hellman, Merkle, Rivest, Shamir, Adelman—and about fifty other cryptographers attended, with many of them meeting in person for the first time. They presented their latest papers, discussed potential improvements to existing schemes, or simply got to know each other a bit better as they spent an evening barbecuing on the beach.

However, this all happened to the stark dismay of the NSA. Like the new wave of cryptographers gathered at Crypto 1981, the government agency, too, recognized the potential of public key cryptography. But rather than sharing in the optimism and excitement at the conference, people within the intelligence community were concerned that strong encryption could jeopardize their entire modus operandi. They wanted to halt this cryptographic revolution in its tracks, and in the wake of the conference, the NSA began issuing warnings to scientific organizations not to facilitate presentations of the kind that Crypto 1981 had so openly showcased.

When he learned about this, Chaum took it upon himself to fight back, personally taking the lead to ensure the conference wouldn't remain a one-time event. Equipped with a list of names and contact information provided by Adleman, the graduate student started reaching out to all the big names in the field of crypto. Careful not to draw any attention from the NSA—he sent out physical letters or met in person, but avoided phone conversations on the topic—Chaum eventually managed to get everyone to return to Santa Barbara for Crypto 1982, while also organizing a European convention (*Eurocrypt*) in Germany that same year.

On top of that, Chaum founded the International Association for Cryptologic Research, a nonprofit organization tasked with furthering research in cryptography, which he announced at Crypto 1982—again, much to the chagrin of the NSA.

Yet, Chaum's greatest contributions to the field of cryptography weren't the events he organized or the organization he founded, but the tools he designed.

Remailers

Public key cryptography allowed two people who'd never met before to exchange messages that only they could read. This offered privacy of communication—a breakthrough.

But it was not in itself a panacea, Chaum realized. Even with public key cryptography, a significant privacy leak remained: traffic analysis could reveal who converses with whom, and when.

Such *metadata* could reveal more about someone than they might feel comfortable with. An investigative journalist might not want to reveal his sources, for example. Or citizens of countries with authoritarian regimes might not want anyone to know that they communicate with a political dissident. Or maybe an employee reaching out to a competing firm to enquire about job opportunities prefers his boss not to find out that he's been in touch with this company.

In his 1981 paper "Untraceable Electronic Mail, Return Addresses, and Digital Pseudonyms," Chaum proposed a solution to this problem, also based on public key cryptography.[78]

This is how it worked.

If Alice wanted to send Bob a message, she'd first take his public key, and encrypt the message with it. This way, only Bob should be able to decrypt it.

But she wouldn't send the message to Bob directly; a snoop monitoring their connections could then see that the two are communicating, which is what Alice is trying to avoid.

Instead, Alice would take the encrypted message and attach Bob's email address to it. She'd then encrypt this whole package—the encrypted message for Bob and his email address—one more time, but this time using the public key associated with a special mixing server. The message would now have two layers of encryption: one layer for the original message, and another layer for the whole package. Alice would then send this encrypted package to the mixer.

The mixing server would in turn decrypt the package with its private key, to find the original encrypted message, and Bob's email address. The mixer would use this to forward the encrypted message to Bob, who'd then decrypt it to read Alice's original message. As an intermediary, the mixer broke the direct link between Alice and Bob, making it harder for the snoop to conclude that they were communicating. And unless it's made clear from the contents of the message, Bob himself would not know it came from Alice, either.

This basic scheme does the job as long as the mixer is honest, and can be trusted not to reveal to the snoop (or to Bob) that it first received the encrypted package from Alice. But Chaum explained that it's not even necessary to trust the mixer.

To mitigate the risk of an untrustworthy mixer, Alice could use several mixers. Alice would in that case send an encrypted package to mixer 1, which mixer 1 could decrypt to find mixer 2's email address and another encrypted message, which mixer 2 could in turn decrypt to find mixer 3's email address and yet another-encrypted message, which mixer 3 could then decrypt to indeed find Bob's email address and one more encrypted message, which Bob could finally decrypt to read the original message. By stripping off one layer of encryption each, and forwarding the package to the next recipient, the mixers would know who they received the package from and where they forwarded it to, but none of them would know where the package originated from and who the final recipient was.

A snoop monitoring Bob's communication, likewise, might know that mixer 3 ultimately sent the message to Bob, but even if mixer 3 shares this information with the snoop on request (or court order), it only helps the snoop one step down the line. If even one of the mixers is unwilling to cooperate, the trail ends. (And if the mixers reside in different jurisdictions, even law enforcement from any particular country might have a hard time tracing the origin of a message.)

With that, Chaum had laid the crucial conceptual groundwork for what would later come to be known as *remailers*.

And his contributions to the field of cryptography wouldn't end there . . .

Chapter 5:
Denationalization of Money

ECONOMIC DEPRESSION AND currency devaluations had paved the way for fascism and, ultimately, to the Second World War.

Yet, Friedrich Hayek sadly observed that many of his peers in academia at the time failed to recognize the harm that monetary policy had done. Instead, many intellectuals of the day attributed the rise of fascism to the failure of free markets. As economists, political scientists, and other academics in the West considered alternative ways to organize society, socialist ideas were gaining popularity—a development that Hayek deemed downright dangerous.

To counter the trend, the Austrian took it upon himself to explain why socialism wasn't the answer, but, rather, part of the problem. The resulting book, *The Road to Serfdom*, took a more political approach, although heavily informed by economic insights like the economic calculation problem. Written and published during the war years, its core thesis was that collectivist ideologies—including *both* fascism and socialism—tend to lead to totalitarianism. It would become the most successful book of Hayek's career.

It was, perhaps, a good time for Hayek to shift more of his time and energy away from economics into the political realm. After two decades of debate and rivalry, it was becoming evident that not his, but Keynes's ideas on monetary policy were winning hearts and minds within universities, policy institutes, and government institutions. If free market ideology was to survive at all, it was probably going to be based on Keynesian doctrine.

This was confirmed when representatives from the Allied nations, confident that they would win the war, met at the Mount Washington Hotel in Bretton Woods, New Hampshire, in 1944. Participants were to design a new monetary order for the postwar period, and Keynes was invited to represent the United Kingdom. Hayek, who had by then attained British nationality as well, was not invited at all.

The main outcome of the Bretton Woods conference could be considered a reinstatement of the gold exchange standard, but in contrast to the prewar classical gold standard it was heavily centered around the US dollar. International trade would be conducted in dollars, while these dollars could in turn be redeemed for gold: one troy ounce per $35. Other national currencies would establish fixed exchange rates against the dollar, and central banks were expected to steer interest rates in order to stabilize their national currencies.

Bretton Woods was also the birthplace of two new international monetary institutions, with Keynes playing an instrumental role in their establishment. The first of these, the International Monetary Fund (IMF), was tasked with overseeing international exchange rates, and could lend money to countries in financial distress. The second, the World Bank, would also make loans, but with a stronger focus on rebuilding postwar Europe (and later other developing countries).

The *Bretton Woods system*, as it was eventually called, started being rolled out shortly after the Axis powers were defeated in 1945—though only in the West. While the Soviet Union had sent representatives to Bretton Woods, the communist state ultimately declined to ratify the agreement, charging that the IMF and World Bank were "branches of Wall Street"[79]; instead, it usurped many Eastern European countries after the war. It represented the beginning of the Cold War, where (a Keynesian variant of) free-market capitalism in the United States and Western Europe would in many ways compete with the socialist doctrine in the East.

Keynes would not be around to study the effects of the Bretton Woods system and the institutions of this new monetary order, however. The economist passed away shortly after the war, in 1946.

Although Hayek had outlived his rival, he recognized that Keynes's ideas were favored over his own, and he didn't feel that the new generation of Keynesian economists were very interested in honest and meaningful debate. The Austrian decided to leave the London School of Economics to join the University of Chicago, where he largely withdrew from the field of economics and indeed shifted his focus towards the realm of politics and philosophy instead.

The Age of Keynes

By the midway point of the twentieth century, the "age of Keynes" had truly arrived in the capitalist West. Economic policy was made by governments, central banks, and other institutions, while economists tried to further work out the theoretical mechanics behind fiscal planning, stabilization policies, and monetary stimuli. London School of Economics Professor William Phillips, for example, introduced the Phillips curve, which showed that inflation and unemployment were inversely correlated. It was exactly as Keynesian doctrine suggested: more government spending meant more jobs.

Politicians were given the theoretical justification to spend the economy out of an economic downturn, and it seemed like a cure-all solution for a while, as Keynesian policies were being rolled out all across the Western world. In the UK, Prime Minister Winston Churchill had in 1944 elevated full employment to a national policy goal. In the United States, Franklin D. Roosevelt's successor, President Harry S. Truman, in 1946 signed the Employment Act into law, making the executive branch of government responsible for managing the economy. And in Europe, the postwar recovery program informally known as the Marshall Plan had turned the entire western half of the continent into something of a Keynesian laboratory.

A little later in the United States, Truman's successor Dwight D. Eisenhower was the first president to truly apply Keynesian economics to its fullest extent. Faced with several short recessions in the mid-1950s, the president fought unemployment by making big investments in interstate highway infrastructure. And after the Soviet Union managed to send satellite Sputnik into orbit, Eisenhower followed it up with significant cash infusions into NASA's space program. It appeared to work as intended; the American economy prospered.

But when, towards the end of his presidency, the time came for Eisenhower to cut back on spending, this almost immediately resulted in a new depression. And the American public was not happy about this. Eisenhower had all the tools at his disposal to curb the trend, they figured, but this time failed to act.

By the time the elections for Eisenhower's successor came around, the economic downturn had become a big theme in the presidential campaigns. Where the young Democratic candidate John F. Kennedy rallied his supporters under the slogan "Let's get this country moving again," Republican candidate and sitting Vice President Richard Nixon was struggling to distance himself from Eisenhower's fiscally conservative approach towards the end of his second term. When Kennedy ultimately won the race with an incredibly short margin, a defeated Nixon was left convinced that he would have won the election if it wasn't for Eisenhower's spending cuts.[80]

In office, Kennedy acknowledged that he would generously invest into the economy on Keynesian grounds. He quickly revitalized Eisenhower's initial spending spree, infusing cash into the American space program, while spending lavishly on the military as well. After the president's assassination just a few years later, in 1963, his vice president and successors Lyndon B. Johnson continued in the same vein, with the Vietnam War representing a major new money sink.

In 1968, by the end of Johnson's presidency, Nixon was ready for another run for office. And this time, he won. As he took over the reins from Johnson, Nixon—a fiscal conservative at heart—initially appeared ready and willing to put a stop to this Keynesian freehandedness, pointing out that the government had for years been spending tens of billions of dollars more than it received in taxes.

But when Nixon's spending cuts immediately resulted in a mild economic recession, the president decided to play ball. He declared himself a Keynesian, announced a full employment plan, and proposed an expansionary budget to stimulate the economy. Nixon had taken away a valuable lesson during his failed bid for the presidency a decade earlier, and was ready to accept the new political reality.[81]

As the president stated in the 1970 State of the Union:

"I recognize the political popularity of spending programs, and particularly in an election year."[82]

Keynesian doctrine actually required government spending as well as spending cuts: spending to give the economy a boost, and cuts when this is no longer necessary, in order to avoid runaway inflation. The problem, it was now becoming clear, was that while increased spending could win elections, spending cuts did not. Nixon had learned the hard way that it was better to stick to the more popular spending stage of the Keynesian cycle, and conveniently ignore the part of the doctrine that prescribed when cuts need to be made.

This problem had, of course, been foreseen. Hayek always contended that Keynes's biggest oversight arguably wasn't in economics, but in politics: elected representatives generally couldn't be expected to apply the level of discipline that a *countercyclical* approach required.

The Nixon Shock

The spurious spending spree by Nixon and several of his predecessors could in some way be explained as an execution of Keynesian doctrine. But by the 1970s, it started to make some of the biggest dollar holders uncomfortable. It was becoming increasingly clear that the United States was living beyond its means, and was issuing and spending far more money than it could account for in gold.

Some of the countries with large dollar reserves therefore eventually decided to start tapering off their paper notes. They wanted to convert dollars into gold—which was easier said than done, since moving and storing large amounts of gold was a serious logistical challenge. French President Georges Pompidou eventually sent a full-blown battleship to New York to retrieve his country's gold from the local Federal Reserve bank. There were strong indications that the British were about to follow suit.

Until on August 15, 1971, Nixon put a stop to it.

Today referred to as the "Nixon shock," the president announced in a tele-vised speech the "suspension" of the convertibility from dollars to gold, "in the interest of monetary stability, and in the best interest of the United States."[83] With no prior warning, Nixon via Executive Order single-hand-edly planted a bomb under the Bretton Woods system: countries that held dollars as part of their reserves could no longer convert the paper notes to precious metal.

Since the dollar was the only currency that was convertible to gold under the Bretton Woods system, this immediately marked the end of gold-backed currency altogether. What remained were national, unbacked currencies— fiat currencies. When six European countries shortly thereafter agreed to tie the value of their currencies together and let them float against the dollar, the Bretton Woods system was effectively abandoned entirely.[84]

Nixon, meanwhile, was set on making the economy boom in time for the 1972 elections, and he figured that he could accomplish this by get-ting the Federal Reserve to lower interest rates. Cheap money would spur inflation, and therefore lead to lower unemployment, the Phillips curve had shown. Nixon appointed his economic councilor Arthur Burns as chairman of the Federal Reserve and, having removed the limitations pre-viously posed by the gold coverage ratio, immediately put the pressure on the new chairman.

Nixon got his way. He won reelection. And by 1973, the official, CPI-based inflation numbers had increased to 9.6 percent, to further rise into double-digit figures in the years that followed.[85]

Inflation

Hayek had argued that artificially low interest rates would result in unsustainable economic booms, and that the following bust merely rep-resented a painful correction, where the market was best left alone to find a more natural equilibrium. Keynesians instead prescribed that the bust should be countered with government spending to get the econ-omy back on track.

Hayek always acknowledged that such Keynesian spending could indeed work in the short term. New money, spent into the economy by the government, could make it appear as if the economy remained fairly stable. But underneath that veneer of extended prosperity, Hayek had warned, would lie a darker economic reality: money creation was merely prolonging the misallocation of resources caused by the initial disturbance.

This was perhaps Hayek's biggest objection to this type of inflation: it would after some time become very difficult to revert. Inflation is addictive, the economist warned; once the economy gets used to easy money, it will only require more of it to sustain its artificially high level of employment.

Indeed, in an early stage, inflation does appear to benefit the economy. When it first sets in, it pushes prices up to higher levels than businesses had foreseen. This would come as a very welcome surprise, as they can sell their products for more money than anticipated and enjoy bigger profits. Businesses that struggled and would otherwise have failed, could keep afloat thanks to the unexpected boom.

But if the inflation persists over a longer period of time, Hayek explained, businesses will eventually have to factor in the expectation of higher future prices. To remain competitive, they will need to increase their investment in the production process, which then drives up the price of capital and labor as well, right up to the point where overall profit margins are back to where they started.

This also means that those businesses that were struggling before inflation set in, once again come at risk of failing.

To prevent these businesses from going under, and to extend the positive effect that the new money had brought, even higher inflation is needed. Higher inflation will push up prices even more than anticipated, thus once again representing a welcome surprise for businesses.

But if this higher inflation also persists, it will of course eventually have to be factored into the production process again, and the businesses that were struggling would once more be at risk of failing.

These businesses could perhaps be saved by even more inflation, but at the end of the day, Hayek warned, new money can only provide short-term stimuli, while more and more of it would be needed over time. It would inevitably result in an economy with both high inflation and economic stagnation.

Hayek:

"And since, if inflation has already lasted for some time, a great many activities will have become dependent on its continuance at a progressive rate, we will have a situation in which, in spite of rising prices, many firms will be making losses, and there may be substantial unemployment. Depression with rising prices is a typical consequence of a mere braking of the increase in the rate of inflation once the economy has become geared to a certain rate of inflation."[86]

In economic terms, this outcome—an economy with both currency inflation and economic stagnation—is called stagflation.

The Cantillon Effect

Hayek had been very concerned about inflation (and the eventual prospect of stagflation) for several reasons.

For one, inflation can distort the intertemporal price system. Perhaps most importantly, it can upset the credit markets, as debtors and creditors are affected very differently by inflation: debtors benefit if the real value of their debts decrease, while creditors suffer because the money they'll later be repaid will be worth less than the money they lent out.

A second, and for Hayek arguably even more devious aspect of inflation, is that it skews accounting practices. Inflation can bloat profit figures, where the return on investment appears higher than it effectively is. And while smart individuals can perhaps include currency depreciation in their profit-loss calculations, the economist pointed out that tax inspectors will still insist on taxing the "pseudo-profits." Inflation essentially results in an implicit tax increase.

But Hayek's biggest concern with inflation was a concern that had already been described in the eighteenth century by the Irish-French economist Richard Cantillon, and had come to be known as the *Cantillon effect*.[87]

The problem, in short, is that new money is first brought into circulation by spending it into the economy. And when the new money is first spent, it is spent into an economy that still uses the "old" prices, which do not yet reflect the additional money created. Spending this money, then, bids up prices of the first goods or services that are purchased with it. The businesses that sell these goods or services enjoy extra profits.

These businesses get to re-spend the new money next, while again, they get to do so in an economy where most prices haven't yet adjusted to reflect the new money supply. The businesses that receive *these* payments, in turn, get to spend it into an economy where some prices have been adjusted, but not all; still a benefit. This goes on until the new money has spread all throughout the economy; prices increase in one part of the economy first, only after which it ripples throughout the rest of society.

This means that those who are "close" to the source of money get to enjoy it before prices are adjusted: they experience an increase in their real income. Those at the outer edge of the ripple, meanwhile, see all prices rise before getting hold of the new money. When they do finally receive some of it, this no longer offers a comparative benefit, And while waiting they experienced a fall in their real income.

As Hayek summarized Cantillon's findings:

"[. . .] only those persons are benefited by the increase of money whose incomes rise early, while to persons whose incomes rise later the increase of the quantity of money is harmful."[88]

Gold producers could historically be found at the heart of the Cantillon effect. But as the role of gold in the financial system was de-emphasized and Keynesianism took hold, governments would increasingly claim their place at the center of the money creation process instead. Whenever governments would expand the money supply to stimulate the economy, it would disproportionately benefit the government itself and, through the Cantillon effect, it would also benefit government employees, government contractors, and those businesses that operate in closest economic proximity to the government, like financial institutions.

This would be reflected in higher prices in the parts of the economy close to the government, which would in turn attract more resources. Importantly, however, these resources wouldn't flow to that part of the economy because that's where they offer the most value to individuals in society. Instead, the Cantillon effect would skew resource allocation towards the source of new money—that is, in practice, towards the government and the financial sector.

As the addictive effect of inflation requires that there is more and more of it, an excessive amount of business activity would over time cluster around the government, utterly dependent on the new money creation, but adding little to no value to society. Hayek foresaw a persistent misallocation of resources in favor of the state—and at the expense of the rest of the economy.

And ultimately, continued excessive money creation can lead to the destruction of whatever remains of the free market system altogether, the economist warned. High inflation could so seriously disturb prices and, therefore, the allocation of resources, that it would eventually create strong public pressure for the imposition of price controls.

A disastrous outcome, in Hayek's view:

"Open inflation is bad enough, but inflation repressed by controls is even worse: it is the real end of the market economy."[89]

Removing the Government

Keynesians—which by that time meant almost all mainstream economists—had not shared Hayek's concern about inflation and, especially, stagflation. They in fact believed that stagflation was impossible. As the Phillips curve had shown, inflation and unemployment were *inversely* correlated; higher inflation would mean lower unemployment.

But Nixon's policies were starting to prove these Keynesians wrong. A combination of low interest rate policies and rising oil prices due to international tensions was by the early 1970s quickly driving inflation up, but now, economic prospects were simultaneously deteriorating all across the Western world. The decade would be characterized by stagflation. With it came a crisis of faith in the Keynesian school of thought.

Hayek had in the leadup to the 1970s mostly focused on politics: he'd for example explained how spontaneous order also applied to the emergence of the body of law, which had made him more of a political moderate compared to some of the more hardline libertarian Austrian economists. But by the mid-1970s, he decided that he couldn't stay quiet any longer. After a long academic career that had brought him from the University of Chicago to the University of Freiburg and finally the University of —Salzburg, Hayek returned to writing about monetary policy.

Keynesian doctrine and its misguided ideas about money were destroying the world economy, the Austrian believed, and making people aware of this had once again become a priority for him. Well into his seventies, Hayek was as determined and uncompromising as ever, now describing inflation not just as harmful, but also as downright unethical, likening it to theft. Money had been broken for a very long time, Hayek contended, and it was time that it got fixed.

Although decades of spurious spending by governments had led to stagflation, Hayek considered it too easy to simply blame the politicians responsible. He believed that the problem lay deeper. Government spending was popular because of the short-term benefits it could provide. All of that currency creation happened in democratic societies, essentially by popular demand. As long as the government and its institutions were the gatekeepers of the currency, influential interest groups would eventually sway politicians to leverage such a powerful tool to their benefit.

Hayek therefore concluded that governments should not be the gatekeepers of money at all:

"A good money, like a good law, must operate without regard to the effects that decisions of the issuer will have on known groups or individuals," Hayek wrote.[90] "Even with the best will in the world, no government can resist this pressure [from such groups or individuals] unless it can point to a firm barrier it cannot cross."[91]

Gold, at least in theory, could offer such a hard barrier. Ideally, gold would then itself be used as currency, rather than stored in bank vaults where it would enable fractional reserve banking. But the impracticality of using gold directly in exchange, and the challenges of storing it securely, probably meant that this ideal was out of scope.

A gold-backed currency—like under the classical gold standard—was more practical, but this requires trust in governments to not devalue the currency against gold, unilaterally alter the coverage ratio, or even scrap convertibility altogether. Indeed, all things that Hayek had seen governments do in his own lifetime.

Hayek had therefore always struggled to come up with the ideal solution to the problem that was money.

But now, in the late days of his career, it finally clicked for him.

"In my despair about the hopelessness of finding a politically feasible solution to what is technically the simplest possible problem, namely to stop inflation, I threw out in a lecture delivered about a year ago a somewhat startling suggestion, the further pursuit of which has opened quite unexpected new horizons," Hayek wrote by the mid-1970s.

"I could not resist pursuing the idea further, since the task of preventing inflation has always seemed to me to be of the greatest importance, not only because of the harm and suffering major inflations cause, but also because I have long been convinced that even mild inflations ultimately produce the recurring depressions and unemployment which have been a justified grievance against the free enterprise system and must be prevented if a free society is to survive."[92]

The idea was that money had to be left to the free market.

Denationalizing Money

Having first made the case in his 1975 Address to the Geneva Gold and Monetary Conference,[93] in 1976 Hayek presented the unconventional proposal at length in his book *Denationalisation of Money*. In essence, the economist argued that banks should be completely deregulated, letting them issue any money they saw fit: backed or unbacked, inflationary or deflationary, loaned into existence or not, and with any level of interest they may want to charge.

Hayek proposed to end the de facto state monopoly on money.

In such a system—a quite radical form of *free banking*—banks would compete to have customers use their money. Hayek believed that such competition was precisely what was needed to develop the best form of money: like in any free market, banks would need to provide customers with a product—in this case, money itself—with better properties than the products offered by their competitors. This competition would drive improvement, Hayek reasoned, as the market would select the best money available.

A particularly important property of any money is indeed the quantity of currency units, or more specifically, the growth rate of its supply—the major cause of inflation. Users of a currency probably would not want the supply to be diluted too fast, as that would harm the purchasing power of the units they held. Hayek believed that competition in this domain would keep currency issuers honest: if one bank would create too much of its money, customers would quickly switch to an alternative instead. Indeed, unwanted inflation would essentially be impossible, because people could simply opt out.

Whereas it had proved to be practically impossible to stop governments from inflating their national currencies to fund their expenses, Hayek reasoned that free market discipline would solve this problem quite naturally.

Speculating what money would look like in a free banking world, the economist imagined that banks would most likely target a precise level of purchasing power—perhaps based on some custom price index—by issuing more currency when a money's purchasing power increased above that target level, and by taking currency out of circulation when its purchasing power dropped below it. A big part of banks' job would be to figure out what people consider a desirable level of purchasing power for their currency, allowing them to select the type of money that best suited their needs.

"It should be in the power of each issuer of a distinct currency to regulate its quantity so as to make it most acceptable to the public—and competition would force him to do so," Hayek wrote. "Indeed, he would know that the penalty for failing to fulfill the expectations raised would be the prompt loss of the business."

He added: "[. . .] the issuing banks, guided solely by their striving for gain, would thereby serve the public interest better than any institution has ever done or could do that supposedly aimed at it."[94]

In *The Argument Refined*, the revised and enlarged version of the book published two years later, Hayek proposed that the most likely outcome of a free banking system wouldn't be a wide range of currencies with various purchasing power targets. Rather, the economist speculated that the vast majority of people would converge on one type of money that has a generally acceptable stability target. This stability target would in turn be adopted by other monies as well, Hayek expected, essentially transforming the stability target itself into something of a meta-currency that other currencies would be based on.

On face value, this could be considered a concession to the use of a consumer price index to define stability—and perhaps, to an extent, it was. But importantly, Hayek's version of the idea was not imposed or binding, nor did it include a government-appointed central body to determine how such an index ought to be established. He believed that this should be left to the free market, allowing people to freely pick whatever target they considered most stable (or otherwise desirable).

This could, indeed, include a currency with a fixed supply, or what Hayek had earlier in his career described as *neutral money*.

Unbacked Money

Hayek's proposal did not immediately win over all of his peers in the Austrian school of economics. Many Austrians believed that the market had already selected the best form of money a long time ago; in a competition spanning thousands of years, gold had won. They maintained that gold was still the best form of money, and that new currencies should at the very least be *backed* by the precious metal.

Although it would in a free banking system of course be possible to offer a gold-backed currency, Hayek did not expect most people to settle on one. While acknowledging that the market had originally selected gold as the best form of money, Hayek believed that governments had since then prevented the further development of money through monopolization and strict regulation. Hayek expected that money would improve drastically if left to the market.

"I believe we can do much better than gold ever made possible. Governments cannot do better. Free enterprise, i.e. the institutions that would emerge from a process of competition in providing good money, no doubt would," he wrote. "Convertibility [to gold] is a safeguard necessary to impose upon a monopolist, but unnecessary with competing suppliers who cannot maintain themselves in the business unless they provide money at least as advantageous to the user as anybody else."[95]

Hayek did, however, consider that new free market currencies might initially need to be backed by fiat currencies, in the same way that fiat currencies had initially been backed by gold until people learned to trust the new money. This could take a while, the economist acknowledged: "The superstition dies only slowly."[96] But eventually, people would come to understand that inflationary fiat currency keeps losing value against the private money. They'd come to realize, through economic incentives, that what they really want from money is scarcity.

That said, in a free-banking system there would be no regulation to guarantee that backed currencies would in fact be exchangeable for whatever was backing them. While specific arrangements could be binding under regular contract law, there'd be no special coverage ratio laws, and no lender of last resort. Banks would bear the cost of their own risks, and so would the customers that opted to trust these banks with their money. But this was arguably a good thing: free banking would remove moral hazard.

And by having free banks operate entirely independently from the existing financial system, Hayek believed the plan was actually feasible as well.

"Not the least advantage of the proposed abolition of the government monopoly of the issue of money is that it would provide an opportunity to extricate ourselves from the *impasse* into which this development [of banking] had led," Hayek wrote. "It would create the conditions in which responsibility for the control of the quantity of the currency is placed on agencies whose self-interest would make them control it in such a manner as to make it most acceptable to most users."[97]

In a world where banks and other financial institutions had over time come to depend on a highly regulated and tightly interwoven financial system, and where it was extremely difficult to make any meaningful changes, Hayek's solution represented a fresh start. He proposed to roll out a market-based monetary system in parallel to the established financial sector, to allow an entirely new currency system to emerge as people adopt it voluntarily.

Hayek envisioned money as spontaneous order.

Realizing Free Banking

While most countries technically did allow alternative currencies—that is, there are usually no laws that explicitly make them illegal—this is often not reflected in practical reality. Banking regulations, money transmitter licenses, AML rules, counterfeiting laws as well as taxes (like capital gains taxes on alternative currencies) offer law enforcement more than enough tools to shut down currency-issuing businesses completely, and get their operators convicted—or at the very least they can make running such businesses practically impossible.

Getting rid of all these legal and fiscal stumbling blocks—true deregulation—would encounter massive opposition, Hayek knew.

He expected that most of this opposition would come from governments: the same entities that would ultimately have to pass this deregulation and legally facilitate currency competition. Governments, Hayek figured, had every incentive not to prevent this: they were the greatest beneficiaries of the fiat currency system and the de facto monopoly on money. Hayek believed that if government money had to start competing with free market currencies, it wouldn't stand a chance; governments were therefore unlikely to welcome free banks.

Making matters even more difficult, most economists would probably protest as well, Hayek foresaw, since free market money would likely kill any possibility of manipulating interest rates to influence the currency's purchasing power and prevent deflation. Most economists in the 1970s maintained that government institutions like the Federal Reserve had an important role in managing the money supply.

"I fear that 'Keynesian' propaganda has filtered through to the masses, [and] made inflation respectable and provided agitators with arguments which the professional politicians are unable to refute," Hayek wrote in frustration.[98]

Adding to the list, the Austrian economist expected that most of the existing banks would oppose the change as well. The "old bankers," as he described them, would be unable to deal with the new challenges that a free banking system would pose on them.

"Especially in countries where competition among banks has for generations been restricted by cartel arrangements, usually tolerated and even encouraged by governments, the older generation of bankers would probably be completely unable even to imagine how the new system would operate and therefore be practically unanimous in rejecting it," Hayek wrote.[99]

With governments, economists, and bankers as anticipated opposition, Hayek certainly expected that realizing free banking was going to be an uphill battle—yet, he strongly believed that it had to be done anyway.

"[Denationalization of money is] the one way in which we may still hope to stop the continuous progress of all government toward totalitarianism which already appears to many acute observers as inevitable," Hayek wrote in the second, refined version of his book. "But the time is short. What is now urgently required is not the construction of a new system but the prompt removal of all the legal obstacles which have for two thousand years blocked the way for an evolution which is bound to throw up beneficial results which we cannot foresee."[100]

And he believed that it was possible. The key was to win over the general population. Drawing a comparison to the Free Trade Movements of the nineteenth century, the economist suggested that a new civil movement—a "Free Money Movement"—could inform people of the harm that inflation and currency manipulation caused; broader public awareness of these issues could form a stable foundation for the cause. Actual political change—deregulation of the banking sector—was presumed to follow in a later stage.

Founded by researchers George Selgin, Lawrence White, and Kevin Dowd a few years later, in the 1980s, the modern free banking school probably came closest to establishing such a movement. The Hayek-inspired advocacy group would research the history and potential for free banking, and published their findings in several books and articles.

But although the Modern Free Banking School gained a small following of like-minded, typically Austrian, economists, it failed to capture the hearts and minds of the public at large. While Hayek lived long enough to see a new generation of politicians and economists rediscover and revitalize his work on free markets and the price system, even winning him the Nobel Prize in economics in 1976, Hayek's call for monetary reform remained unanswered. Fiat currency reigned supreme until, in 1992, Hayek passed away at ninety-two years of age.

Still, his ideas were not entirely forgotten.

Hayek's work on money would soon after his death inspire a California-based group of hackers and cryptographers. But these hackers and cryptographers weren't going to try to convince politicians, economists, and bankers to change the law.

They were going to build a future without them. . .

Chapter 6:
eCash (and Trustless Time-stamps)

SINCE WHITFIELD DIFFIE and Martin Hellman introduced the Diffie-Hellman key exchange in 1976, cryptographers knew how two people who never met before could mask the content of messages between them for anyone but each other. Meanwhile, David Chaum's mix networks had by the early 1980s laid the groundwork for remailers: digital infrastructure to obscure metadata. Combined, such tools could go a long way towards offering privacy for most types of electronic communication.

But it was also Chaum who recognized that it could not yet offer privacy for a very particular type of communication: communication of *value*.

Throughout the 1970s and early '80s, banking was increasingly becoming automated. Paper bills and metal coins—by that time no longer backed by gold—were starting to be displaced by payment cards, while banks were settling debts between them electronically. With the advent of the personal computer, and in its trail, the internet, Chaum expected the digitalization of money to only accelerate. This would allow financial institutions to cut costs and improve their security, while enhancing consumer convenience.

But Chaum realized that this trend, too, could lead to dark places. If payment rails would become digital, the banks that provide them could be required by financial regulation to make users identify themselves before allowing access to these rails. Banks, and by extension the government institutions overseeing them, could then learn exactly who sends how much money to whom, where, and when.

Chaum found the prospect of mass surveillance of payments as worrisome as the mass surveillance of any other type of communication. And for good reason: someone's transaction history arguably reveals as much personal information as their text communication does, if not more.

"The foundation is being laid for a dossier society, in which computers could be used to infer individuals' lifestyles, habits, whereabouts, and associations from data collected in ordinary consumer transactions," Chaum warned. "Uncertainty about whether data will remain secure against abuse by those maintaining or tapping it can have a 'chilling effect', causing people to alter their observable activities. As computerization becomes more pervasive, the potential for these problems will grow dramatically."[101]

But, he proposed, an alternative future was possible.

"The choice between keeping information in the hands of individuals or of organizations is being made each time any government or business decides to automate another set of transactions," Chaum explained. "In one direction lies unprecedented scrutiny and control of people's lives, in the other, secure parity between individuals and organizations. The shape of society in the next century may depend on which approach predominates."[102]

A society with or without anonymous transactions would ultimately mean the difference between democracy and dictatorship, Chaum believed. What was needed, he therefore concluded, was a type of digital money that offered users a similar level of privacy as physical cash.

The world needed *electronic cash.*

The Double-Spend Problem

As Chaum started considering designs for an electronic cash system, he quickly encountered the first challenge for anyone that wants to create a digital form of money: *the double-spend problem.*[103]

Simply, if currency consists purely of digital information—ones and zeroes—it is trivial to copy. A single "digital dollar" can be replicated and sent to two different recipients . . . or even to a million different recipients, to the point where the money suffers from hyperinflation. Needless to say, this type of counterfeiting would fundamentally harm the integrity of the currency and render it worthless.

Conventional digital money systems solve this double-spending problem through a trusted party, like a bank or payment processor.

The most straightforward solution, then, is to use an account system. In such a system, all of a bank's customers have an electronic account at the bank. When one of them wants to pay another, they simply send a message to the bank with the payment details. Assuming the payer has enough funds, the bank subtracts the amount from his or her account and adds it to that of the payee.

If the payer does not have enough funds to complete the payment, the transaction is rejected. So in the event that someone tries to double-spend their balance by sending two conflicting payment requests to the bank (while not having enough funds to make both payments), the bank will simply choose which transaction goes through (presumably the first request it received).

This solves the double-spend problem... but it also exemplifies the privacy issue that Chaum was concerned about: the bank would know exactly who's paying whom, how much, and when. On top of that, the bank would have total control over everyone's balances, and could potentially block or revert payments, and even confiscate or delete funds.

Chaum therefore set out to find a way for such a third party—the bank—to detect double-spending, without the ability to trace how each "digital dollar" moves through the economy.

Blind Signatures

The talented cryptographer solved the problem in 1983. Having just earned his doctorate in computer science at Berkeley to be hired as a professor at the same university, Chaum published his design for an electronic cash system in his paper "Blind signatures for untraceable payments."

As the title of the paper suggests, key to his design for a privacy-preserving payment system was his invention of *blind signatures*.

Chaum's blind signatures were an extension of public key cryptography and, more specifically, the RSA cryptographic signature algorithm. To recap, a cryptographic signature is essentially a piece of data (like a message) encrypted with a *private* key, which can be decrypted with a *public* key. If Alice sends Bob a message and a corresponding cryptographic signature, Bob should be able to decrypt the signature with Alice's public key, converting it into that same message, thereby mathematically proving that the signature was really created with her private key.

A blind signature, then, adds one layer of encryption to the mix.

To have Alice create a blind signature, Bob would first generate a special type of encryption key, called the *blinding key*, and encrypt a message using this blinding key. Bob would then give the encrypted message to Alice, for her to cryptographically sign with her private key. When she signs the encrypted message, she doesn't know what the original message actually is: she's *blind signing*.

The resulting signature is mathematically linked to Alice's public key, as any signature would be. That is, her public key can be used to reproduce the exact encrypted message she signed. (The message itself would still be encrypted; it would reproduce the same encrypted blob she received from Bob.)

But interestingly, Bob could also use the blinding key *first*, in order to remove the layer of encryption created with it. This should essentially result in a new, valid signature from Alice, this time corresponding to the original message. This signature is called the *blind signature*. With the first layer of encryption removed by Bob, anyone can now use Alice's public key to reproduce the original message from the blind signature.

In other words, anyone with the original message can at that point use Alice's public key to verify that the blind signature corresponds to the message. This includes, of course, Alice herself. If Bob gives her the original message and the blind signature, she can use her own public key to verify that she indeed blind-signed an encrypted version of that original message.

As a real-world analogy used by Chaum in his paper, it'd be as if Bob put a letter in an envelope laced with carbon paper and handed this envelope to Alice, who'd sign the outside of the envelope, and give it back to Bob. If Bob then removed the envelope and showed Alice the letter with a carbon copy of her signature, she'd know that the letter had indeed been in the envelope she signed.

Anonymous Payments

To use the blind signature scheme for an electronic cash system, Alice from the example above would actually be a bank: let's call this bank Alice Bank. Alice Bank is a regular bank, where customers have bank accounts with dollar deposits. And let's say Alice Bank has four customers: Bob, Carol, Dan, and Erin.

Now, Bob wants to buy something from Carol with electronic cash.

First, Bob would need electronic cash. So he'd request a "withdrawal" from Alice Bank. (Ideally, he had already made this withdrawal before he wanted to pay Carol—but that's a detail.) Counterintuitively, to make the withdrawal, Bob actually creates "digital dollars" himself, in the form of unique serial numbers. He'd then encrypt these digital dollars (serial numbers) with a blinding key, and send them to Alice Bank.

Alice Bank would then blind-sign each encrypted dollar, and send the signatures back to Bob. For each blind-signed encrypted dollar that Alice Bank returns to Bob, Alice Bank subtracts a regular dollar from Bob's bank account.

Bob would then remove a layer of encryption using his blinding key, so Alice's signatures are converted into blind signatures. To pay Carol, he'd simply send her the digital dollars and the associated blind signatures. Carol then uses Alice Bank's public key to verify these signatures, and if they check out, she immediately forwards the digital dollars and blind signatures to Alice Bank.

Alice Bank would have never seen these digital dollars before; the first time it received them, they were encrypted. However, importantly, Alice Bank would be able to confirm that they were signed with its own private key. Alice Bank would then check the serial numbers against a local database to make sure that the same digital dollars hadn't already been deposited by someone else, thus ensuring that they weren't double-spent.[104]

The digital dollars pass both checks if they contain a valid signature and were previously unused. Alice Bank then records them in its local database to prevent future double-spending, adds the equivalent amount of regular dollars to Carol's bank account, and confirms this to her. With this confirmation, Carol would know she'd been paid a valid digital dollar by Bob, and give him whatever he was buying from her.[105]

Because Alice Bank would have seen the signed banknotes for the first time only when Carol deposited them, Alice Bank would have no way of knowing that they originally came from Bob. They could have just as well come from Dan or Erin. By extension, after Alice Bank issued the "digital dollars" to Bob, it could not have stopped him from spending them, since she'd have no idea which digital dollars to render invalid.[106]

Indeed, Chaum had designed a form of electronic cash.[107]

In the years following the publication of his first paper on untraceable payments, Chaum expanded on the potential of electronic cash in presentations at the Crypto conferences and in several other papers. These follow-ups fleshed out exactly how to implement an electronic cash scheme, with the best detailed example of this being his 1985 paper with the descriptive title "Security Without Identification: Transaction Systems to Make Big Brother Obsolete."[108]

"The large-scale automated transaction systems of the near future can be designed to protect the privacy and maintain the security of both individuals and organizations," its one-sentence introduction triumphantly declared.

DigiCash

A few years later, by 1989, Chaum had settled in Amsterdam. During one of his earlier visits to the Netherlands, local academics offered him a job as chief cryptographer at the Dutch Centre for Mathematics and Computer Science (CWI), which he had gratefully accepted; it allowed him to live close to his Dutch girlfriend.

Around this time, the government of the Netherlands was considering a new road toll project that would have cars pay for the privilege of driving on certain highways through a smart card affixed to their windshield, to be scanned by high-speed card readers positioned around the roads. The idea was controversial, however: the Dutch didn't like the idea of their cars being tracked.

When the government came to the CWI research center to ask if they knew of any privacy-preserving solutions to realize this kind of toll system, Chaum saw the opportunity he'd been waiting for. He had patented his blind-signature technology, but to his own bewilderment, interest in developing digital cash schemes had been limited since the publication of his papers. He now recognized that there was a unique chance to help put the technology to use himself.

Chaum rallied a group of students from the nearby Technical University Eindhoven, promising them a trip to the International Collegiate Programming Contest (ICPC) in Washington DC on his expense (and a vacation to Disney World in Florida to boot) if they helped turn his blind signature scheme into a proof of concept. With time of the essence—the Dutch government already had a development team in mind for the project and wasn't too keen on delaying the process—Chaum and the students worked around the clock from one of their living rooms.

They succeeded within ten days and their proof of concept earned Chaum the contract.

With this initial job secured, the cryptographer decided to found Digi-Cash, an Amsterdam-based startup that would specialize in digital money and payment systems. These payment systems of course included the government toll project,[109] but Chaum, now heading his own company, wanted to realize his bigger vision as well.

It had by the early 1990s become increasingly clear that the internet was about to go mainstream, and Chaum believed that electronic payments would eventually be an essential part of this emerging digital realm. Like many internet experts at the time, he expected micropayments to become ubiquitous: web-services had to generate revenue somehow, and the obvious solution was indeed to charge people small amounts of money to use them.

"As payments on the network mature, you're going to be paying for all kinds of small things, more payments than one makes today," Chaum predicted. "Every article you read, every question you have, you're going to have to pay for it."[110]

DigiCash's flagship project was a digital payment system that would let people make such payments privately, using electronic cash—*eCash*.

CyberBucks

DigiCash quickly began attracting international attention. In an era where Netscape and Yahoo! confirmed that the big money was moving into early internet startups, many tech entrepreneurs in the early 1990s considered Chaum's startup a rising star of this fast-growing industry.

It was going to take Chaum and his team—which included some of the students he began the project with—several years to turn their initial proof of concept into a full-fledged payment system, however. With the ultimate goal to sell their eCash technology to banks, it also required bank-grade security.

In the meantime, they did release an early version of their technology. DigiCash's first implementation of Chaum's electronic cash design was rolled out from inside the company office itself—but instead of American dollars, Dutch guilders, or another fiat currency, this early electronic cash system used *CyberBucks*.

CyberBucks was a "made-up" currency, not backed by anything—play money, if you will. But the company did promise to never issue more than a million units into circulation. The virtual bucks were generally given away for free, and anyone could store the digital currency on their computer, or load it onto a smart card to buy a soda or some phone credit in the DigiCash building itself. These smart cards were essentially tamper-proof, credit card-sized computers specifically designed to make these kinds of payments, and they became a big focus for DigiCash; Chaum believed that the smart cards were integral for payment privacy, as in-person payments with credit cards presented an even larger privacy problem than online payments.

The idea behind CyberBucks was that DigiCash employees could fiddle with the eCash technology, while visitors could get a taste of the future. And when Chaum and his colleagues decided to give away 100 CyberBucks to any merchant that would accept the internet currency as payment, a small group of enthusiasts eventually started to use CyberBucks outside the Digicash offices as well. Although it could typically just be spent on gimmicky products like digital pictures or small puzzle games for Apple's Macintosh computer, the company currency enjoyed some wider adoption.

What's more, when CyberBucks eventually started being traded on an unofficial CyberBucks exchange, users could convert the electronic cash units into actual fiat currency and back. CyberBucks, after some time, commanded a real market price, while some users even started holding on to a little bit of the digital currency as a form of savings or speculation.

This did require a lot of trust in DigiCash. While the company promised to cap the CyberBucks supply at one million, there was no inherent way to enforce this limit. Chaum and his colleagues could technically issue far more than a million CyberBucks if they wanted to, and due to the system's strong privacy features there would be no way for outsiders to check whether or not this had happened.

On top of that, the currency system entirely depended on DigiCash's continued support: the company server prevented double-spends. And while CyberBucks was a fun and interesting experiment, DigiCash's top priority was in the end to prepare their main electronic cash product for prime time. . .

eCash

eCash approached the benchmark of bank-grade security after four years of development. Real-money trials began in 1994, at which point financial institutions could acquire a license from Chaum's startup to use the new technology.

The first bank to jump on the opportunity was the Mark Twain Bank in St. Louis—not exactly an international powerhouse, but it was a start. Customers and businesses with accounts at Mark Twain could enjoy privacy in their electronic transactions by making and receiving payments in eCash.

Others soon followed suit. Banks in several countries, including Norske Bank and Bank Austria[111]—at the time the largest banks in Norway and Austria respectively—as well as the Australian Advance Bank,[112] began eCash trials shortly after Mark Twain. And by early 1996, one of the largest financial institutions in the world got on board as well: Deutsche Bank started using Digicash's technology.[113] Credit Suisse, another major international player, joined the trials, too.[114]

Yet, what was perhaps even more notable than the collaborations Chaum established, were the business deals that he failed to finalize—though this is where the story of what exactly happened at DigiCash starts to diverge, depending on who you ask.

According to several DigiCash employees,[115] there had been great interest from major players in the tech and finance industry. Two of the three major Dutch banks—ING and ABN Amro—were said to have made Digi-Cash partnership offers worth tens of millions of dollars. Payment giant Visa, similarly, would have proposed Chaum an eight-figure deal. And Netscape is said to have shown interest as well; eCash could potentially have been included in the most popular web browser of that era, but the partnership never materialized.

But the biggest offer of all is said to have come from none other than Microsoft. Bill Gates wanted to integrate eCash into the Windows 95 operating system, the story goes, and offered DigiCash some 100 million dollars to make it happen. Chaum would instead have asked for two dollars for each version of Windows 95 sold, which was too rich for the American software colossus, and the deal was off.

DigiCash employees initially accepted Chaum's rigid strategy, but each time they heard of another multimillion deal falling apart, they grew more wary of his business instincts. Speaking with a Dutch reporter, one employee later suggested that the same distrustful personality trait that made him a great cryptographer, got in the way when Chaum wore his business hat. His "paranoid" nature would have made him unable to build up business relationships, causing him to back out of business deals at the last moment.

It became a growing source of frustration at the DigiCash offices. Besides recognizing that their own job security was at stake if the company didn't start making money, Chaum's inability to get eCash into the hands of more people also frustrated them on an ideological level. Digicash had a way of attracting developers with a commitment to furthering digital privacy, and at a time when e-commerce started to catch on with the general public, they worried that DigiCash was being left behind.

Chaum himself, however, strongly dismisses these allegations as malicious slander. He contends that the various multimillion dollar offers weren't as concrete as these employees seemed to think. Rather than his personal failings as a businessman, he maintains there simply wasn't a large market for digital cash—a reading that some of the more commercially focused DigiCash employees have attested to as well.

Regardless of which version of the story is closer to the truth, it is clear that by the end of 1996, patience had run out in the DigiCash office. Chaum's employees demanded a change in company policy.

Bankruptcy

Change ultimately came from Chaum's home country.

In search of new funding, his company turned to American venture capitalists; US investment culture was better acquainted with, and had a bigger appetite for, these types of high-risk tech startups. DigiCash got a fund injection, while MIT Professor Nicholas Negroponte was made chairman of the board, and Chaum was replaced by a new CEO: Visa-veteran Michael Nash.[116] Illustrative for the new direction, the company's headquarters were also moved from Amsterdam to Palo Alto, California, in the heart of Silicon Valley, where tech startup valuations were going through the roof. Chaum did remain part of DigiCash, but now as CTO.

This wasn't exactly the type of change most of the Dutch DigiCash employees had been hoping for, however. Several of them at this point decided to leave the company.

And perhaps more importantly, it proved not to make much of a difference.

eCash simply wasn't catching on with the greater public. The banks that trialed the technology weren't really pushing it to their customers, and it probably also didn't help that eCash was relatively expensive to use, typically costing several percentages of the transaction value in fees. Mark Twain bank had in a couple of years time only enrolled 300 merchants and 5,000 users, while other banks weren't doing much better.

And, perhaps supporting Chaum's reading of DigiCash's history, the company's new leadership was unable to strike major deals as well. While a collaboration with CitiBank came close—this could perhaps have given DigiCash some much-needed momentum—the major American financial institution ended up walking away, too.

By late 1997, DigiCash had burned through most of its funds. After one last reshuffle of the company's organization and leadership, Chaum's startup in 1998 filed for bankruptcy.

After eight years of operation, DigiCash had not been able to live up to the hype it generated among the early generation of internet entrepreneurs. Perhaps Chaum's inability to build business relationships were to blame for the failure, as some former employees had concluded. Or maybe demand for anonymous digital cash—while a sexy selling point in the early '90s—just wasn't as high as the pioneering cryptographer initially expected: instead of micropayments, much of the web instead ended up being funded through advertisements, and privacy just didn't seem to rank very high on the average consumer's priority list.

On top of that, DigiCash had struggled with a chicken-or-egg problem. eCash was only useful if people could spend it somewhere, so without places to spend the digital cash, there was no incentive to get it in the first place. At the same time, accepting eCash was only useful for merchants if there were enough people that wanted to spend it.

"It was hard to get enough merchants to accept it, so that you could get enough consumers to use it, or vice versa," Chaum recalled in 1999. And: "As the Web grew, the average level of sophistication of users dropped. It was hard to explain the importance of privacy to them."[117]

Chaum's electronic cash startup went under. With it, the CyberBucks double spend server went offline as well. And without this server, there was no way to know which currency units were still valid. It meant, bluntly, the end of the experiment. Those still holding CyberBucks were left with nothing but a bunch of worthless numbers on their computer.

With that, anyone who'd been involved with the niche digital cash side project learned a valuable lesson. Although blind signatures guaranteed a level of privacy, CyberBucks' reliance on a trusted party in the form of DigiCash had turned out to be the project's fatal flaw.

Around this time, someone else, incidentally and for a very different reason, had been trying to fix a very similar type of flaw . . .

Scott Stornetta

Fresh out of Stanford with a PhD in physics, Scott Stornetta was excited to start his new job at what was in 1989 an epicenter of computer science innovation: the New Jersey-based telecom research center Bellcore.

Effectively responsible for the architecture of much of America's telecommunications systems in a time when information technology was developing at breakneck speed and the internet was growing every day—and the field of cryptography had been experiencing nothing short of a renaissance—Bellcore was in the middle of what Stornetta later described as a "golden age of research." New hires weren't even assigned specific tasks; the thirty-year-old physicist was instead instructed to find out what was important *himself*, and then go and work on that.

It happened to be the case that Stornetta had something important in mind even before he'd set foot in his new work environment.

Before his move to the East Coast, Stornetta spent the last few years at Stanford working from the Xerox PARC research center in Palo Alto. It was a revolutionary environment—the Xerox division had facilitated groundbreaking innovations like the personal computer, Ethernet, and laser printing—but Stornetta had in recent years also started to encounter an ugly new problem at the highly digitalized research center: forgery.

Forgery itself wasn't a new phenomenon, of course. Humans have essentially tried to forge documents since the invention of writing. But digital forgeries were a relatively new concept, and Stornetta had come to believe that they represented an even more challenging problem. Whereas physical forgery tends to leave marks, a digital document—whether that's an employment contract, insurance papers, or a university degree—can be altered spotlessly.

Digital authentication did solve part of that problem: cryptographic signatures could prove that an electronic document was vetted (signed) by the right person. However, this would not prevent that same person from creating and signing altered documents later on. There is no way to tell the difference between an old bit and a new bit, so how could anyone ever be sure that they're looking at an original document instead of a later forgery?

Stornetta foresaw a crisis of credibility, and decided to dedicate his first period at Bellcore to solving this problem.

He already had a possible solution in mind as well. Stornetta wanted to design a time-stamping system for digital records: getting away with a forgery is much harder when people can prove that the original document existed at an earlier point in time.

Stornetta had not yet figured out how such a time-stamping system would work, exactly, though he suspected that cryptography could be a key part of the answer. And while he wasn't a cryptographer himself, he was lucky enough that Bellcore cryptographer Stuart Haber—who was also the person who hired Stornetta at Bellcore—agreed to team up with him for the job.

Over the following weeks, Stornetta and Haber brainstormed ideas, speculating on potential strategies to solve the challenge before them.

Hash Chains

One of their most promising schemes made use of a hash function,[118] a type of one-way function that scrambles data into a unique and seemingly random string of numbers of a fixed length. Any digital data can be hashed, whether it's a single letter or an entire book, a music file or a program's source code. Importantly, the same data will result in the exact same hash every time, but if the original data is altered even a tiny bit, the resulting hash would change unrecognizably. If a single comma is removed from a book, the resulting hash would look nothing like the hash of the original book.

Stornetta and Haber considered that documents could be time-stamped by a special time-stamping service. A document would be hashed together with a timecode indicating when the time-stamp service received it, and this hash would be cryptographically signed by the time-stamping server as a form of proof. To show that a document existed at a certain point in time, the owner of the document could provide the original document and the time-stamp, which anyone could then put through a hash function and verify that an identical hash was indeed signed by the time-stamping server.

Further, Stornetta and Haber speculated that different documents could be chronologically linked in a hash chain. That is, each new document that the time-stamping server received would not only be hashed together with a timecode, but also with the hash of the previous document. This new hash, in turn, would be hashed together with the next document to create the next hash, and so forth. The resulting "chain" of hashes could prove exactly which documents were time-stamped in what order; it would form a chronological "backbone record" of all processed documents.

This did mean, however, that the time-stamping service itself would have to be trusted not to tamper with the backbone record. In theory, this service could make forgeries by hashing and signing the same documents with different time-stamps, and it could recreate a new hash chain to change the chronological order of the documents, or even delete documents from the record altogether.

Relying on such services was quite common in the field of computer science; public keys were typically distributed by a certificate authority that linked these keys to specific identities, for example. Yet, for Stornetta and Haber, this was no ideal solution. They believed that security in the digital realm shouldn't require trust in any particular person or entity; much like the cryptographic tools at their disposal, time-stamping would ideally stand on its own.

This turned out to be the most challenging part of the problem.

As long as any single entity acted as a time-stamping service, it required trust in that entity, while solving this by adding more entities to create a system of security checks also seemed like a dead end. Even if someone would be tasked with overseeing that the time-stamping service remains honest, everyone would still have to trust that this person doesn't collude with the time-stamping service to change the records. For the same reason, it wouldn't really help to add a third person to keep both of them honest, or a fourth, or a fifth . . . This would at best increase the scale of collusion required to forge historic records—but it wouldn't altogether preclude the possibility.

Stornetta and Haber appeared to have run into a fundamental problem that cryptography could not solve. After weeks of fruitless spitballing, the Bellcore colleagues ultimately saw no other option but to conclude that what they really wanted to achieve could not be done.

As a kind consolation, they decided to publish their findings. Although Stornetta and Haber hadn't solved the problem of trust, they could now at least show that the problem was unsolvable . . .

Distributing Trust

It had only been in the process of making the case that the problem was unsolvable that Stornetta realized that they were, in fact, wrong—at least technically.

Stornetta and Haber had concluded that adding more entities to perform checks on the time-stamping service doesn't solve the problem of trust—it just changes how big the collusion would have to be. Indeed, this seems logically true, and in most cases is indeed true.

But Stornetta now realized there is an exception to this rule: if *everyone* checks the time-stamping service, no one can collude: there would not be anyone left to collude against. As long as everybody watches everybody else, there is no trusted party at all!

Or as Stornetta put it:

"If we can essentially create a conspiracy so large that it included the entire world, then we would have in fact inverted the problem and created a trust-free system."[119]

Now of course, making the group that checks for forgeries so big that it literally includes everyone on earth is rather implausible. Nevertheless, the fresh insight did represent a real breakthrough in Stornetta and Haber's thinking.

It eventually led to the publication of their 1990 paper "How to Time-Stamp a Digital Document."[120] Breaking new grounds in the field of digital time-stamping, the paper outlined two slightly different proposals.

The first proposal closely resembled their hash chain backbone record idea, where the time-stamping service would cryptographically sign and chronologically link each update to the record to prove that it was really the time-stamping service that added the new document, and in what order. But importantly, instead of trusting only the time-stamping service with the backbone record, this backbone record would now be shared with every participant.

The brilliance of this solution was that if the time-stamping service were ever to try to backdate, delete, or otherwise change a previously time-stamped document, any user that kept a copy of the backbone record would notice the change. If the content or the timecodes of a document was altered even slightly, this would completely change the corresponding hash, which would in turn also change every hash that came after it, making it entirely incompatible with the widely distributed record: the time-stamping service would never get away with its attempted forgery.

The second solution described by Stornetta and Haber even eliminated the time-stamping service altogether. In this variant, a group of participating users would take turns to add a new document to the hash chain. Whenever someone would want to time-stamp a document, the randomness of the hash of that document itself would be used to determine which participant should sign it, as if it were some type of hash lottery.

Featuring not one, but two ingenious proposals—one even more trust-minimized than the other—Stornetta and Haber's paper represented a big leap forward for digital time-stamping.

That said, hash chains did present a new problem: they didn't scale particularly well, especially when considering the modest computational resources available to an average computer user in the early 1990s. With one new hash for each document added to the backbone record, the participating users would over time need to store quite a lot of data if these systems were to catch on in a big way.

And as these users would need to store increasingly more data in order to participate, more of them would likely opt out and instead just trust the record held by the time-stamping service and other users, which would in turn reintroduce trust into these systems: to really be secure, the time-stamping scheme explicitly depended on broad participation.

It was mathematician Dave Bayer who helped resolve this conundrum, with *Merkle Trees*.

Merkle Trees

In the years after completing his internship with Martin Hellman, Ralph Merkle had gone on to make a name for himself as one of the preeminent cryptographers of his generation. Among other innovations, he'd designed a new one-way function, introduced a faster encryption protocol, proposed his own signature algorithm, and although he technically didn't coauthor the paper, many cryptographers had come to regard Merkle as the third inventor of the Diffie-Hellman key exchange.

But perhaps most notable of all, Merkle had in 1979 invented the Merkle Tree.[121] Originally designed as part of a system for producing authentication certificates for a public key directory, Merkle Trees offer a compact and secure check on the contents of all sorts of data sets by combining hashes in a clever mathematical structure.

Specifically, a Merkle Tree cryptographically aggregates different pieces of data using a few simple steps. First, all the different pieces of data are hashed individually, so each piece of data has its own unique hash. Next, all these hashes are paired in groups of two. Each pair of hashes is then hashed together, which produces one new hash per pair. All the new hashes are then paired again, and these pairs are again hashed together. This process repeats until there is only one hash left, called the *Merkle Root*. (Visualized, the resulting data structure looks something like a family tree, but for large numbers instead of people.)

Merkle Trees facilitate checks to see whether the hash of a specific piece of data is included in the tree. Importantly, this can be done without needing to see any of the other data that was hashed, nor even most of the other hashes. All that's needed is a *Merkle proof*, consisting of the relevant "branches" of the tree: this essentially serves as a compact set of "directions" to find the path from the Merkle Root to the hash of the specific piece of data.

Meanwhile, it's strictly impossible to edit or remove anything from a tree without changing the entire tree, or, more precisely, without changing the Merkle Root. If a piece of data is altered or removed, the corresponding hash would change as well, which in turn necessarily affects what its "child" hash looks like, which of course affects the next hash, and so on, all the way down to the Merkle Root. Not unlike hash chains, Merkle Trees unequivocally show whether data was altered, but in a much more compact format.

It would prove to be a valuable property in the battle against digital fraud.

A Chain of Roots

Well versed in the many cryptographic proposals that were introduced in the decade and a half prior to the publication of Stornetta and Haber's first paper, Bayer suggested to the Bellcore researchers that they could use Merkle's hash structure for time-stamping—a suggestion that the duo gladly accepted. Their second paper, "Improving the Efficiency and Reliability of Digital Time-Stamping," was published in 1993, and included Bayer as a third author.[122]

Stornetta, Haber, and Bayer proposed to time-stamp many documents at once by including them all in one big Merkle Tree, with one such tree created per day or so. Instead of a hash for each time-stamped document, users would only need to keep the daily Merkle Root as a backbone record, and just their own Merkle proofs to locate the hash of their time-stamped documents in the relevant tree.

It represented a dramatic efficiency improvement, which allowed more users to participate in the time-stamping process. It would even be possible to publish the daily Merkle Root in a newspaper, where it'd be very public and preserved in physical newspaper archives. (Stornetta and Haber later founded the time-stamping startup Surety, which indeed included Merkle Roots in *New York Times* classified ads.)

Furthermore—and as elaborated on in Stornetta and Haber's third paper "Secure Names for Bit-Strings"[123]—each new Merkle Tree could also include the previous Merkle Root. As such, the series of Merkle Roots would themselves create a chronological hash chain. If one Merkle Tree is created per day, yesterday's Merkle Root would be included in today's Merkle Tree, while today's Merkle Root would be included in tomorrow's Merkle Tree, and so on.

In this way, the order of Merkle Trees would be cryptographically linked, too. This would make forgery harder, still: even if someone for example managed to forge one *New York Times* edition in the physical archive to include a different Merkle Root somehow, it wouldn't add up with the Merkle Roots published in all newspapers published since then—nor, of course, with people's personal records.

Indeed, if someone would try to backdate a document, it wouldn't just alter the Merkle Root of that specific day, but it would be incompatible with every time-stamping record that was published since then. Forgery, practically speaking, would be impossible. In effect, Scott Stornetta and Stuart Haber designed a form of historic data authentication.

The key to their success, had been the distribution of trust.

Chapter 7:
The Extropians

FRIEDRICH HAYEK WANTED to denationalize money and David Chaum wanted to make it private. While the economist and the cryptographer each had a revolutionary idea, they never quite shared the same goal.

They did, however, inspire the same man.

Max O'Connor grew up in the small British town of Bristol in the 1960s and '70s. His imagination was sparked early on by real events—like the moon-landing that he witnessed on television at age five—as well as fictional stories from the comic books he devoured. He dreamed of a future where humanity expanded its potential in sci-fi-esque ways, a world where people would possess X-ray vision, carry disintegrator guns, or could walk straight through walls.

By his teenage years, O'Connor had acquired an interest in the occult. He thought that the key to realizing superhuman potential could perhaps be found in the same domain as astral projection, dowsing rods, and reincarnation. To explore these possibilities, he founded the Psychic Development and Research club at his school, where he and his fellow junior occultists studied the supernatural.

But O'Connor, who around this time became interested in life extension in particular, wasn't exactly finding what he was looking for. What was consistently missing, he began to realize, was compelling evidence that any of the mystical practices actually worked.

The teenager eventually changed his mind on the occult entirely, and concluded that there was no value to be gained from these beliefs and practices. Instead of the supernatural, he figured that human progress was best served by science and logic.

And even without supernatural powers, O'Connor could at least maximize his own potential through hard work. In school, he was a keen student, and ambitious, too—at least as long as the topics in class were compelling. He was especially interested in subjects concerning social organization, and he eventually graduated top of his economics class in school.

The hard work paid off when O'Connor in 1984 was accepted to the University of Oxford, and his drive to achieve and make the most out of himself only seemed to grow at this prestigious university. He worked diligently for three years straight, following courses in politics, economics, and philosophy. By age twenty-three, he'd earned degrees in all three.

At that point, it was time for a change of scenery. As a young adult, the fresh Oxford graduate aspired to be a writer, but the old university town with its wet climate, dark winters, and traditional British values wasn't providing him with the energy or inspiration that he was looking for. It was time to go somewhere else, somewhere new . . . somewhere exciting.

O'Connor found that new destination when he in 1987 was awarded a fellowship to enter a PhD program in philosophy at the University of Southern California. He was moving to Los Angeles.

Upon arrival in the Golden State, O'Connor immediately felt at home. The sunny LA weather was an obvious upgrade from Oxford's dreariness, and in stark contrast to the conservative mindset that was prevalent in Great Britain, the cultural vibe on America's West Coast encouraged ambition and to aspire for success: Californians celebrated achievement, they respected risk-taking, and they praised movers and shakers.

Here, O'Connor would start a new life, as a new man.

To commemorate the fresh start, he even decided to change his name; from then on, Max O'Connor would go through life as "Max More."

"It seemed to really encapsulate the essence of what my goal is: always to improve, never to be static," he later explained. "I was going to get better at everything, become smarter, fitter, and healthier. It would be a constant reminder to keep moving forward."[124]

FM-2030

Expanding the human potential, and life extension more specifically, had never really been popular topics in England. But in California, Max More found that he wasn't alone in his interest.

One of More's colleagues at USC, a Belgian-born, Iranian-American author and teacher born as Fereidoun M. Esfandiary but who went by the name "FM-2030," had throughout the '70s and '80s been popularizing a radically futurist vision for mankind.

Inspired by the worldwide protest movements of the 1960s, where he saw everyday people from around the world speak out against government corruption and social injustice, FM-2030 began envisioning a future where humanity would transcend borders to establish a universal dialogue free from nationality, politics, and heritage. To realize this, he started advocating high-tech homes and lifestyles, for people to live in an interconnected global society.

Furthermore, development of new technologies would give engineers the tools to dramatically change the world for the better, FM-2030 predicted. He believed that any risks associated with technological innovation would be offset by the rewards of progress: solar and atomic power would bring energy abundance, humans would colonize Mars, robot workers would increase leisure time, and people could earn a living from the comfort of their own homes thanks to the advent of teleworking.

Even more interestingly, FM-2030 predicted that technology would soon reach the point where it could drastically improve humans themselves. Health standards would advance considerably as more diseases could be cured while genetic flaws could be corrected; future pharmaceuticals could boost the human potential by, for example, enhancing brain activity.

Ultimately, he expected that medical science would even "cure" aging, and therefore, do away with finite human lifespans. By FM-2030's estimation, humanity would conquer death around his hundredth birthday in the year 2030; it's what the number in his name referred to. ("FM," meanwhile, variously stood for Future Man, Future Marvel, or Future Modular—and sometimes something else, depending on his mood or who asked.)

As traditional limitations on the human potential, like finite lifespans, would be removed while bionic body parts and other artificial enhancements increasingly unlocked new possibilities, FM-2030 predicted that humans would eventually transform most radically, and turn themselves into synthetic post-biological organisms:

"It's just a matter of time before we reconstitute our bodies into something entirely different, something more space-adaptable, something that will be viable across the solar system and beyond."[125]

Transhumanism

FM-2030 believed that technological advancements would ultimately alter the human condition: humanity would upgrade itself to create a new and improved version of the species. Technology would realize a post-human condition.

To most, these predictions sounded rather fantastical. But when a research affiliate at the MIT Space Systems Laboratory named K. Eric Drexler around the same time described a technique for manufacturing machinery on a molecular level, the fantastical was already starting to sound a little less implausible. Nanotechnology, Drexler believed, could fundamentally change industries including computing, space travel, and production—as well as warfare.

And indeed, Drexler believed that nanotechnology could revolutionize healthcare, too. He explained that physical disorders are typically caused by misarranged atoms, and he instead imagined a future where nanobots could enter the human body to fix this damage with exact precision—in effect restoring the body to full health from within.

As such, nanotechnology would be able to cure just about any disease, and, Drexler speculated, ultimately extend life itself.

"Aging is fundamentally no different from any other physical disorder," Drexler wrote in his 1986 book *Engines of Creation*, "it is no magical effect of calendar dates on a mysterious life-force. Brittle bones, wrinkled skin, low enzyme activities, slow wound healing, poor memory, and the rest all result from damaged molecular machinery, chemical imbalances, and mis-arranged structures. By restoring all the cells and tissues of the body to a youthful structure, repair machines will restore youthful health."[126]

These were the types of ideas that captivated Max More like nothing else.

Moreover, for More, these ideas weren't just fun speculation. He believed that the sort of predictions that FM-2030 and Drexler were making deserved to be considered as something more fundamental. He was convinced that they offered a perspective on human existence, and even on reality itself. As More collected, studied, and thought about the concepts that these futurists had been sharing, the PhD candidate ultimately formalized them into a new and distinct philosophical framework: *transhumanism*.

The general idea and term "transhumanism" had already been used by evolutionary biologist Julian Huxley in the 1950s, but it was More who now really established it as an updated version of the humanist philosophy. Like humanism, transhumanism respects reason and science, while rejecting faith, worship, and supernatural concepts like an afterlife. But where humanists derive value and meaning from human nature and the existing human potential, transhumanists would anticipate and advocate transcending humanity's natural limitations.

"Transhumanism," More summed it up, "differs from humanism in recognizing and anticipating the radical alterations in the nature and possibilities of our lives resulting from various sciences and technologies such as neuroscience and neuropharmacology, life extension, nanotechnology, artificial ultra-intelligence, and space habitation, combined with a rational philosophy and value system."[127]

Extropianism

All transhumanists want to enhance the human potential. However, even if they have the same goal, Max More recognized that different transhumanists could favor very different approaches to realize this goal.

More himself believed in a positive, vital, and dynamic approach to transhumanism; he favored a message of hope, optimism, and progress. But he did not believe that this progress could be forced or even planned. He rejected the Star Trek-like version of the future where humanity settles under a single, all-wise, world government to guide the species forward.

Instead, More believed that transhumanists could benefit from the insights of Friedrich Hayek.

Technological innovation requires knowledge and resources, and Hayek had explained that the former is naturally distributed throughout society, while the latter is best allocated across the economy through free-market processes. If people are simply allowed the liberty to experiment, innovate, and collaborate on their own terms, More figured, technological progress would naturally emerge.

In other words, a more prosperous *tomorrow* was best realized if society could self-organize as a spontaneous order *today*.

More found an early ally in fellow USC graduate student Tom W. Bell. Like More, Bell adopted the transhumanist philosophy and favored More's joyful and free approach to achieve it. He decided that he would help spread the rather novel ideas by writing about them under his own new pseudonym: Tom Morrow.

And to encapsulate their vision, Morrow coined the term *extropy*. Serving as an antonym of "entropy"—the process of degradation, of running down—extropy stood for improvement and growth, even infinite growth. Those who, like Max More and Tom Morrow, ascribed to this transhumanist vision, would be regarded as *Extropians*.

More then went on to outline the foundational principles for the Extropian movement in a few pages of text called "The Extropian Principles: A Transhumanist Declaration." It included five main guidelines or, indeed, principles: *boundless expansion, self-transformation, dynamic optimism, intelligent technology*, and—as an explicit nod to Hayek—*spontaneous order*. Abbreviated, the principles formed the acronym B.E.S.T. D.O. I.T. S.O.

"Continuing improvements means challenging natural and traditional limitations on human possibilities," More summarized the movement's goals in The Extropian Principles. "Science and technology are essential to eradicate constraints on lifespan, intelligence, personal vitality, and freedom.

It is absurd to meekly accept 'natural' limits to our life spans. Life is likely to move beyond the confines of the Earth—the cradle of biological intelligence—to inhabit the cosmos."[128]

Like the transhumanist vision that drove it, the Extropian future was ambitious and spectacular. Besides life extension, which arguably represented the central pillar of the movement, Extropian prospects included a wide array of futurist technologies, ranging from AI to space colonization and mind uploading, to human cloning, fusion energy, and much more.

Importantly, however, Extropianism had to remain rooted in science and technology—even if often quite speculative versions of it. Rather than dwelling off to the domain of science fiction, Extropians had to consider how to actualize a better future through critical and creative thinking, be proactive, and perpetually learn.

This called for "rational individualism" or "cognitive independence," More wrote. Extropians had to live by their "own judgment, making reflective, informed choices, profiting from both success and shortcoming," which, he explained, in turn required free and open societies where diverse sources of information and differing perspectives are allowed to flourish.

Conversely, states and their governments could, in the Extropian view, really only hinder progress. Taxes deprived people of the resources to produce and build; borders and other travel restrictions could prevent people from being where they are of most value to the global society, and government regulations only limit people's ability to experiment and innovate.[129]

"Centralized command of behavior constrains exploration, diversity, and dissenting opinion," More concluded.[130]

The Subculture[131]

In the fall of 1988, Max More and Tom Morrow published the first edition of a new journal called *Extropy*, marking the de facto launch of the Extropian movement.

Even though More and Morrow had printed only fifty copies of this first edition, the journal was quickly connecting scientists, engineers, researchers, and other future-minded Californians from a variety of backgrounds. Its subscribers included computer scientists, rocket engineers, neurosurgeons, chemists, and more. Among them were also some notable names, like the pioneering cryptographer Ralph Merkle, or Nobel Prize-winning theoretical physicist Richard Feynman.

What they shared in common was a science-based optimism about the future. With *Extropy*, they finally had a magazine to learn about the most radically futurist ideas out there; or they could share their own radical ideas as guest contributors.

What's more, Extropianism offered them a unique perspective on life itself.

Equipped with a superior tool belt to explain the previously unexplained, science had over the past couple of centuries chipped away much of religion's stronghold in society. But More didn't believe that science alone would be enough to get rid of religion in its entirety, because religion serves another important purpose: it offers meaning. People cling to religion despite all evidence in large part, argued More, because they rely on their faith to get through tough times and endow themselves with a feeling of purpose. And while he found that most religions actually did not offer that great a form purpose—they tend to place humans beneath some powerful being(s) or downplay this life in favor of an afterlife—this represented *some* form of purpose nonetheless.

In order to get rid of religion entirely, people had to be given an alternative source of meaning, More believed:

"The Extropian philosophy does not look outside us to a superior alien force for inspiration. Instead it looks inside us and beyond us, projecting forward to a brilliant vision of our future. Our goal is not God, it is the continuation of the process of improvement and transformation of ourselves into ever higher forms. We will outgrow our current interests, bodies, minds, and forms of social organization. This process of expansion and transcendence is the fountainhead of meaningfulness."[132]

This Extropian perspective on life would over the next couple of years manifest itself as a small and local Californian subculture with distinct habits and rituals. The Extropians had their own logo (five arrows spiraling outward from the center, suggesting growth in every direction) and they congregated at an unofficial club house (or "nerd house") called Nextropia. They developed their own handshakes (shooting their hands with intertwined fingers upwards to only let go when their arms stretched all the way up: the sky's the limit!), they organized events (where some of them wore Extropian-themed costumes, for example dressing up as space colonists), and, following the lead of Max More and Tom Morrow, a number of Extropians changed their names: there was an MP-Infinity, a Skye D'Aureous, and someone calling himself R.U. Sirius.

As the Extropian community grew from a few dozen to a couple hundred people, More and Morrow in 1990 also founded the Extropy Institute, with FM-2030 joining as its third founding member. The non-profit educational organization would produce a bimonthly newsletter, organize Extropian conferences, and—cutting edge for its time—host an email list to facilitate online discussion. While email was still a niche technology, the tech-savvy and future-oriented Extropians generally knew how to navigate the newly emerging internet.

Some of them even worked on a particularly ambitious internet navigation project themselves . . .

The High-Tech Hayekians

K. Eric Drexler, whose work had been a major inspiration for Max More, had joined the Extropian community shortly after it was established, as had several of his friends—fellow technologists who liked to work on some of the most innovative and challenging projects of the day.

One of them was Mark S. Miller, at the time the main architect of Xanadu, the world's first-ever hypertext project. (Hypertext is the text you can click on to take you to different parts of the internet.) Originally founded as early as 1960, the ambitious Xanadu project was still a work in progress thirty years later.

As part of the project's development, Drexler and Miller had throughout the 1980s published several papers on allocating processing power across computer networks. In short, they proposed that computers could essentially "rent out" spare CPU cycles to the highest bidder. Self-interested computers would allocate their resources across the network through virtual markets to maximize efficiency, all without the need for a central operator. It would allow computing power to be utilized wherever it was valued the most, while encouraging investment in more hardware if there was sufficient demand for it.

Indeed, Drexler and Miller were using Hayek's free-market insights to design computer networks.

Drexler and Miller had studied Hayek's work on the advice of another Xanadu contributor and mutual friend of theirs called Phil Salin. A futurist with economics degrees from UCLA and Stanford, Salin liked to merge free-market insights with the cutting edge in technology: most notably, he had by the mid-1980s concluded that the time was right for the establishment of a private space transportation industry, and launched one of the most ambitious startups of the decade in the form of private space launch company Starstruck.

The three of them—Drexler, Miller, and Salin—had been dubbed the "high-tech Hayekians" by economics journal *Market Process,* a shared nickname that the trio accepted with pride.[133]

AMIX

Despite successfully launching a rocket into space, Starstruck ended up a commercial failure: Salin found that the US government made it practically impossible to operate a space transportation business because the taxpayer-subsidized Space Shuttle was consistently undercutting the market.

But luckily, this wasn't Salin's only project. Besides advising Drexler and Miller, he'd also been publishing papers and essays about the economic effects of the computer revolution of his own,[134] and these came to form the basis for yet another ambitious endeavor: Salin would create an online marketplace for buying and selling information. Although perhaps not as spectacular as launching rockets into Earth's orbit, he believed that this project had the potential to change the world in an even bigger way.

Called the American Information Exchange, or AMIX for short, the type of information to be sold on this marketplace could be just about anything people were willing to pay for. It could include advice from a mechanic on how to get an old car running again, or a few lines of computer code to automate the accounting at a dentist's office, or maybe a blueprint design for a new vacation home in the Florida Keys. If it was information, it could be sold on AMIX.

Salin believed that AMIX's greatest benefit would be a sharp reduction of transaction costs in the broadest sense of the word. That is, all the costs associated with making a purchase, including opportunity costs (the "cost" of having to miss out on other things). A transaction cost could for example be the opportunity cost of doing market research to find out which insurance provider offers the best deal, or the cost of calling different liquor stores in order to find out which one of them sells a specific brand of wine.

On AMIX, people could instead pay someone else to find the best insurance option for them, or purchase information about liquor stores and their inventories. If anyone on the information market offered these services for less money than it would have effectively cost the prospective buyers to find the information themselves, trading for it over AMIX would decrease the transaction cost of the actual purchases. AMIX could make buying insurance, wine, and many other goods and services cheaper by slashing transaction costs.

Society would benefit tremendously from such an efficiency gain, Salin believed, because lower transaction costs would make certain trades worthwhile that otherwise wouldn't have been. If someone doesn't have the time to call a dozen liquor stores, the option to instead pay someone else a small fee to do it for them could result in the sale of one more bottle of wine, leaving the wine connoisseur, the liquor store as well as the AMIX researcher better off.

In short, more trade means a better allocation of resources across the economy—spontaneous order.

Cryonics

AMIX was a visionary concept. But it was also way ahead of its time. When AMIX went live in 1984, Salin and his small team had built the marketplace from scratch. The reputation system they developed was the first of its kind, as was their dispute resolution tool, and since no online payment processors were operational yet, they had to implement this themselves as well. Even websites didn't exist at the time, which meant that AMIX users had to establish their own network—a network they had to access via dial-up modems since there was no broadband internet yet. Unsurprisingly, the project was off to a slow start.

And sadly, Salin didn't get to develop AMIX much further: shortly after the project's launch, he was diagnosed with stomach cancer. Salin ended up selling AMIX to software company Autodesk in 1988, which eventually shut down the project in 1992—just after the high-tech Hayekian had passed away at the age of forty-one.

Still, for Extropians, there is always hope . . . even in death.

If indefinite lifespans are really within reach for mankind, as the Extropians believe, dying just before this transhuman breakthrough is achieved adds a bitter layer to the tragedy. To stumble with the finish line in sight—perhaps just a few decades early—would mean the difference between dying like all humans have done throughout all of history so far, and experiencing eternal life by partaking in the transformation of the human condition. Dying a twenty-odd years too early might just mean missing out on eternity.

This is why Extropians developed a fallback plan—an escape route to bridge the gap. The Extropians embraced *cryonics*.

Today, five facilities across the US, China, and Europe[135] cryopreserve a couple hundred human bodies and heads of dead individuals. Before passing away, those people signed up to have their bodies (or just their heads) frozen as soon as possible after clinical death, to be stored in subzero temperatures. Over a thousand more people have signed up to have their bodies or heads preserved after their deaths as well.

The Extropian prediction is that those individuals might, at some point in the future, be brought back to life. Although clinically dead, the people kept in biostasis are essentially waiting for science and technology to advance to the point where they can be unfrozen, resurrected, and cured from whatever ills got the best of them. They would wake up a few decades into the future in good health, all set to participate in the transhuman future that awaits.

. . . or so goes the theory. There is, of course, no actual guarantee that such resurrections will ever be possible. With today's technology, it certainly isn't. But with tomorrow's technology, who knows?

Even if one estimates that the chance of success is (very) slim, the odds of eventual revival may reasonably be estimated as greater than zero, and that's a bet that Salin and other Extropians were willing to make.

The remaining—living—Extropians will just have to keep the transhumanist flame burning in the meantime.

Digital Cash

The Extropian movement, like Max More himself, was naturally at home in California. Silicon Valley was by the early 1990s increasingly recognized as the global hotspot for innovation, which in turn attracted some of the most ambitious technologists, scientists, and entrepreneurs to the American West Coast.

But there was a notable exception. By the early 1990s, some of the Extropians had become convinced that one particularly interesting and important technology was actually being developed by a small startup halfway across the globe. They believed that the realization of electronic cash was critical, and David Chaum appeared to be holding all the cards.

For at least one Extropian, a computer scientist named Nick Szabo, it was reason to head to Amsterdam and work for DigiCash himself. Game developer Hal Finney, meanwhile, started advocating the importance of digital cash to his fellow Extropians in hopes of getting more of them involved. Spread across seven pages in the tenth edition of *Extropy*, published in early 1993, Finney detailed the inner workings of Chaum's digital cash system, and—tapping into the group's libertarian ethos—explained why Extropians should care.

"We are on a path today which, if nothing changes, will lead to a world with the potential for greater government power, intrusion, and control," Finney warned. "We can change this; these [digital cash] technologies can revolutionize the relationship between individuals and organizations, putting them both on an equal footing for the first time. Cryptography can make possible a world in which people have control over information about themselves, not because government has granted them that control, but because only they possess the cryptographic keys to reveal that information."[136]

Finney turned out to be right: the Extropian community came to generally share his concerns, and they understood why electronic cash offered an important part of the solution. Moreover, as they learned about cryptographically secured money, some Extropians started toying with the idea that the potential benefits of electronic cash could be even greater than privacy alone.

Where Chaum had mainly been concerned with the anonymous features of digital currency, these Extropians also began to consider its potential in the context of *monetary* reform.

By 1995, the newfound Extropian interest culminated in a special *Extropy* issue: the fifteenth edition of the journal was all about digital cash. The magazine cover prominently featured a blue-reddish mockup currency bill where instead of some head of state Hayek's portrait appeared on the note. "Fifteen Hayeks," the denomination read, and it was supposedly issued by the "Virtual Bank of Extropolis."

Inside the journal, about half of all articles discussed the potential of electronic cash, with different authors exhibiting various views relating to the digitization of money. These ideas of course included the well-known privacy features that Chaum's design offered. But most authors explored additional ideas as well.

In his "Introduction to Digital Cash," software engineer Mark Grant for example speculated that digital money could be used to establish local currency schemes, while also suggesting one particularly spicy alternative way of backing Chaumian cash.

"Just as the personal computer and laser printer have made it possible for anyone to become a publisher, digital cash makes it possible for anyone to become a bank, whether they are a major corporation or a street-corner drug dealer with a laptop and a cellular telephone," Grant explained. "Indeed, as national debts continue to increase, many people might see an advantage in using cash backed with, say, cocaine instead of cash backed solely by a government's ability to collect taxes."[137]

Another contributor, web engineer Eric Watt Forste, wrote a raving review of modern free banking school researcher George Selgin's *The Theory of Free Banking*. The book, which offers an elaborate account of how banking infrastructure could develop in a free-banking environment, could offer a blueprint for the digital domain as well, Watt Forste suggested:

"While crypto mavens are busy explaining how these banks could function technologically, the theory of free banking explains how they could function economically," Watt Forste concluded his review.[138]

Lawrence White, Selgin's closest ideological ally in the free-banking movement, had even contributed an article to the journal himself. Although mostly offering a more technical comparison between electronic cash schemes and existing payment solutions, White slipped in a hint of how digital currency could dramatically upset international banking dynamics: "One major potential advantage of electronic funds transfer via personal computer is that it may give ordinary consumers affordable access to off-shore banking."[139]

But perhaps most notable of all, Max More took it upon himself to summarize and present Hayek's seminal book on competing currencies.

More Denationalizing Money

Hayek's work had shaped Extropianism. The Austrian's insights regarding distributed knowledge, free markets, and spontaneous order represented a core source of inspiration for Max More when he formulated the movement's organizational principles. Now, More asked his fellow Extropians to also consider one of Hayek's much more recent proposals; a radical idea that had until then gained limited traction.

The founder of the Extropian movement argued for the denationalization of money.

In his article, More proved himself a well-grounded student of Hayek's work and an effective communicator of it. He offered a compact summary of Hayek's contributions to the greater monetary policy debate, and explained how the fiat currency system was responsible for four "economic ills": inflation, instability, undisciplined state expenditure, and economic nationalism.

Inflation is caused by government expansion of the money supply in a Keynesian attempt to lower unemployment, More explained, but it actually distorts the economy, increases effective taxes, and has an addictive effect to boot.

Instability, meanwhile, is caused by central bank interest rate manipulation—More summarized Hayek's business cycle theory—not by an inherent instability in the market (as he pointed out both Keynesians and Marxists claim).

Economic nationalism (or what Hayek had actually called monetary nationalism), furthermore, unnecessarily affects different parts of the economy in unpredictable and detrimental ways, More wrote.

And last but not least, the monetary system enabled undisciplined state expenditure, More explained; fiat currency helps grow the scope of government.

"The state expands its power largely through taking more of the wealth of productive individuals," wrote the Extropian. "Taxation provides a means for funding new agencies, programs, and powers. Raising taxes generates little enthusiasm, so governments often turn to another means of finance: Borrowing and expanding the money supply."[140]

Each of these ills hampered economic growth, which in turn therefore curtailed human progress. More summed up the problem succinctly: fiat currency frustrated the Extropian mission.

But, More argued, the ills could be remedied. As Hayek had described in *Denationalisation of Money*, the solution was to leave money to the free market. If the (de facto) state monopoly on money could be abolished, currency competition would incentivize private currency issuers to actually offer the most desirable form of money. Inflation, instability, undisciplined state expenditure, and monetary nationalism would be a thing of the past.

That said, More, too, knew that this wouldn't come easily. Whereas Hayek had always believed that convincing governments to adopt his proposal was going to be an uphill battle, the Extropian was probably even more pessimistic about this prospect than the Austrian economist had been in his book. Since governments benefit from their monopoly the most, they had no incentive to abolish it and every reason not to.

Yet, More now saw a new opportunity. He believed that Hayek's vision could be realized by leveraging the recent interest and innovation around electronic cash. It was trivial for governments to enforce a money monopoly when banks were easy to locate, regulate, tax, penalize, and shut down—but when banks can be hosted on personal computers on the other side of the world and operate with anonymous digital currency, the dynamic would change dramatically.

Governments wouldn't formally abolish the money monopoly, More figured, but the right set of technologies could make this monopoly much harder to enforce.

Through his article in the journal, the founding father of the movement called on Extropians to consider transactional privacy and currency competition in tandem.

"Competing currencies will trump the present system by controlling inflation, maximizing the stability of dynamic market economies, restraining the size of government, and by recognizing the absurdity of the nation-state," More wrote. "Pairing this reform with the introduction of anonymous digital money would provide a potent one-two punch to the existing order—digital cash making it harder for governments to control and tax transactions."

Concluding:

"I deeply regret Hayek's recent death. [. . .] Not having been placed into biostasis, Hayek will never return to see the days of electronic cash and competing private currencies that his thinking may help bring about. If we are to remain the vanguard of the future, let's see what we can do to hasten these crucial developments. Perhaps we will yet see a private currency bearing Hayek's name."[141]

PART II

CYPHERPUNKS

Chapter 8:
The Cypherpunk Movement

TIM MAY COULD see glimpses of the future. He had a knack for recognizing the potential of new technologies, and could predict how they would impact society before almost anyone else could.

Most notably, May was early to foresee how important personal computers and the internet would become. He scored himself a primitive DARPA account as early as 1973 at the UC Santa Barbara college campus where he studied physics, and one year later, at age twenty-two, landed a job at Intel, where he'd work in the Memory Products Division.

Offering a major contribution early in the company's history, the young physicist solved the *alpha particle problem*: May discovered that Intel's integrated circuits had been unreliable due to slightly radioactive packaging material. It set him up for a big career at the rapidly growing semiconductor chip manufacturer.

Because he received part of his job compensation in the form of stock options, the Intel physicist had about a decade later, by the mid-1980s, made a small fortune: at just thirty-four years of age, May concluded that he'd amassed enough wealth to sustain himself for the rest of his life. He decided to retire early, and moved to Santa Cruz, a coastal town some thirty miles south of San Jose, California. He spent most of the following year in a comfortable beach chair reading books on economics, technical papers, as well as cyberpunk novels.

A relatively new genre at the time, cyberpunk stories were typically set in high-tech dystopias. The books generally conveyed a grim version of the future, but one where the internet (or some evolved version of it) offered a refuge for their freedom-minded protagonists. In Vernor Vinge's *True Names*, a group of hackers hide from government strongmen by freely roaming their pseudonymous avatars through a colorful and three-dimensional representation of the internet itself. In Neil Stephenson's *Snow Crash*, nation-states lost most of their power to large corporations and the mafia, while people escaped their meager existence by enjoying alternative lives in a virtual reality world. And William Gibson's *Neuromancer* similarly presents a globally connected, virtual-reality environment as a colorful alternative to an unfriendly underworld society.

May was planning to eventually write a cyberpunk novel himself, modeled after Ayn Rand's *Atlas Shrugged*. In Rand's story, originally published in 1957, a United States in decline embraces socialist doctrines, as the American people turn against the country's most successful entrepreneurs. Some of these entrepreneurs eventually decide to go on "strike": a small community of can-do innovators set up base in a remote mountain range called "Galt's Gulch," using a screen of heat rays and reflectors to hide from the outside world. Rather than demonized, America's most industrious entrepreneurs should be cherished and celebrated, was the book's not-so-subtle message.

Having read Rand's magnum opus as a teenager, *Atlas Shrugged* had set May on a path to explore and learn more about free markets and libertarianism. He'd eventually study Austrian economics, and specifically, the theories of Friedrich Hayek.

All this made the aspiring author fit in naturally with a niche Californian subculture that was emerging in the 1980s; having been introduced to it by some of his local friends, May found an ideological home with the Extropians. Even if he wasn't entirely on board with some of the more outlandish transhumanist far-sights—ideas like eternal life, brain uploading, or an AI singularity—he did share a commitment to freedom and technological advancement.

It was in this context that Tim May became acquainted with Phil Salin, the "high-tech Hayekian" who'd unsuccessfully tried to establish a private space transportation industry with his startup Starstruck. May and Salin shared a passion for both Austrian economics and technology, and both believed that the former could be furthered through the latter.

BlackNet

May had spent about a year reading on the beach when Salin told him about AMIX, the ambitious internet project he was working on.

AMIX, Salin explained to his friend, would be an online marketplace for buying and selling information. He told May how this could drastically reduce a wide array of transaction costs, tremendously benefiting the free market. He asked May what he thought of the idea; Salin was interested to hear his friend's feedback.

The concept sounded interesting to May, indeed. But, as he mulled over the pitch for a bit, he concluded that he found it interesting for very different reasons than Salin did. May told his friend that expert advice or shopping tips—the types of information that Salin had had in mind—probably wouldn't actually be all that valuable. But he did believe that a very different category of information would be in high demand.

Secret information.

People would be willing to pay good money for corporate secrets, classified government documents, military intel, credit data, medical records, banned religious material, or illegal pornography, May suggested.[142] And, importantly, some of those with access to this kind of information would almost certainly be willing to sell it for the right price if they could do so anonymously.

Of course, buying and selling this kind of information would in many cases be illegal, May knew. If hosted on AMIX, Salin would presumably be forced to ban trading of it. But May foresaw that this ultimately wouldn't make a real difference. The developments in the field of cryptography he'd been reading about in academic journals would eventually make their way into people's hands, he explained to Salin, so it was only a matter of time until a fully anonymous AMIX variant would emerge where users are only known by their pseudonyms, and purchases were done with anonymous digital cash.

May dubbed this type of information market a *BlackNet*.

In the months following this first discussion with Salin, May kept thinking about the broader implications that a service like a BlackNet embedded. As he kept pulling on some of the threads his own ideas had laid bare, May figured that anonymous information markets could eventually make it fundamentally unsafe for large corporations to have their employees handle sensitive information at all: these employees would always be tempted to make an extra buck by selling the data online.

This could introduce something of a catch-22, May speculated. Trade secrets would presumably give businesses an edge over their competitors if used widely within the company—but in that case it would probably only be a temporary edge before the information was leaked to competitors. *Or*, the trade secrets could be used on a very limited scale to try to prevent leaks—but in that case the edge over competitors also wouldn't be as big.

Perhaps, May therefore suggested, the mere existence of a BlackNet could fundamentally shake up the economic incentives that make large corporations viable in the first place. Instead of billion-dollar multinationals, radical transparency could usher in a more dispersed and vibrant economy, characterized by a much more diverse range of smaller businesses.

And May ultimately realized that this dynamic wouldn't just affect large corporations, either. It could equally affect governments and their militaries, as well as other public institutions that handle confidential information. A single rogue government official with a profit motive would be enough to distribute all sorts of classified files to the internet's top bidders. Unable to secure sensitive data, government power could be weakened significantly. May loved the idea.

So would another local friend of his . . .

Eric Hughes

When Eric Hughes in the late 1980s—then in his mid-twenties—studied mathematics at Berkeley, the cryptographic revolution had already made its way into the curriculum. By the time he graduated, he was well versed in the recent innovations by the likes of Whitfield Diffie, Martin Hellman, Ralph Merkle, and David Chaum. And like them, Hughes intuitively understood the promising potential of their breakthroughs in the context of an increasingly digitized society.

Hughes found that fundamental human rights, like the right to privacy, were under constant threat from governments. Even if some of these rights were legally guaranteed, governments seemed to always have a way of encroaching on them if and when they were able to do so.

For Hughes, modern cryptography offered a way to safeguard individual privacy without having to rely on law or legislation, or the interpretation of them by politicians and judges. The right to private communication could instead be secured through technologies like public key cryptography and mix networks.

The level of privacy that could be obtained with strong cryptography, he realized, might ultimately offer immunity from physical threats and force altogether. As long as anonymous internet users could keep their real-world identities a secret, nothing they'd do or say online could possibly subject them to bodily harm.

When the young mathematician heard that Chaum had founded a company in the Netherlands to implement an electronic cash system, the Berkeley graduate decided to apply for a job. Like Chaum, he believed that money would become digital one way or another, and a privacy-preserving form of currency could mean the difference between a free society and a totalitarian dystopia. And Hughes believed that Chaum's cryptographic protocols had the potential to make that difference. Chaum, in turn, believed that Hughes would be a good fit for his company; he was hired.

But when Hughes in 1991 arrived in Amsterdam to begin his new endeavor, he rather quickly became disenchanted by what he found at the DigiCash offices. Chaum, Hughes discovered to his dismay, had made smart cards—the tamper-proof, credit card-sized computers specifically designed for payments—the centerpiece of his design. Rather than relying purely on the power of mathematics and perfecting the cryptographic protocols needed to deploy electronic cash for the internet, he found that DigiCash was focusing on expensive and unauditable hardware products to facilitate offline payments.

Hughes believed Chaum was making a gross strategic mistake by undervaluing pragmatism and cost efficiency in favor of experimental features, and the young mathematician eventually concluded that DigiCash wasn't the place for him after all. He left the startup after only six weeks in Amsterdam.

Back in California, Hughes considered finding a place to live that was a bit closer to the sea. He decided to spend a few days house hunting in Santa Cruz, where he could stay with an old friend who'd moved there a few years prior: Tim May.

When Eric Hughes arrived in Santa Cruz in 1991, May shared his vision for anonymous information markets with him. He explained how BlackNets would leverage the kind of privacy tools that Hughes had been studying and wanted to build, and how they could bring down (or at least drastically reduce the size of) big corporations and government institutions.

Although Hughes didn't consider himself a free market libertarian to the same extent as Tim May did, the concept of anonymous information markets intrigued him just as much, and for the next couple of days, the far-reaching potential of modern cryptography was all the two of them could talk about. As they philosophized about the implications of anonymous networks, the viability of pseudonymous reputation systems, and the prospects of borderless payments, house hunting had to wait.

But after a few days of discussing potentially game-changing use cases for public key encryption, remailers, and digital cash, their conversations kept leading back to the same nagging question.

Why were there still no software tools that implemented these protocols?

None of the breakthrough crypto innovations proposed since the 1970s were actually being put to practice by real people, because there were no computer programs available that implemented these protocols. While academic papers detailed how Alice and Bob could communicate privately thanks to the Diffie-Hellman key exchange or RSA encryption, this was, at the end of the day, completely useless as long as there was no software that performed these tasks for Alice and Bob.

Granted, a few such projects were in development. Indeed, Chaum was working on an electronic cash system—even though he wasn't quite developing it in the way that Hughes would have liked. In addition, one of May's fellow Extropians, the local Bay area computer scientist and cryptographer Phil Zimmermann, was working on RSA-based public key encryption software called Pretty Good Privacy (PGP).

Still, this seemed like very meager results when considering the magnitude of the breakthroughs that made May and Hughes so excited for the future. While the new wave of crypto had been spreading across academia for about fifteen years, and a series of successful Crypto conferences had showcased a range of groundbreaking concepts, actual software development was lagging far behind.

The Meeting

Hughes wouldn't move to Santa Cruz in the end. Yet, the trip wasn't wasted. During his visit to the beach town, Hughes and May had come to agree that it was time to start closing this gap between academia and the real world, and they concluded that they were going to have to take the initiative to make this happen themselves. May and Hughes committed to gathering an assembly of some of the brightest and most competent cryptographers and hackers from the Bay area, and got to work.

The first person they involved with their plan was John Gilmore, an early Sun Microsystems employee and cofounder of the digital rights group Electronic Frontier Foundation (EFF) who had already been speaking about bringing cryptography to the masses for some time within local hacker circles. The three of them—May, Hughes, and Gilmore—then started inviting more like-minded individuals who they believed wouldn't shun some hands-on tech activism.

A couple of months would go by, until on a Saturday in September about two dozen such like-minded individuals showed up at Hughes's new—and at the time still unfurnished—apartment in Oakland. Most of the attendees were sourced from the Bay area hacker community, while May also brought in a small Extropian delegation. It made for an especially tech-savvy group of people.

May opened the assembly with a primer on cryptography. He pitched the attendees on the promising potential of public key crypto as well as some of the innovative schemes that had been proposed since Diffie and Hellman's breakthrough, before handing out a booklet (composed by himself) explaining the basics and defining important terms. The group proceeded to discuss the potential implications for society if crypto tools became widely available and, conversely, the unsettling implications of a future without such tools.

In the afternoon, the whole gang, seated on the floor for lack of furniture, proceeded to playfully experiment with analog representations of crypto protocols. They created the paper-based "crypto-anarchy game," where envelopes represented an anonymizing message relay protocol, a bulletin-board served as an information market, and monopoly money was passed around like digital cash. In a fun way, everyone got a feel of how these systems would work.

The meeting was a success. By the end of a day filled with mini-seminars, brainstorm sessions, and games, everyone who made it to Hughes apartment for this special occasion was infected with the same sense of enthusiasm that had moved May, Hughes, and Gilmore to gather the unique group of people in one place. More importantly, they now shared the organizers' assessment that the crypto protocols they'd been learning about had to be implemented as working software, and be made available as far and wide as possible. To further the cause, they agreed to make the gathering a monthly event.

At this point, the group also concluded they needed a catchy name to describe themselves with. Hughes had until then been calling it the Cryptology Amateurs for Social Irresponsibility (or CASI for short), but they were now debating suggestions like "The Crypto Freedom League," "Privacy Hackers," and "The Crypto Cabal." It was amid all this banter that Hughes's girlfriend at the time, hacker Jude Milhon, jokingly exclaimed: "You guys are just a bunch of cypherpunks!"[143]

With the clever portmanteau of "cipher" and "cyberpunk," the group had found their name.

The Cypherpunks

Hosted in alternating locations—often at one of their homes or at someone's workspace—the meetings that followed represented a central point for information sharing, discussion, and project coordination. It also gave everyone a chance to get to know each other a bit better, of course, while new people were welcome to join and learn more about the initiative and how to participate.

The Cypherpunks during these early meetings outlined future goals, and formulated their strategies to realize these goals.

First and foremost, the Cypherpunks set out to prevent a dystopian future, a future where digital communication can be monitored, analyzed and, ultimately, abused. Like the cryptographers that inspired them, they were concerned that such loss of privacy could empower despots and tyrants, at grave loss of individual liberty; May at one point half-jokingly announced that George Orwell's *Nineteen Eighty-Four* was required reading for all of them.

But the Cypherpunks weren't just going to promote or even demand privacy. They would not limit themselves to lobbying elected officials, or otherwise work through the political and legal process, as some existing interest groups (like the EFF) were already doing.

Key to their strategy, Cypherpunks were going to claim privacy themselves.[144]

"We must defend our own privacy if we expect to have any," Hughes wrote in "A Cypherpunk's Manifesto," which the group's cofounder read out loud at a Cypherpunk meeting in early 1993. "We must come together and create systems which allow anonymous transactions to take place. People have been defending their own privacy for centuries with whispers, darkness, envelopes, closed doors, secret handshakes, and couriers. The technologies of the past did not allow for strong privacy, but electronic technologies do."

They were going to build these electronic technologies, distribute it as free software, and per the hacker ethic, they weren't going to ask anyone for permission to do so.

"Cypherpunks write code," Hughes declared. "We know that someone has to write software to defend privacy, and we're going to write it."[145]

Cypherpunks write code. It would become the group's unofficial battle cry.

The Mailing List

The monthly Cypherpunk meetings had an open character. Besides the core group of regular participants, curious newcomers would show up to get a taste of what was going on. To help coordinate this, Hughes set up an email list, hosted on Gilmore's computer, where he announced upcoming events. Every subscriber conveniently received a message with the date and location in their inbox.

But the Cypherpunks mailing list would soon serve a broader purpose. It didn't take long before the list was used to continue discussions from the physical meeting. Not long after that, whole new topics were introduced for the first time on the mailing list, not relating to anything that had been on the agenda of the in-person gathering at all. As the volume of messages increased, the Cypherpunks mailing list began to lead a life of its own.

Email of course had the added benefit that anyone could participate, regardless of geographical distance, and from the comfort of their own homes. Perhaps unsurprisingly, therefore, growth of the Cypherpunks mailing list quickly outpaced that of the actual Cypherpunk events. Just weeks after its launch, the list already had 100 subscribers—significantly more than the few dozen hackers and cryptographers who attended the monthly gatherings.

And the popularity of the mailing list started to really explode when tech magazine *Wired* in May 1993 dedicated its cover story to the Cypherpunks. "Rebels with a Cause (Your Privacy)," the cover read, just above a photo of three masked men holding the American flag. (The expressionless white masks with codes scribbled on them hid the faces of May, Hughes, and Gilmore.) Thanks to this cover story, just about anyone with an interest in computers had now heard about the group of privacy activists, and with its global reach, hundreds of people from all around the United States and the rest of the world were flooding in to subscribe to their email list.

Over the next couple of years, the Cypherpunks mailing list became a small phenomenon on the early internet. With up to 2,000 subscribers and sometimes almost as many emails per month, the Cypherpunks discussed a broad range of topics: from cryptographic protocols, to government policy, to software implementations, and tips for books or films, as well as periodic rants and flame wars. The list offered a platform for public discussion between some of the most talented hackers on the planet, while Silicon Valley CEOs and mainstream journalists liked to read along as well.

Tim May proliferated himself on the mailing list through his many emails: no one was more active than he was, and no one offered a more diverse range of contributions. He painted future scenarios, shared ideas, engaged in discussions, offered technical explainers, proposed strategies, commented on current affairs, linked to relevant articles, and he regularly shared "quickly written" essays—sometimes several a day.

But he also distinguished himself with his unique wit. He'd sometimes sarcastically argue against the Cypherpunk agenda from the perspective of an Ingsocian government, berating other list contributors as "citizen units." Other times, he made purposefully politically incorrect jokes to challenge the boundaries of what was considered socially acceptable, at one point for example turning his email signature into a "Bible excerpt awaiting review under the Communications Decency Act," with the accompanying text describing an incestuous orgy.[146] (Or perhaps he downright overstepped socially acceptable boundaries, depending on who you'd ask; May didn't seem to care much either way.)

And his presence on the mailing list served another valuable purpose, too. Although the list was completely unmoderated, May often acted as a de facto moderator, guiding conversations when needed. If a discussion was at risk of derailing, he had a habit of weighing in with his signature analytical take, explaining why he believed certain comments or topics were or were not appropriate for the list, but without actually forbidding anything; he didn't want anyone to have that power, not even himself. Rather than imposing on others how to behave, May had a way of leading by example, and when other subscribers would complain about the content on the mailing list, he encouraged them to lead by example as well.

For many of its subscribers, May had over the months and years that the list was active probably come to embody what the Cypherpunk philosophy represented. Due to his strong presence—both content-wise and in his guiding role—he'd become a leading and characteristic voice of the movement.

May himself, however, regularly made sure to point out that he did not, in fact, represent all Cypherpunks. In the same way that he did not want any moderator to be in charge on the mailing list, he strongly rejected the idea that he or anyone else should be considered a formal leader or spokesperson of the movement.

"While it may be the case that each of us has his or her own personal [hierarchical] ratings of others, it is important that we never have tried to formalize or 'vote on' these ratings. Or voted to elect a Great Leader," May at one point argued. "Our strength is in our numbers and in our ideas, not in the guy we have ensconced in an office in Washington so he can give press conferences and sound bites for journalists. Our strength is in our multi-headed (dare I mention 'Medusa'?), multinational, informal lack of structure."[147]

Indeed, the Cypherpunks were not an organization in the traditional sense. It was an intentionally informal, unstructured, and open collective. The Cypherpunks had no voting procedure, no representatives, and they didn't even issue collective statements. Anyone could become a Cypherpunk, but all Cypherpunks ultimately engaged as individuals. They were not tasked with responsibilities or subject to rules—nor could anyone hold others responsible for their own actions.

Still, action *was* encouraged. If someone believed the Cypherpunks should build a specific technology, attend some event, or contribute something else to the cause, it was up to them to take the initiative and see if others wanted to help.

In effect, the Cypherpunk movement did not just work towards a different type of future. For May, it already represented that future. He considered the open, permissionless, and nonhierarchical mode under which the Cypherpunks and their email list operated as a model for an upcoming *crypto-anarchist* society.

Crypto-Anarchy

The Extropians would sometimes speculate about carving out areas of freedom to subvert, hide, or escape from state control over their lives. Some of them proposed that building cities on big floating islands in the sea—*seasteading*—was the way to go. Others believed it might be possible to purchase a small island on which to found a libertarian society. Yet others suggested they should all move to a specific jurisdiction and try to influence local political structures to get rid of as many laws and regulations as possible.

But Tim May didn't really feel like moving. He had a better idea.

Ever since May had connected the dots to see the disruptive potential of anonymous information markets, he'd begun envisioning a future that resembled the worlds from his cyberpunk books, while at the same time drawing analogies with *Atlas Shrugged*. The type of society he wanted to write about in his upcoming novel, he'd realized, could be made a reality.

In Rand's novel, the productive entrepreneurs manufacture their escape using futuristic technology. Heat ray screens were still delegated to the realm of science fiction, May knew, but the cofounder of the Cypherpunk movement had come to see that—like in cyberpunk stories—the internet and strong cryptography could eventually facilitate a very similar escape from state power.

May outlined this vision in "The Crypto Anarchist Manifesto."[148] Originally written for the 1988 edition of the Crypto conference, he read the short manifesto at the very first Cypherpunks gathering at Hughes's apartment, and later shared it with the Cypherpunks mailing list as well.

"A specter is haunting the modern world, the specter of crypto anarchy," the manifesto opened with a nod to Karl Marx's and Friedrich Engels's *Communist Manifesto*, before predicting that computer technology and cryptographic protocols "will alter completely the nature of government regulation, the ability to tax and control economic interactions, the ability to keep information secret, and will even alter the nature of trust and reputation."

To conclude a few paragraphs below:

"Just as the technology of printing altered and reduced the power of medieval guilds and the social power structure, so too will cryptologic methods fundamentally alter the nature of corporations and of government interference in economic transactions."[149]

The internet had not (yet) morphed into a colorful 3D-world, as Vinge's, Stephenson's, and Gibson's novels imagined the future to be like. But taken as more metaphorical representations of online domains, May had come to appreciate the stories as visionary regardless. As the internet continued on its inevitable path towards mass adoption, and people would step-by-step learn to self-organize online, May believed that real-world state institutions would eventually be replaced by cyberspace-equivalents. The internet would increasingly facilitate a parallel, digital society, with its own communities, companies and, ultimately, its own economies.

"This allows for rapid experimentation, self selection, and evolution," May proposed on the Cypherpunks mailing list. "If folks get tired of some virtual community, they can leave. The cryptographic aspects mean their membership in some community is unknown to others (vis-a-vis the physical or outside world, i.e., their 'true names') and physical coercion is reduced."

Continuing:

"The electronic world is by no means complete, as we will still live much of our lives in the physical world. But economic activity is sharply increasing in the Net domain and these 'crypto anarchy' ideas will further erode the power of physical states to tax and coerce residents."[150]

This was all made possible, indeed, by the power of cryptography. Not only would crypto tools help users shield their real-world identity, protecting them from physical force, but the same tools would let any two individuals conduct business without either of them ever knowing who they dealt with.

"[. . .] strong crypto is the 'building material' of cyberspace," May wrote to his fellow Cypherpunks, "the mortar, the bricks, the support beams, the walls. Nothing else can provide the 'permanence'… without crypto, the walls are subject to collapse at the first touch by a malicious person or agency. With crypto, not even a 100 megaton H-bomb can breach the walls."[151]

May foresaw that Cypherpunk tools would help people hide that economic activity from the state and create a "Galt's Gulch in cyberspace," and he looked forward to a future where this would ultimately lead to the collapse of governments altogether. Without forced redistribution of wealth, this future economy would self-organize around voluntary interaction and free markets; *spontaneous order* would emerge through the internet.

"Indeed, Hayek has had a _lot_ to do with the Cypherpunks!" May wrote on the Cypherpunk mailing list. "From 'The Road to Serfdom' to 'Law, Legislation, and Liberty,' his works have exerted a profound influence on me, and on many others. [. . .] In fact, I would say Hayek would've been a candidate for being a cover boy for 'Wired'… assuming of course he was 60 years younger, had some of his body parts [pierced], and, even better, was a Netchick."[152]

Code

Tim May was well aware that the crypto-anarchist ideas he spread weren't exactly appealing to a general audience; not everyone hopes for the collapse of governments. Worse, when they'd learn that unbreakable encryption and anonymous mix networks could enable large-scale distribution of child pornography and facilitate secure communication for terrorist cells, many people would probably look at these new tools with fear and anger.

Yet, May refused to downplay the risks that these new technologies introduced.

"Privacy has its price," he simply argued. "The ability of people to plot crimes and commit crimes behind closed doors is obvious, and yet we don't demand secret cameras in homes, apartments, and hotel rooms!"[153]

Besides, for May, crypto-anarchy was not some faraway utopia that required widespread support for his ideas anyways: rather, he almost considered it a fait accompli. He understood that the road to get there could be riddled with setbacks and repressive laws, justified by policy makers that stoke fears about the "Four Horseman of the Infocalypse": terrorists, pedophiles, money launderers, and pornographers. But Cypherpunk tools were cheap to distribute, easy to use, and they couldn't be un-invented. In the long run, May believed, success was virtually guaranteed.

This did not mean that every Cypherpunk shared May's rather radical vision, though—nor did they need to. More often than not Cypherpunks were libertarians, but many also subscribed to a more moderate world-view than May did. Some Cypherpunks were in fact not libertarian at all, with several of them even identifying as socialist.

"I am not a libertarian, nor is it likely that I ever will be," Hughes wrote to the mailing list. "The agenda of privacy is orthogonal to most partisan political positions. As strong as the libertarian presence is on this list, it is by no means the only view. It is precisely because cypherpunk issues cut clean across the political spectrum that they are so powerful."[154]

What mattered, May and Hughes agreed, was that Cypherpunks could work towards a common goal regardless of their political affiliation:

the goal of developing and distributing privacy tools. *Cypherpunks write code.*

Indeed, the group had barely gotten started when Hughes developed an early version of the first-ever remailer, based on David Chaum's mix network proposal. The early implementation of this remailer would accept emails, scrub any details referring to the sender, and forward it to either the next remailer or to the intended recipient of the email. Hughes's implementation did not yet include encryption tools, however; it was still a work in progress.

Lucky enough, Hughes soon got help from another Cypherpunk. Hal Finney, one of the Extropians that had joined Tim May to the Cypherpunk gatherings, had just started contributing to Phil Zimmermann's PGP implementation. Leveraging his newfound knowledge of public key cryptography, it wasn't long before Finney rolled PGP into Hughes's remailer code.

Just a few weeks after the first meeting, Cypherpunks had developed a fully functional remailer. And they would operate it, too. Finney and several other Cypherpunks took it on themselves to run the remailer programs, and distributed software and starter guides so others could join them. With that, remailers were operational. Anyone with a computer and an internet connection could by late 1992 send emails without revealing their metadata.

Around that same time, Zimmermann was about to release PGP 2.0. Finney's contributions to this release had resulted in significant improvements over the first version, and the software now included a web-of-trust system to let users cryptographically vouch that a public key really belongs to a specific individual.

With Hughes's brand-new remailer software and Zimmermann's upgraded encryption tool, the Cypherpunks were off to a good start.

But it wouldn't be long before they were forced on the defensive . . .

The Crypto Wars

When Bill Clinton took office as the 42nd President of the United States in January 1993, his new administration was quick to share its concerns about potentially nefarious use of personal computers and the internet.

They announced that law enforcement was going to require new tools in order to keep up with the recent pace of technological innovation.

It turned out to be a harbinger of the Crypto Wars of the 1990s; the US government was going to try to limit the use of cryptography.

The first shot was fired when Zimmermann became the target of a criminal investigation. In the United States at this time, cryptographic protocols that used keys larger than 40 bits were classified as munitions within the definition of the Arms Export Control Act. Sending or bringing a strong cryptosystem abroad required a license—the same type of license you'd need for international transport of firearms, ammunition, or explosives.

Zimmermann had no such license, but he did share his free software over the internet. Since the internet knows no borders, the government insinuated that Zimmermann had been illegally exporting the software and the crypto protocols it included.

And then there was the Clipper chip, a chipset developed by the NSA and supported by the Clinton administration. The Clipper chip used public key cryptography to encrypt data, but the NSA had added a special decryption key to the protocol. The plan was to have telecommunication companies like AT&T adopt the chipset, which would let users encrypt their phone calls. The telecom companies would hold on to a decryption key, however, which could be handed to the government on request. Such *key escrow* was needed for national security reasons, the Clinton administration insisted: authorities had to be able to listen in to the phone calls of potential and suspected terrorists.

The Clipper chip faced opposition from privacy advocates and civil liberties interest groups across the country, including the EFF, the Electronic Privacy Information Center (EPIC), and the American Civil Liberties Union (ACLU), as well as tech publications like *Wired*, cryptography startups like Ron Rivest, Adi Shamir, and Leonard Adleman's RSA, and some politicians (both Democrat and Republican). Critics believed that key escrow could subject citizens to increased and possibly unlawful government surveillance.

The Cypherpunks of course rejected the Clipper chip as well; opposition against the NSA chip became one of the first regularly recurring topics on the mailing list. It was obvious that handing decryption keys to telecoms (and, by extension, to government bodies regulating the telecoms) would render these cryptographic protocols all but useless.

For Cypherpunks, privacy in no small part meant privacy from governments; that's how they could prevent an Orwellian future. And of course, the crypto-anarchist vision probably wouldn't get very far with their Galt's Gulch in cyberspace if the cryptographic building blocks that shielded them from the state turned out to be porous.

At the same time, mandating the use of compromised or weak encryption protocols would not make the world a safer place in any meaningful sense, cypherpunks argued. Nefarious actors could still use proper encryption underneath the weak Chipper chip layer of encryption to hide the contents of their communication, so even if government agents would use their designated decryption key, all they'd find is more ciphertext.

Tim May believed that the Cypherpunks could serve a key role in the ensuing crypto wars. Where established interest groups were better organized, better funded, and better connected with policymakers and regulators, May saw the Cypherpunks's more anarchist organizational model as a strength in its own right. Scattered throughout the United States and beyond, with no formal leader or organization, the Cypherpunks were impossible to co-opt. Whereas the EFF, EPIC, and ACLU could engage in gentle negotiation, the Cypherpunks weren't going to adopt anything resembling a position of moderation.

"In a sense, Cypherpunks fill an important ecological niche by being the outrageous side, the radical side… perhaps a bit like the role the Black Panthers, Yippies, and Weather Underground played a generation ago," May wrote.[155]

Indeed, the Cypherpunk opposition took shape in various forms; exactly because they had no formal organization, Cypherpunks ultimately acted on their own accord. Some of them distributed flyers with information about the Clipper chip at local malls. Others analyzed how the chip worked to try to find flaws in its design. And, of course, the Cypherpunks's main strategy was writing code.

"One real world intrusion could be the outright banning of strong crypto, with government approved ciphers mandated," May speculated about further escalation of the Crypto Wars. "Such a ban will have a chilling, devastating effect on our privacy, on our ability to set up the cyberspace worlds I have described, and on computer-mediated markets in general."

Concluding:

"Our immediate goal must be to make sure the 'genie is out of the bottle,' that enough crypto tools and knowledge are widely disseminated so that such a government ban is futile."[156]

Successes

The Cypherpunks were motivated and driven, but facing the full force of the US government, few would have expected them to come out of the Crypto Wars as victors.

Yet, they started booking one success after another.

One of the most notable wins could be attributed to Matt Blaze, a Bell Labs security researcher and regular on the Cypherpunks mailing list. In 1994, Blaze dealt a painful blow to the Clipper chip by publishing a paper that exposed a flaw in the chip's design that would let users disable the special decryption key. Already suffering some reputational damage from the fierce opposition it faced, it now turned out that the Clipper Chip didn't even do what it was supposed to.

It was enough for telecom companies to decide against adopting the NSA technology. The project would be entirely defunct by 1996.

In a similar vein, Cypherpunks Ian Goldberg and David Wagner in 1995 managed to break Netscape's closed source and export-grade encryption standard as part of a contest designed by Hal Finney, and did so within just a few hours. It represented a blow to the image of one of Silicon Valley's premier flagship companies.

In response to the breach, Netscape claimed that they were barred from offering stronger encryption standards abroad, and although this was only part of the problem, it did little to reassure potential customers outside the US. The affair highlighted another problem caused by the classifying encryption as munition: American tech companies risked losing market share to foreign competitors.[157]

Yet another Cypherpunk, Brad Huntting, had in 1994 came up with a clever idea to challenge export restrictions on such crypto protocols: to publish code in a physical format to demonstrate that bans on software distributions are in conflict with fundamental rights.

"The right to free speech is protected by the US constitution. We need only show that encryption software == speech," he wrote to the mailing list. "This shouldn't be to [sic] difficult (a bit painful perhaps, but not difficult). The act should involve a published work (preferably in the printed sense)."[158]

About a year later, Zimmermann published *PGP: Source Code and Internals*: he had printed the complete PGP source code in a book. As indeed pointed out by Huntting, books (including the export of books) are in the US protected under the First Amendment. By freely and legally distributing in hardcover the exact same information that had made him subject to criminal investigation, Zimmermann highlighted the absurdity of crypto exports regulations.

Although it was never confirmed that it had anything to do with the publication of his book, the US government dropped Zimmermann's case in early 1996.

Moreover, the export bans would by the end of that year be lifted altogether. A combination of legal challenges, economically harmful limitations on the American tech sector, and the by then already irreversibly widespread distribution of crypto protocols outside of the United States moved the Clinton administration to scrap commercial encryption from the Munition List entirely.

The Cypherpunks hadn't done it alone: the movement to defend cryptography during the Crypto Wars was broader than just them. But, they had undeniably played an important part. The loose collective of hackers and cryptographers united by little more than a mailing list on the internet had taken on the US government, and won.

Chapter 9:
Cypherpunk Currency

CYPHERPUNKS HAD SET out to defend privacy in the digital age, and they understood that the privacy offered by physical cash was at risk. If electronic payments were to replace paper bills and metal coins, banks and other transaction processors (and by extension the governments that regulate them) could monitor all economic activity.

Echoing David Chaum's warnings—the cryptographer and his eCash system served as a great inspiration—Cypherpunks believed that this could ultimately mark the end of human freedom.

"[. . .] if the government creates this cashless society, then the government will have unprecedented control over nearly all aspects of our lives," Tim May would argue on the Cypherpunk mailing list.

"All transactions, no matter how trivial, will be recorded, stored, and subject to analysis. A complete audit trail of all purchases, food preferences, entertainment choices, liasons [sic] with others, etc., will exist," he wrote. "Furthermore, transactions which are deemed to be politically incorrect, and there are dozens of obvious examples to choose from, can be _outlawed_ by the mere typing of a few lines of instructions into the appropriate data bases."[159]

May in his post offered some relatively mundane examples to support this point. Someone who'd been arrested for driving under the influence could be barred from purchasing beer at a liquor store, he suggested, or pregnant women ("and under Clinton's computerized health care system this will all be known") could be refused to buy cigarettes. State oversight over transactions wouldn't just affect dangerous criminals or fringe political dissidents, the Cypherpunk wanted to stress, it would ultimately facilitate total control over all citizens: "Make no mistake, a government-run cashless society will be worse [than] Orwell's worst."[160]

It's why May had at the very first Cypherpunk gathering presented the concept of electronic cash, and why the loose collective of hackers and cryptographers who gathered in Eric Hughes's unfurnished apartment immediately embraced the idea. The creation of a digital payment system with strong privacy guarantees, Cypherpunks believed, could help prevent such a dystopian future.

But this wasn't the only reason why Cypherpunks wanted to create digital cash; they believed that cash for the internet could benefit their movement in more ways than one.

Besides privacy, some Cypherpunks were very interested in other features that electronic money could potentially offer—like fast transaction settlement, non-reversibility, or cost efficiency. They were excited about new possibilities that such features might unlock: internet cash could benefit online services and games, they speculated, or enable machine-to-machine payments. This could in turn perhaps facilitate innovative new types of markets, like the markets for allocating computer resources proposed by the high-tech Hayekians.

Even closer to home, digital cash could benefit Cypherpunk projects like remailers. The remailers developed by Eric Hughes and Hal Finney were initially operated by Cypherpunks as free services, but it wasn't obvious that this arrangement could last. As these services would grow more popular over time, operating a remailer could eventually become too resource-intensive for hobbyist volunteers; Hughes expected that operators would one day have to start charging fees. For obvious reasons, such payments would have to be anonymous: users shouldn't have to reveal their identity to use remailers.

Similarly, the development of anonymous information markets—BlackNets—depended on the existence of a privacy-preserving form of digital money. For people to be willing to sell classified documents or secret reports over the internet, they'd have to be confident that superiors at their government agency or corporation couldn't find out it was them who sold these records for a little extra cash: indeed, this meant that this little extra cash needed to be void of any identifying properties.

And electronic cash was ultimately a critical building block in Tim May's crypto-anarchist vision for the future. Establishing a parallel society in the digital realm—a "Galt's Gulch in cyberspace"—required that people could hide their income and wealth from their governments. An anonymous digital currency would allow people to escape taxation.

May knew that electronic cash would not by itself immediately put the taxman out of a job. Those people with visible participation in the economy—"the guy who works for Lockheed or behind the counter at Safeway"—would still be footing the bill to pay for Uncle Sam. But May argued that if some notable segment of the economy successfully and consistently escaped taxes, a change in public sentiment would eventually trigger a much bigger social change.

"[T]he effect will be [. . .] an erosion of _support_ for taxation, as word spreads that many consultants, writers, information sellers, and the like are sheltering much of their income via use of networks and strong crypto," May wrote. "The tax system is already shaky--$5 trillion national debt, growing every year—and it may not take much of a push to trigger a 'phase change'; a tax revolt."[161]

And last but not least, there was the potential for monetary reform.

In particular, some of the Cypherpunks who, like Tim May were also part of the Extropian community, saw in electronic cash a tool to help realize Friedrich Hayek's free banking economy. Since electronic cash can be denominated in whatever the market wants, they figured it could make currency competition significantly more practical, and much harder to stop: free banks could be located anywhere in the world, while anyone with an internet connection could use their currency, anonymously.

"[. . .] the strong crypto used allows more flexibility in bypassing normal currency rules and can allow users to mutually agree on whatever currency they wish,"[162] May wrote on the Cypherpunks mailing list. And: "one of the potential advantages of strong crypto is the oft-discussed 'denationalization of money.'"[163]

Altogether, it posited electronic cash as something akin to the Cypherpunk's holy grail.

Chaum's Compromise

When the Cypherpunks were just getting started in the early 1990s, the only electronic cash project that offered strong privacy was David Chaum's eCash. So when they discussed digital cash at their meetings or on the Cypherpunks mailing list, Tim May and other Cypherpunks typically referred to Chaum's design, either implicitly or explicitly. His blind signature scheme had solved a crucial part of the privacy puzzle.

Several of the Cypherpunks would even go to Amsterdam themselves, to work at Chaum's digital currency startup for a while. Besides Cypherpunk cofounder Eric Hughes and computer scientist (and Extropian) Nick Szabo, this for example also included security specialist Bryce "Zooko" Wilcox-O'Hearn, and early Cypherpunk Lucky Green.

Chaum, however, wasn't particularly charmed by the more radical crypto-anarchist aspirations that May and some of the other Cypherpunks espoused. The cryptographer wasn't working on a digital cash system to facilitate digital black markets, and he had no desire to help people bring down governments through mass tax evasion. For Chaum, privacy was needed to save democracy—not to get rid of it. While not all Cypherpunks shared May's more radical vision, Chaum preferred not to be associated with their movement at all, and he never joined their mailing list.

Meanwhile, not all Cypherpunks were unequivocally happy with Chaum and his work, either.

Hughes had of course decided to leave DigiCash after just a few weeks at the company; his disappointment in Chaum's business strategy had ultimately served as an impetus to found the Cypherpunk movement. In the following years, Hughes asserted himself on the Cypherpunks mailing list as a consistent and sometimes harsh critic of his former employer: he regularly lambasted the startup's continued focus on hardware products.

Cypherpunk hopes that Chaum would deliver on the promise of digital cash crumbled further when they learned that eCash was being designed without strong privacy guarantees for sellers (eCash transaction recipients). Whereas DigiCash's electronic cash system offered robust privacy for buyers (transaction senders), the true identity of an eCash recipient could be uncovered if the sender and the bank cooperated to do so. (In short: the sender would need to share the unblinded digital cash with the bank, so when the recipient deposits the eCash notes, the bank could link this to the real name associated with the recipient's bank account.)

To the surprise of many Cypherpunks, Chaum considered this a desirable feature. The DigiCash CEO reasoned that having the option to deanonymize recipients could prevent that eCash would be used for extortion, kidnapping, or other nefarious criminal activity. By extension, this would probably also make the digital cash system more acceptable for banks and other financial institutions, and (especially) for the regulators overseeing them.

Privacy Hardliners

For most Cypherpunks, the compromise on seller anonymity in eCash was a big disappointment.

Their goal was, first and foremost, to preserve the level of privacy that was already offered by physical cash, which included anonymity on both sides of a transaction: neither buyers nor sellers reveal personal information when they exchange a dollar bill. May's crypto-anarchist vision, furthermore, *required* full buyer and seller anonymity: no one would put stolen army documents up for sale on a BlackNet if it was trivial for the purchaser to learn their real name.

Most Cypherpunks therefore had no desire or intention of making compromises on privacy for the sake of making electronic cash technology less attractive for criminals. Nor were they interested in designing software tools to make digital cash more acceptable for regulators: governments were *themselves* considered the greatest potential threat to their privacy, at least in the dystopian future they had set out to prevent. They believed that any weaknesses in privacy systems were bound to be abused.

"_any_ system which allows government to act to trace a transaction, or to trace a message, or to gain access to keys, essentially throws away the liberty-enhancing advantages of cryptography completely," May argued on the mailing list. "[A]sk yourself whether the government of Myanmar, known as SLORC, would not use its 'Government Access to Keys' to round up the dissidents in the jungle. Would Hitler and Himmler have used 'key recovery' to determine who the Jews were communicating with so they could all be rounded up and killed? Would the East German Staasi have traced e-cash transations? [sic] For every government extant on the planet [. . .] one can easily think of dozens of examples where access to keys, access to diaries, access to spending records, etc., would be exploited."[164]

And although it was true that extortionists, kidnappers, and other criminals would benefit from a fully anonymous payment system as well, May did not believe that the kinds of privacy compromises pursued by Chaum could even realistically solve anything. The scenario where a kidnapper is caught because his identity is revealed through cooperation between the payer and the bank would probably never actually occur, he pointed out, because the kidnapper would not use this system with compromised privacy features in the first place.

Rather, as long as *any* private payment solution existed anywhere in the world, the kidnappers would probably demand that the money is simply sent to them through that system instead . . . and some private payment solution would likely always exist *somewhere*.

"It could be a physical bank, a la the Bank of Albania, or it could be an underground payment system, a la the Mafia, the Tongs, the Triads, whatever," May suggested. "Unfortunately for [financial regulators], and unfortunately for the victims of such crimes, no such worldwide stoppage of all such systems seems possible, even with draconian police state measures. There are just too many interstices for the bits to hide. And too much economic incentive for some persons or banks to offer such funds transfer methods."[165]

Chaum had through eCash helped shape how May and his fellow privacy activists thought about online privacy and electronic payments, but a few years into his digital cash project, the pioneering cryptographer was making fundamentally different trade-offs than most of the Cypherpunks would.

Disappointed, May wrote to the Cypherpunks mailing list:

"As to fully untraceable digital cash--the real e-cash--we may be the carriers of the torch for this."[166]

Patents

Some of the Cypherpunks did come up with solutions to make an eCash-like system with complete privacy for both buyers and sellers.

Zooko, for example, pointed out that the problem was easily solved if users were allowed to have pseudonymous bank accounts: banks can't link an eCash payment to a real identity if they don't know the real identity of their account holders to begin with. (The Cypherpunks sometimes discussed offshore banking in this context.)

Nick Szabo, alternatively, suggested that sellers could perhaps swap the eCash they received with someone else's eCash, and send this new eCash to the bank instead. This would prevent the original payment from being linked to the recipient's real identity—though it might require trust in the eCash exchanger. (The exchanger could still cooperate with the bank to reveal the eCash recipient's identity, and possibly even steal the eCash by abandoning the trade halfway through.)

A third option was proposed by an anonymous mailing list contributor who came up with a scheme where the seller was involved with the initial creation of the eCash. Where in the original eCash protocol only the buyer and the bank are involved with the generation of blinding keys and blind signatures, this protocol would let the eventual recipient of the electronic currency add a layer of encryption as well.

But for all of these solutions, there was one big problem: David Chaum held the patent for the blind signature algorithm. And the Cypherpunks believed that he would only license his product to "respectable" organizations that would not, in his view, make his technology look bad. Suffice to say, the Cypherpunks concluded he wouldn't license it to their ragtag group of crypto-anarchists and privacy fundamentalists.[167]

It represented a source of frustration for the Cypherpunks, perhaps best articulated in a lengthy mailing list post by Tim May. Channeling both the hacker ethos and the Extropian philosophy, the group's cofounder argued that technological progress was best achieved through experimentation and competition, and made the case that software patents hinder both.

Physical products, even if patented, can at least be used to the buyer's desire after purchase, May pointed out. For example, patented microchips were in the 1980s freely used by independent technologists to build their own computers, kicking off the personal computer revolution. Software licensing schemes, in contrast, imposed all kinds of restrictions on how the software is used even after it is purchased, effectively killing further innovation.

"[. . .] the issue of concern is that the patents on the software ideas and concepts mean that experimenters, developers, and hackers cannot buy a license for digicash the way they would buy some ICs and then experiment, develop, and hack," May explained. "The guy in the garage trying to develop a 'digital postage stamp,' for example, can't use the Chaumian blinding protocols without hiring lawyers, paying Chaum his up-front fee, and laying out his designs and business plans (which he very probably doesn't even have!)."[168]

As a result, May expected the evolution of digital cash to grind to a halt.

While David Chaum was unquestionably a pioneer in the field, Cypherpunks increasingly came to see the cryptographer as someone who hindered rather than helped the future of electronic cash.

Alternatives

If Cypherpunks wanted to improve on the eCash protocol, they would have to wait another decade for Chaum's patents to expire—but this seemed like an eternity. Tim May, Eric Hughes, and John Gilmore had started the Cypherpunk movement exactly because they'd already grown frustrated by the lack of progress in the crypto domain, and that was itself over ten years after Chaum had published his first digital cash papers.

An electronic form of cash was due, and *Cypherpunks write code*; they would have to work around the patents.

One way to do this was by looking for alternatives. Chaum's proposals from the 1980s had marked the start of a stream of publications in the 1990s: in just a few years' time, some 200 papers were published on the topic of electronic money, and several dozen new patents were filed.[169] As one of the more notable examples, in 1996 Ron Rivest and Adi Shamir (of RSA fame) designed two micropayment schemes called PayWord and MicroMint, while in that same year the NSA would describe an electronic cash scheme, too.[170]

From time to time, various Cypherpunks proposed alternative electronic cash designs on the mailing list as well. As an early—and quite original—example, computer science student Hadon Nash presented a digital currency scheme he called "Digital Gold." In his post, Nash described a system where users would "own" numbers; any number goes, but lower numbers would have a lower value. Claiming a number was as easy as producing a cryptographic signature with that number, and the first person to claim it would "own" it. Transferring ownership of a number was done with a message that included the new owner, as identified (only) with a public key, and a cryptographic signature proving that the original owner approved of the transfer. The history of ownership of any number could then be tracked through a chain of cryptographic signatures.[171]

Most electronic cash designs didn't introduce anything groundbreaking, however. In regards to privacy features in particular, many—including the scheme proposed by the NSA—were just variations on (or iterations of) Chaum's design. And those that did introduce an innovative approach tended to have other fundamental limitations. Rivest and Shamir's electronic cash schemes, for instance, could only really be useful for rather specific kinds of low-value payments because the validity of currency units would quickly expire.

Yet other ideas were broken on a more fundamental level—like Nash's Digital Gold solution, which didn't account for the double-spending problem. As pointed out by Hal Finney on the Cypherpunks mailing list, if the same number was transferred to multiple public keys, different users may end up with diverging ownership records. (Nash did suggest a system where users would have to check with "agencies" to see if a coin would be accepted by them before accepting it themselves—which would prove the number wasn't double-spent—but this part of the proposal hadn't been worked out very well.)

"I have to say, though," Finney nonetheless wrote, "that although I don't really think the digital gold proposal is technically feasible, the proposal to own numbers shows tremendous chutzpah and is quite creative."[172]

The Experiments

Because there didn't seem to be many promising alternatives, a more popular way to work around Chaum's patents was therefore to stay under the radar.

A number of Cypherpunks would eventually implement their own versions of eCash, but to avoid lawsuits, these digital cash systems were intended for testing purposes only. They assumed that their experimental projects would be tolerated as long as they had no commercial intentions, and wouldn't be used to transfer real value.

By mid-1994, the play money schemes represented a small Cypherpunk trend. Mailing list contributor Matt Thomlinson, for example, launched an implementation of eCash named Ghostmarks. Meanwhile, Pr0duct Cypher, a pseudonymous individual who also contributed to PGP, launched Magic Money. And Mike Duvos, another regular on the mailing list, ran a Magic Money implementation which he called Tacky Tokens.

Further, someone going by the name Black Unicorn even presented the "fully backed" DigiFrancs system:

"DigiFrancs are backed by 10 cases of Diet Coke, located at the UniBank 'vault' reserves in Washington, DC. DigiFrancs are redeemable for their equivalent value in 16 oz Diet Coke cans (unchilled) on demand FAS

Washington, DC. This arrangement implies no agreement between any of the parties and Coca-Cola company."[173]

While of course intended as a joke—even the Diet Coke-backed Digi-Franks were not actually intended to be used as money—the various types of electronic cash actually did gain minor traction as media of exchange. Some of the Cypherpunks accepted these play currencies in exchange for digital knickknacks like GIFs.

Indeed, these weren't exactly large value transfers, but it did raise an interesting question.

"Now, if you're still awake, comes the fun part," Pr0duct Cypher announced, after explaining the technical details of Magic Money on the mailing list, "[H]ow do you introduce real value into your digicash system? How, for that matter, do you even get people to play with it?"

Chaum wanted to deploy his eCash system through existing financial institutions, where digital cash units would be redeemable for real dollars (or other fiat currencies). eCash would effectively be backed by money in the bank, which should—hopefully—make people comfortable enough to start accepting the new type of money as payment.

But Pr0duct Cypher now suggested that maybe this dollar redeemability wasn't actually necessary. Perhaps, he mused, digital cash wouldn't need to be backed at all.

"What makes gold valuable?" he asked, rhetorically. "It has some useful properties: it is a good conductor, is resistant to corrosion and chemicals, etc. But those have only recently become important. Why has gold been valuable for thousands of years? It's pretty, it's shiny, and most importantly, it is scarce."

Pr0duct Cypher concluded:

"Your digicash should be scarce."[174]

Backing Digital Cash

Throughout the next couple of years—the mid-1990s—topics like the nature of money, value, and currency backing would pop up on the

Cypherpunks mailing list with some regularity. It made sense that Cypherpunks were discussing these issues; in order to create electronic cash, they had to understand what would actually give it value. Why would anyone give up real products or services in exchange for a number on a screen?

It turned out that various list members had very different ideas about this.

Some didn't really consider digital cash to have any value at all, and even thought that it was a bit of a misnomer to speak about it in monetary terms. Software developer Perry Metzger, one of the more active list contributors on topics related to digital cash, for example argued that something along the lines of "digital anonymous bank drafts" would actually be a more accurate description.

"Just as a check can be USED for money but is in fact a way of TRANSFERING [sic] money, so digicash isn't in and of itself the source of value — its [sic] a bookkeeping system for something that is," he wrote. "That something could be dollars, gold, cocaine futures contracts on the Bogota Commodity Exchange, girl scout cookies, or anything else people decide is a good medium of exchange."[175]

Others, like Eric Hughes, didn't have an issue considering digital cash a form of money, but did agree that the bits and bytes had to be backed by *something* of value; in most cases a conventional fiat currency like the dollar or pound would be the obvious choice. He believed that for electronic currency to catch on, users would need a guarantee that they'd be able to exchange their digital cash for a fixed amount of "real" money.

Yet another perspective came from Robert Hettinga, a Cypherpunk who (in his own words) used to work in "Morgan Stanley's cage in Chicago."[176] As another very active participant in discussions about money and electronic cash on the Cypherpunk mailing list, Hettinga argued that the need for convertibility to "real" money would disappear over time, as people would slowly learn to trust the new digital currency.

Drawing an analogy from evolutionary biology, he wrote:

"Remember, proto-wings were evolved by pond-skimming insects so they could skim across ponds faster. Eventually, when those proto-wings evolved into actual wings, flying insects didn't need ponds anymore. With that idea in mind, digital bearer certificates are going to have to interface with the book entry world of meatspace for a while, in order to be [convertible] into other assets."

But, Hettinga predicted: "Eventually, at some point, those assets won't be book-entries anymore."[177]

Tim May, meanwhile, didn't believe money needed to be backed in the first place. In line with Hayek's freebanking far-sight, he argued that it ultimately all came down to future expectations: people just needed to have confidence that money would maintain its purchasing power.

"I believe _all_ forms of money, whether hard, fiat, whatever, come from the expectation that the money will be of the same value, more or less, in the future," he wrote. "Call it the 'greater fool theory of money.' All one cares about is that a greater fool will take the money."[178]

Still, May didn't quite view electronic cash as being money in its own right. Rather, he considered it something new, a means to transfer funds from one bank account or place of holding to another—more akin to checks or wire transfers. So although he didn't believe digital cash had to be "backed" in the way it was commonly understood, May did assume that currency-issuing banks or bank-like entities would ultimately control the actual currency underlying the electronic cash: "What really backs [digital cash] up is the reputation of the entities."[179]

And then, there was a British Cypherpunk who thought electronic cash did not need to be backed *at all* . . .

Adam Back

Adam Back, a computer science postdoc at the University of Exeter in his mid-twenties, had never attended an in-person Cypherpunk meeting. But he had found the mailing list online. He'd become particularly interested in electronic cash, and quickly became one of the most active participants in discussions on this topic.

Having dabbled with CyberBucks for a little bit himself, Back experienced firsthand that people could attribute value to purely digital, unbacked coins. Based on little more than a promise about the total supply, Cyber-Bucks were traded for real money, and used in actual commerce—even if only within a small niche in an obscure corner of the internet.

Although CyberBucks had become worthless the instant that DigiCash's server went offline, Back saw no reason why a new and improved electronic cash system couldn't attract value in a similar way—and do better.

"How about this, rather than interface your ecash system with US dollars yourself through credit cards/ debit cards/ cheques / cash, just set up an entirely disconnected system," he proposed on the Cypherpunks mailing list in April 1997.[180]

"What we want is fully anonymous, ultra low transaction cost, transferable units of exchange. If we get that going [. . .] the banks will become the obsolete [dinosaurs] they deserve to become," Back added a few days later in a follow-up email. "I think this would be a good outcome, and I'd rather see this happen than see anyone go to any great effort to get the banks involved."[181]

Back believed that, just like any other product traded on the free market, the forces of supply and demand would regulate the value of a digital currency, as users would buy and sell it for fiat currencies as well as accept it in exchange for goods and services. Once a market value was established, this electronic cash could be used to send value over the internet with a click of a button, and—importantly—without having to deal with financial institutions whatsoever.

To what extent people would value an unbacked digital form of money ultimately depended on its properties, Back predicted. A digital currency that can be used anonymously—like cash—would presumably be valued more than an otherwise-similar digital currency that leaves traces of users' spending patterns, for example. A digital currency that can persist regardless of any specific company going bankrupt, meanwhile, would probably be valued more than a currency that risks becoming useless overnight due to a single server going offline. And so forth.

Back eventually shared a shortlist of six desirable properties for electronic cash[182]:

1. *anonymous (privacy preserving, payee and payer anonymous)*

2. *distributed (to make it hard to shut down)*

3. *have some built in scarcity*

4. *require no trust of any one individual*

5. *preferably offline (difficult to do with pure software)*

6. *reusable*

Any system that could offer these six properties would attract real value, Back foresaw, and would thus become an actual, unbacked, digital currency.

It sounded simple enough, perhaps—though the computer science post-doc knew that it really wasn't. Some of the properties were difficult enough to realize even in the most general computer science context, while integrating them into a digital currency scheme would almost certainly be significantly harder. Successfully combining all six into a single system would be much harder, still.

Regardless, in true Cypherpunk fashion, Adam Back didn't just talk about electronic cash.

He wrote code . . .

Chapter 10:
Hashcash

GROWING UP IN the East Midlands of England, Adam Back had at thirteen years old saved enough money to buy the popular Sinclair ZX81 home computer. First released in January 1981, the black fax machine-sized device with built-in keyboard could be plugged into his family's home television set, bringing its 8-bit magic to the boy's fingertips right in the middle of his own living room.

As he played with the machine in his after-school hours—besides actual video games, this could also just mean having it do calculations to achieve some effect he found interesting—the young Adam Back became fascinated with the potential of computing.

And he had a knack for it, too. Lacking a native assembler to turn human-readable source code into machine-readable binaries (ones and zeroes), the youngster figured out how to code one up for the ZX81 himself. It required him to reverse-engineer the most basic inner workings of the computer, even having to convert binaries back to source code to understand how other programs worked.

By the time Back headed to college around age sixteen, he'd gained an advanced grasp of the operation of computers, and he knew that this was the field he wanted to keep exploring. Although computer science wasn't a formal course at his school at the time, the campus did have a computer lab. Back gratefully made use of the facility, often spending long days in the lab teaching himself more advanced programming languages.

After college, Back went on to study computer science at the University of Exeter, in the southwest of England. During his studies, he became particularly interested in distributed computing, where several computers connect through a network to collaborate on the same problem, typically by dividing the problem into smaller parts ("parallel computing").

Intrinsically motivated to master the curriculum, Back would regularly top his class throughout his three years as undergraduate student, which would by the early 1990s set him up to really pursue his interest in-depth. At twenty-one years old, the University of Exeter allowed him to skip his Masters, and accepted Back straight into a PhD program focused entirely on distributed computing. For the next four years, he'd study various coordination methods for networked computers—and their potential failure modes.

It was here that Back was introduced to long-standing challenges in distributed computing like the Byzantine Generals Problem, which computer scientists had struggled with since the late 1970s. The essence of this problem was that coordination across multiple computers could be tricky on open networks, where malicious (or even just unintentionally unreliable) nodes could join and frustrate the efforts of honest participants to reach a consensus.

The classic allegory, first described by computer scientist Leslie Lamport, was that of a group of (indeed) Byzantine generals surrounding a city.[183] As each of them staked out the situation, they'd communicate through messengers to coordinate whether to attack or retreat. Although either of these options would be acceptable, they'd have to all agree on which option to take; it would be a disaster if some of the generals were to attack, while others decide to retreat.

The problem, however, is that there are also some treacherous generals (and/or treacherous messengers, depending on the version of the allegory), who might send conflicting messages—"attack" or "retreat"—to various generals, causing discord. Since instant communication across different parties is impossible, some would see one instruction first ("attack"), while others would initially see the other instruction ("retreat").

The challenge, therefore, was to design a protocol that each honest participant could independently follow, so that they would all reach the same conclusion, whether that would be the conclusion to attack a city or not, or find consensus on how to coordinate some shared computational task.

These were the types of challenges that Adam Back loved to rack his brain on.

The Cypherpunk

As a PhD candidate, Back got acquainted with a master's student at the same university who was trying to optimize the RSA encryption protocol for parallel computing. It seemed like an interesting project to Back, and close to his own field of research, so he decided to help. This meant that he had to familiarize himself with the RSA algorithm, which in turn also led him to study Phil Zimmermann's new PGP project.

By now, Back had also developed an interest in free markets, and he was sympathetic to anarcho-capitalism. The hyper-libertarian ideology in which all functions of the state are entirely replaced by market-based solutions resembled the future society described in one of his favorite books: cyberpunk classic *Snow Crash*.

As such, Back found the cryptographic tools he was learning about very interesting on a sociological level.

"Less privacy is a bad thing in market economics terms, because as privacy takes a downward spiral, which leads to ever increasing government intervention, increasing sizes of governments, fascism, etc. the free market economy will go to hell," he would later explain. "Poverty, and food shortages will result, a la the former USSR, which is slowly recovering from the decline caused by statist, facist [sic] policies."[184]

Additionally, the graduate student was quick to realize that these kinds of technologies could offer individuals the means to exercise fundamental rights, like freedom of speech and freedom of assembly. In essence, Back found that cryptography could have significant implications for the balance of power between individuals and the state.

As he went looking for places on the internet to discuss these kinds of topics, the young PhD candidate from Exeter learned that he wasn't the only one to have come to this realization.

Halfway around the world, the Cypherpunks had just started organizing their regular meetings and—more importantly—launched the Cypherpunks mailing list. A coder since a young age, Back was very inspired by their motive of writing software to have a positive social impact, and was quick to subscribe.

"That was an interesting outlet," Back later recalled his first interactions with the Cypherpunks mailing list, "because people were working on other things [than] PGP, other things you could build with encryption and cryptography. I spent a good part of my PhD actually not working on distributed systems but learning about cryptography protocols, mainly with an applied interest to think about what a given cryptography paper would enable you to build."[185]

Back would over the years become one of the more active participants on this list, sometimes contributing dozens of emails in a single month. He was passionate about philosophical topics like privacy, free speech, and libertarianism, and engaged in in-depth technical discussions pertaining to anonymous remailers or encrypted file systems—technologies to which he contributed as well.

Back also engaged with the crypto wars that broke out not too long after he joined the mailing list, and was in some ways very directly affected by it. When the United States government regulated cryptography under the US Munitions List, Americans were by law no longer allowed to share, say, the RSA algorithm with Back—or with any of his countrymen. (In the case of RSA, Back of course already knew the algorithm.)

The ban struck a chord with the newfound Cypherpunk. He believed that the cryptographic protocols in question really just allowed individuals to exercise the rights they should already have on a legal basis: if private conversations are allowed, why should public key cryptography not be? And perhaps even more importantly, cryptography was ultimately just math. Back found it both absurd and worrying that the US essentially made sharing certain numbers and equations illegal.

It inspired the British Cypherpunk to prove his point in a unique way. In line with the activist ethos of the group, Back produced "ammunition" shirts: black t-shirts with the RSA protocol printed on them in white letters. According to the law, anyone wearing Back's apparel while crossing the border to exit the United States was technically a munitions exporter.

He would sell the shirts to his fellow-Cypherpunks and, fittingly, accepted DigiCash's pilot currency CyberBucks as payment.

Fittingly, because perhaps more than anything else Adam Back was very interested in electronic cash.

Taking Action

When Adam Back joined the Cypherpunks mailing list, DigiCash was really the only game in town when it came to anonymous digital currency. But progress on eCash was moving slower than he and many others would have liked.

Back shared the Cypherpunks' assessment that this was to a large extent because David Chaum was using his patents to keep his technology exclusive. He found that DigiCash's policy of convoluted licensing schemes and restrictions on what users could and couldn't do with the eCash technology was preventing hackers and tinkerers from playing around with and improving the technology, and technical progress had all but grinded to a halt.

Succinctly encapsulating the Cypherpunk philosophy, Back wasn't one to sit around and wait until things changed, however.

In the hopes that it would help speed things up, Back initially wrote software libraries (source code to be used by other developers) for both eCash and Brands Cash, the latter being an eCash-inspired electronic cash system designed by former DigiCash employee Stefan Brands. While he was at it, Back also figured out how to extend Brands's system to facilitate offline transactions, with no need to check with the bank for double-spends for each payment. (Though when Back discussed his solution with Brands, it turned out that someone else had already solved that problem before him.)

When eCash still wasn't really taking off by the mid-90s, however, Adam Back started to grow rather impatient.

"Blind signature technology has been around for a long time now, and there is not one on-line instance of a practical real world use of this

—technology," Back wrote to the Cypherpunks mailing list in October 1995, frustrated.[186]

He saw that non-anonymous internet payment systems were quickly claiming market share, which meant that the future of digital transactions was drifting in a dangerous direction. Once these privacy-violating alternatives would entrench themselves into people's habits as their standard online payment solutions, he believed it would be significantly harder to get internet users to switch to anonymous digital cash.

It was time to take action. Since he wasn't confident in DigiCash's progress, and no one else seemed to be working on viable eCash alternatives, Back concluded that the fastest route to success was perhaps to play ball with Chaum. He proposed that a group of Cypherpunks could found a startup bank, and actually license the technology from DigiCash to issue fiat currency-backed eCash themselves.

"I'm serious, and would want to invest in it," Back made clear on the Cypherpunks mailing list. "So what say? 1st digicash bank, 'run', and owned by a group of cypherpunks?"[187]

The only person who replied to his proposal pointed out that this plan probably wouldn't work either: after all, Chaum didn't want to license his technology to a band of Cypherpunks.[188] The idea died a quiet death.

Two years later, in the summer of 1997, Back returned to the list to propose the idea of a distributed bank. Having successfully completed his PhD program and now working at the university as a postdoc researcher, he really leveraged his field of expertise this time, as he explained that bank operations could be fragmented across a network of different people or entities. They'd be able to simulate a virtual computer by exchanging messages and computing encrypted functions, Back posited, where the virtual computer would essentially operate as a regular bank.

By splitting the bank up into several interdependent parties, no single entity would need to be trusted with the bank's operations. And although the Byzantine Generals Problem had still not been solved completely, the system could only be cheated if some threshold number of participants would collude.

"The bank would live in the network in this virtual CPU," Back wrote. "Individual nodes may come and go, yet the secured software entity which is the bank and it's [sic] account information would live on."[189]

His email received no response.

Spam

By the second half of the '90s, every email service on the internet had to deal with seemingly ever-increasing amounts of junk mail, or *spam*: unsolicited messages mailed in bulk, typically sent by advertisers. The Cypherpunks were not spared; promotion for weight-loss pills, penis enlargement products, and quick money-making schemes were cluttering the mailing list more and more each year.

The problem was especially serious for remailers. The anonymizing services run by a number of Cypherpunks were easily and often abused to distribute spam. Some of the operators in fact suspected that their remailers were specifically targeted in a type of denial-of-service (DOS) attacks; the goal would've been to overwhelm the remailers with garbage emails to make these services unavailable for genuine use.

Adam Back, who ran a remailer as well, was part of a group of Cypherpunks that set out to solve the problem. And to solve it, it should be added, without falling back on solutions that required internet users to identify themselves; for remailers, privacy was the point.

Nor did they want to rely on laws and regulation. While there were calls to simply make spam email illegal, involving the government to solve their problems wasn't the Cypherpunk way.

This was also important because it would not always be clear what exactly constituted spam in the first place. Granting the state the authority to make that distinction would effectively let governments determine which forms of communication between internet users are OK and which are not. This could open the door to politically motivated censorship, Cypherpunks like Tim May warned.[190]

Adam Back, furthermore, pointed out that in order to hold spammers accountable before the law, they would also need to be identified. If some anti-spam government agency was tasked with catching the perpetrators, Back warned his fellow Cypherpunks, remailers would probably become a huge target, with potentially dire consequences for online privacy in general.[191]

"The danger with using government to attack spammers, is that this is the net, and we don't want governments involved in regulation of content, nor in attempting to enforce 'identity escrow', 'internet drivers licenses' or anything else," Back wrote to the Cypherpunk mailing list. "We can sort them out ourselves without the need of government intervention, thanks kindly."[192]

A much better solution, Cypherpunks generally agreed, would be some kind of digital equivalent of postage. If sending an email came at a cost, it would strongly disincentive spam, especially because spammers usually had to send out many thousands if not millions of junk emails to profit from their endeavor. Similarly, overwhelming remailers required tons of garbage emails.

Digital postage could work in different ways. Remailers could, for example, charge postage to forward emails. This wouldn't just discourage spam emails from being sent through these services but, as a nice bonus, it would also introduce a financial incentive to run remailers. Alternatively, or in addition to that, postage could be awarded to the recipient whose email software could be programmed to reject messages with insufficient fee.

The actual postage itself could also be designed in several ways, but most ideas involved an issuer of electronic stamps. This issuer could for example generate unique large numbers and sell these (perhaps for digital cash). The unique number would then have to be included in an email, and once a remailer or the recipient's email program receives the message, it would check with the issuer if the number is indeed a valid piece of postage. If it is, the remailer or recipient might get some money (digital cash?) in return from the issuer, depending on the system's design specifics. If the postage wasn't valid, the email would simply bounce.

An alternative option would be to simply use digital cash as postage directly. An email could in this case include a tiny bit of digital currency in a dedicated field, for the intended recipient to strip out. For some time, it seemed like this could be a good use case for eCash.

Unfortunately, it turned out to be more complicated in practice. For one, the early eCash releases were not yet capable of handling the very specific types of transfers that were required for postage. On top of that, the lack of payee anonymity in Chaum's electronic cash system would mean that the sender of a message could (be coerced to) collaborate with the bank to reveal the real identity of a remailer operator and/or the email recipient.

It made DigiCash's eCash largely unsuited for postage, after all.

The First Electronic Postage

What Adam Back did not know was that the problem of postage had already been solved a few years prior, and in a very different way than the Cypherpunks had been considering.

By the early 1990s, the advantages of an electronic mailing system over its paper equivalent had become obvious to Cynthia Dwork and Moni Naor, two computer scientists at IBM: email was much faster, much cheaper, and much more versatile than the postal service could ever be. But they'd also realized that email presented its own challenges. As electronic mail gained in popularity, which they indeed foresaw, so would spam.

"In particular, the easy and low cost of sending electronic mail, and in particular the simplicity of sending the same message to many parties, all but invite abuse," the duo explained in their 1992 paper "Pricing via Processing of Combatting Junk Mail."[193]

A solution was needed, they posited, and a solution was what the paper offered. Dwork and Naor proposed a system where senders would have to attach a little bit of additional data to their email. This data would be the solution to a math problem, derived from the properties of the email itself, and therefore unique to that email. Without the correct solution attached, email clients should reject the email altogether.

In their paper, Dwork and Naor suggested three candidate puzzles that could be used for the purpose, all based on cryptographic algorithms like signature schemes. In all cases, adding the correct solution to an email wouldn't be all too difficult (for a computer); it would perhaps require a couple of seconds of processing power. Still, this would represent a small cost. Checking whether the solution is correct, meanwhile, would be very easy and barely cost any processing power at all.

The key idea behind the scheme was that calculating a correct solution to a puzzle wouldn't be much of a pain for individual users who'd send the occasional email to coworkers, family, or friends—but it would quickly add up for spammers. To send thousands or even millions of messages on a single day, they'd have to solve as many puzzles, which in aggregate would require significant amounts of processing power.

"The main idea is to require a user to compute a moderately hard, but not intractable, function in order to gain access to the resource, thus preventing frivolous use," Dwork and Naor explained. Spamming, they proposed, could be made expensive.

Although Dwork and Naor did not propose the term themselves, the type of solution they introduced would later come to be known as a "proof-of-work" system. The solution to the math problem would prove that actual work was performed.

It was a nifty solution. But whether it's because it was slightly ahead of its time, or because it just wasn't advertised broadly enough, outside a relatively small circle of academics this early-90s proposal never attracted too much attention. Dworn and Naor's postage scheme was never implemented, let alone used, and many of the Cypherpunks were probably unaware of the idea.

Luckily enough, the concept would soon be reinvented.

Hashcash

[ANNOUNCE] hash cash postage implementation

On March 28, 1997, the now 2,000-or-so subscribers of the Cypherpunks mailing list received an announcement in their inbox.[194] Sent by Adam

Back, the email included a description and early implementation of what he described as "hashcash": a "partial hash collision based postage scheme." He had successfully designed a postage solution for email.

Like Dwork and Naor's scheme, hashcash postage wouldn't be paid to remailer operators, or the recipients of an email, or to anyone else for that matter. Instead, it would only add a cost for senders.

Back had considered solving spam by increasing the cost of bulk email in a different discussion on the mailing list about one week earlier—though only loosely: "A side benefit of using PGP, is that PGP encryption should add some overhead to the spammer—he can probably encrypt less messages per second than he can spam down a T3 link," he commented in a discussion about adding more privacy to remailers.[195]

Back's new proposal made this general idea even more explicit: it would require that senders attach a proof of work to their emails. Indeed, hashcash was in several ways similar to Dwork and Naor's postage scheme: the proof of work would be unique to the email, and it would require a little bit of processing power to produce.

As the name suggests, however, Back's proposal was based on hashing.

Hashing—the cryptographic trick that turns any data into a unique and seemingly random string of numbers of a specific length—is a completely unpredictable process. Although the same data will result in the same hash every time, the only way to find out what the hash of a piece of data will look like in the first place, is to actually hash it. It's this unpredictability that hashcash leveraged in a smart way.

To generate hashcash, a user had to generate a hash out of an e-mail's metadata (the sender's address, the recipient's address, the time, etc.) and a random number—a nonce. But here's the trick: not every resulting hash would be considered "valid." Instead, the (binary version of) a valid hash had to start with a predetermined number of zeroes. And there would only be one way to generate a hash that starts with enough zeroes: the user would have to try different nonces and create new hashes until he'd find one that happened to meet the threshold. Simple trial and error.

The amount of leading zeroes required would determine how difficult it'd be to find a valid hash. More zeroes would make it more difficult, because computers would on average need to make more guesses.

"The idea of using partial hashes is that they can be made arbitrarily expensive to compute," Back explained the advantage of using hashes, "and yet can be verified instantly."

Like Dwork and Naor's solution, the idea was that regular users shouldn't have a problem finding a valid hash to send along with an email fairly quickly—within a few seconds—but spammers shouldn't be able to do it thousands or millions of times and still remain profitable.

"[. . .] if it hasn't got a 20 bit hash [. . .] you have a program which bounces it with a notice explaining the required postage, and where to obtain software from," Back explained on the Cypherpunks mailing list. "This would put spammers out of business overnight, as $1,000,000 \times 20 = 100$ MIP years which is going to be more compute than they've got."

A subtle difference from Dwork and Naor's solution was that their proof-of-work system wasn't subject to randomness. The duo's postage scheme essentially required solving a rather straightforward puzzle, which meant that a more powerful computer would solve the puzzle faster than a weaker computer every time.

Producing a valid hash, on the other hand, is a guessing game. And while a more powerful computer would be able to make more guesses per second, a weaker computer could still get lucky from time to time and find a valid hash faster. (Though since spammers would have to generate thousands or millions of valid hashes per spam session anyway, the little bit of variance involved with generating a single hashcash proof of work wouldn't make a meaningful difference—at least not in the context of stopping junk mail.)

"Hashcash may provide a stop gap measure until digicash becomes more widely used," Back concluded his announcement. "Hashcash is free, all you've got to do is burn some cycles on your PC. It is in keeping with net culture of free discourse, where the financially challenged can duke it out with millionaires, retired government officials, etc on equal terms."

And:

"Hashcash may provide us with a fall back method for controlling spam if digicash goes sour (gets outlawed or required to escrow user identities)."

Digital Scarcity

Hashcash enjoyed some adoption in the years following Adam Back's announcement. The solution would be implemented in Apache's open source SpamAssassin platform, while Microsoft gave the idea a spin in its incompatible Postmark system. Back himself as well as several other academics meanwhile came up with some alternative applications for the proof-of-work system, including anti-DOS solutions.

But hashcash postage never went truly mainstream. The innovative nature of the solution probably wasn't enough to overcome the bootstrapping hurdle: someone couldn't really start demanding hashcash for incoming emails if no one else was using it, as this would result in their email client rejecting all incoming messages. At the same time, there was no incentive to start using hashcash for outgoing emails if no one was demanding it. Like David Chaum's eCash, Back's electronic postage system, too, suffered from a chicken-and-egg problem for which there did not appear to be an easy solution.

It wasn't a great concern for Adam Back, however. The University of Exeter researcher—his day job by now was to work on an encrypted messaging system for medical data—had been thinking beyond hashcash almost immediately after he published the proposal to the Cypherpunks mailing list. Postage was a good problem to solve, but the computer scientist was even more interested in creating digital cash for general use.

And while many Cypherpunks still assumed that an electronic cash system would have to be layered on top of existing financial infrastructure, like eCash was, Back had a different vision. He believed that hashcash could offer a whole new direction of research to help realize that vision.

Hashcash's key innovation was that it tied purely digital data (numbers, essentially) to real resources in physical reality. Producing proof of work required computing cycles, and computing cycles themselves use up electricity, which in turn costs energy to produce. Whereas most things digital can be copied ad infinitum at virtually no cost, proof of work could, in a way, bridge the fundamental scarcity of energy in physical reality into the digital realm.

Indeed, hashcash was digital, yet scarce. The total number of hashcash "currency units" (for lack of a better word) was to some extent limited: there would never be more hashcash than however much could be produced with the amount of energy people would be willing and able to spend on producing it.

This was a key insight, because built-in scarcity represented one of the six properties that Adam Back had put on his shortlist for an ideal electronic cash system. Until recently, digital scarcity could only be created as a promise, like DigiCash's promise to put a hard limit on the total amount of CyberBucks they would create. But promises, of course, could be broken. Back believed that proof of work embedded the potential to guarantee scarcity on a much more fundamental level.

At the same time, he knew that hashcash could not function as a fully fledged digital cash itself. Although it could be used anonymously, was hard to shut down, did not require trust in any individual, and also had some modicum of scarcity, this really only ticked three of the six boxes on Back's shortlist.

The main problem was that hashcash wasn't reusable. Each currency unit was custom made to fit with a specific email, so it couldn't be re-spent elsewhere, and was of no further benefit to recipients.

Back was therefore thinking that hashcash—or proof of work more generally—could form the basis of a different type of electronic cash design.

One of his first suggestions was, for example, a *Chaumian* system where the bank would issue electronic cash upon receipt of hashcash: users would create proof of work and get unbacked digital cash in return. This cash would be anonymous, reusable, and somewhat scarce—though this scarcity would admittedly be rather weak in practice as people could always create more proof of work if they wanted to. And with computer processors getting more powerful each year, producing valid proof of work would get cheaper and cheaper over time.[196]

Indeed, hashcash's fundamental scarcity was more of a technicality. If it were to really form the basis of an electronic currency, newer and more powerful computers would eventually flush the market with fresh currency units, and the currency would hyperinflate.

In addition, users would need to trust the bank not to create money out of nothing. Like any electronic cash system following Chaum's design, the entity that issues the digital currency and prevents double-spending, would *itself* need to be trusted to not erroneously enrich itself.

Though, Back believed free market competition could potentially help solve this problem.

"So, perhaps you could have multiple banks and let reputation sort them out, if you could arrange the protocols so that it would be apparent if a bank was minting more cash than it had received hash collisions for. [. . .] But if you've got multiple banks then you've got to have an exchange mechanism. The market could probably take care of this, setting exchange rates based on banks reputations," he suggested, in what now very closely resembled a free-banking system as described by Friedrich Hayek.

Still, the young Cypherpunk from Exeter believed that they could maybe do even better than that:

"it would be nicer to have something which required no trust and which had no posssibility [sic] of cheating rather than relying on reputation to sort them out."[197]

Chapter 11:
Bit Gold

NICK SZABO'S FATHER was one of 200,000 Hungarians to have fled their country after Soviet troops crushed the anti-communist revolt of 1956. As tens of thousands of his fellow freedom fighters were being imprisoned or interned, and in some cases even executed, he'd decided to leave everything behind, and eventually found a new home all the way across the Atlantic, in *the land of the free*.

Although this had happened almost a decade before he was born, his father's experience would shape Nick. As the son of a refugee, growing up far from the oppressive Soviet stronghold over Eastern Europe, the second-generation American boy was instilled early on with a deep distrust of anything that even resembles communism or government overreach.[198]

Szabo eventually found a great source of inspiration in the works of Friedrich Hayek. *The Road to Serfdom* seemed to have quite accurately described how the Soviet Union morphed into a totalitarian state, with the repression of the Hungarian revolution serving as one of the first great examples of this outside of the Russian homeland. And Szabo would later name Hayek's 1988 book *The Fatal Conceit*—another, more political, refutation of socialism, which emphasized the historical importance of private property—as one of the most important books he ever read.[199]

Meanwhile, the young Szabo was finding an interest in computers which, perhaps fittingly, was a relatively new technology that was rapidly developing in the US and the rest of the Western world, while the communist East lagged far behind. When the first personal computers started spreading to American homes and offices in the late 1970s and early 1980s—his mother regularly brought her Apple II home from work—he was quick to recognize the potential of the machines. By the mid-1980s, this made him decide to study computer science at the University of Washington in Seattle.

During his studies, Szabo did a year's internship at NASA's research center for jet propulsion, JPL, before earning his computer science degree in 1989. Now in his mid-twenties, he decided to move some 800 miles south, to the San Francisco Bay Area, where his skillset was in particularly high demand. He landed a programming job at IBM, which had throughout the 1980s set the standard for home computing with its relatively inexpensive microcomputers.

Szabo's personal interests were always broader than just computer science alone, however. A true polymath, he liked to study a wide range of topics in his free time: from politics to biology, and from history to economics, indeed with a particular focus on free-market economics. Not unlike Hayek, who especially in this later phase of his career used economic concepts to explain persistent political realities, Szabo appreciated how combining cross-disciplinary knowledge could help him gain new insights. He loved leveraging such insights to speculate about the future of technology, society, and humanity.

It made him fit in perfectly with the Extropians.

The techno-utopian futurist movement had been gathering momentum in and around Silicon Valley during his first years in the Bay Area, and Szabo would proliferate himself as a prominent member of the Extropian community. The computer scientist published essays and letters in the *Extropy* magazine on topics like space colonization (inspired by his experience at JPL), artificial intelligence, nanotech, and more.

It was also through the Extropian community that Szabo became acquainted with Tim May.

The Crypto-Anarchist

One day May invited Szabo to join a Cypherpunks gathering. Szabo was happy to join; he, too, had been concerned with the apparent decline of privacy in the forthcoming digital age.

When Szabo a few weeks later met the group of hands-on privacy activists, he knew he'd come to the right place.

Throughout the next couple of years, Szabo helped the Cypherpunk cause where he could. Notably, he took an early lead in opposing the NSA's Clipper Chip, both on the Cypherpunks mailing list and in real life: he gave talks on the topic at various events, and sometimes handed out flyers to inform people of the risks associated with this type of surveillance technology. He had a way of conveying the unsettling implications of the looming privacy infringements to nontechnical audiences, and was happy to share his approach with the other Cypherpunks so they could learn to do the same.

But Szabo's interest in digital privacy was ultimately part of an even bigger picture. He embraced the promise of a "Galt's Gulch in cyberspace." As detailed in the many mailing list posts by his friend Tim May, Szabo had realized that the tools needed to protect individuals from state power were no longer reserved to the domain of fictional literature. The computer scientist with Hungarian roots agreed that cryptography could bring the ideal of truly free markets, immune to physical force or state coercion, closer to reality.

"If we step back and look at what many cypherpunks are trying to achieve, a major idealistic theme is a Ghandian cyberspace where violence can only be make-believe, whether in Mortal [Kombat] or 'flame wars'," he wrote to the Cypherpunks mailing list. "Cypherpunks want our telephone networks, Internet businesses, etc. to be both protected from force, and not dependent on force for their existence. Our 20th century information commerce systems, from publishing to credit cards, have often been very dependent on the threat of violence, usually law enforcement, to protect intellectual property rights, deter fraud, collect debts, etc."

He proposed:

"There is no utopia in sight where such threats can be completely eliminated, but we can recognize that they exist and carefully work to reduce our dependence on them."[200]

Smart Contracts

Perhaps more than anyone else, Szabo was very aware that in order to realize May's vision of crypto-anarchy, private communication was merely a first step.

As a student of Hayek's work—including the Austrian's later, more political writings—the Cypherpunk had come to understand that prosperous societies had done so well because they'd adopted certain rules, in the form of laws, that regulated human behavior. Likening it to the layered design of computer protocols, Szabo recognized that the laws that formed the bedrock of society (like constitutional laws) were the most basic, but also the most important rules of all. All other rules are based on this foundation.

Szabo found that two of the fundamental building blocks in the "base layer" of any prosperous society were—indeed—property rights and contract law. Property rights facilitate and incentivize investment, production, and expansion, while contract law enables trade and specialization. He believed that a society that enforces property rights and contract law can ultimately evolve into a modern capitalist society.

But property rights and contract law are in modern capitalist societies enforced by the state, Szabo knew. Ownership, and the change of ownership, is ultimately enforced by courts and police leveraging the state's monopoly on violence, either implicitly through (the threat of) fines or jail time or explicitly by protecting or returning someone's property by force.

To create a stateless and nonviolent cyberspace economy, Szabo therefore concluded, crypto-anarchists would have to first lay a new foundation.

The first part of this foundation—property rights—could be realized with public key cryptography, as extensively explained by Tim May; personal data would be secured with math instead of physical force.

But it was not immediately clear how two people could trade this data without *counterparty risk*. One party in the trade would always have to send their data or otherwise finalize their part of the deal first, at which point their counterparty could disappear and default on its obligation. In cyberspace, there were no courts or police to enforce contract law.

One potential solution was to use arbitration for settling disputes, where an arbitrator would be given the means to transfer the data in question from one of the trading partners to the other (either at its own discretion, or perhaps in cooperation with either one of the trading partners). This would, however, require that both parties trust the arbitrator not to steal, or collude with their counterparty. This trust could, perhaps, be established through reputation over time: an arbitrator's spotless record of past behavior could in a way serve as a viable alternative to state enforcement—even if it would never be completely risk-free.

But by the mid-1990s, Szabo believed he had a better idea. He envisioned a solution that could not be cheated by either trading party, and required no trusted arbitrator. Szabo proposed *smart contracts*—digital contracts that would autonomously enforce their own terms, as embedded in computer code.[201]

As a simple example, let's say Alice wants to buy a secret number from Bob for $10. A smart contract could then be programmed so that as soon as Bob enters the secret number in some agreed-upon spot where Alice can find it (perhaps by adding it to the contract itself, not unlike a digital signature), the contract's code would recognize and verify this, to then *automatically* withdraw $10 from Alice's account and transfer it to Bob. (Szabo used a vending machine as a primitive analogy: the "contract" between a consumer and a vending machine says that if the consumer inserts a coin, the machine—through an automated response—dispenses a can of soda or a candy bar, without any further human involvement.)

Smart contracts could in theory be made arbitrarily complex, and they could in principle embed all kinds of contractual clauses, including liens, bonds, or delineation of property rights. This would even enable whole new business arrangements, Szabo suggested, offering the example of a smart contract for a car loan that would, upon failure to repay the loan, automatically return control of the digital car keys to the bank.

Most properties and features that a smart contract should contain could be implemented by drawing from the ever-growing Cypherpunks toolkit, Szabo believed: "Protocols based on mathematics, called *cryptographic protocols*, are the basic building blocks that implement the improved tradeoffs between observability, verifiability, privity, and enforceability in smart contracts," he wrote.[202]

The biggest challenge, however, was to make sure that the contract would be executed automatically, reliably, and unconditionally. Most obviously, this meant that none of the parties to the contract should be responsible for its execution.

As a general starting point, Szabo suspected that the best solution was to be found in the realm of distributed computing, where participating computers had to follow strict protocols to stay in consensus with each other. Although the Byzantine Generals Problem (the coordination problem that Adam Back learned about in university) indeed hadn't been solved completely—some risks remained if there were too many unreliable participants—he believed that robust *enough* protocols had been designed for most scenarios.

"The terms of contractual relationships can often be formalized and standardized, and then performed via network-based protocols," Szabo explained on the Cypherpunks mailing list. "These protocols, along with economic incentives, protect the performance of the contract from both fraud by the principals and attack from third parties."[203]

That said, most smart contracts would presumably also require a form of money: at least one of the parties involved usually has to make a payment as their part of the deal. Furthermore, this had to be a type of currency that could be transferred across the internet, and that could be sent autonomously by a computer program . . . ideally anonymously.

Smart contracts required electronic cash.

Trusted Third Parties

If the digital equivalents of property rights and contract law were two of the foundational building blocks needed to realize a "Galt's Gulch in cyberspace," a digital equivalent for money was the third.

Nick Szabo had been among the first of the Extropians and Cypherpunks to recognize this. Back when Hal Finney first began advocating the benefits of electronic cash in the *Extropy* magazine, Szabo was the Extropian who'd moved to Amsterdam to work for David Chaum. Around the same time that the first webshops began popping up online, Szabo joined DigiCash as an internet programmer.

As he spent some time working at the company's offices in the early 1990s, Szabo got to experience firsthand what went on in the world's most promising electronic cash startup. He saw how DigiCash introduced the first Chaumian digital cash product in the form of CyberBucks, the unbacked prototype eCash implementation for which the startup promised to never issue more than one million units. And he witnessed how CyberBucks even attained a bit of purchasing power, as some Cypherpunks and other interested techies were willing to buy small amounts of the digital cash with conventional currencies, or accepted it in exchange for low-value goods or services.

The CyberBucks system depended entirely on the company DigiCash, however: Szabo realized that Chaum's startup could simply issue more than one million of the electronic cash if they'd have a change of heart, or were lying all along, or if a rogue employee would try to cheat the system, and so forth. Moreover, there would be no way to detect it if they did. (Not to mention that CyberBucks would become instantly worthless if DigiCash's servers ever went down, as indeed ended up happening.)

Szabo considered these to be substantial problems.

"One of the things I learned there was how easy it was to mess with peoples' balances in a centralized currency," the digital currency pioneer later recalled. "Who would trust their wealth to some scraggly Frank Zappa fans in far-off Amsterdam?"[204] (They loved playing Frank Zappa records at the DigiCash office.)

Like Scott Stornetta and Stuart Haber a couple years earlier, it spurred Szabo to analyze and consider the role of trusted parties in the rapidly evolving online ecosystem more generally. Although cryptography could offer a level of privacy and security on par with (or even better than) the physical domain, Szabo found that protocol developers had a tendency to assume away a particular type of risk—the risk inherent to relying on a *trusted third party* (TTP).

The typical example is a certificate authority that provides a registry of real-world identities coupled with their public keys. While a convenient way to find someone's public key, these public keys are really only as safe to use as the certificate authority itself. If a public key listed by a certificate authority actually belongs to an attacker, Szabo would point out, this attacker can decrypt any messages intended for whoever is associated with the public key in the registry.

In an essay on this topic, aptly titled "Trusted Third Parties are Security Holes,"[205] Szabo later explained that TTPs were often not included in the cost of a design, and why he believed this to be a mistake. Trusted third parties are security holes, the Cypherpunk argued, *even* if they are themselves truly honest: they could become hot targets for malicious hackers, or perhaps even for nation-states and their regulatory bodies during times of political instability or oppression.

A compromised TTP could, then, prove to be tremendously costly. Szabo argued that the cost of a potential breach should be factored into protocol design, which he believed would in turn mean that many protocols would have to be redesigned to get rid of the trusted third parties altogether.

Once more, Szabo proposed that solutions could perhaps be found in the realm of distributed computing.

"The best 'TTP' of all is one that does not exist, but the necessity for which has been eliminated by the protocol design, or which has been automated and distributed amongst the parties to a protocol," he concluded in his paper.

Free Banking

Like Chaum before them, most Cypherpunks were for the most part interested in electronic cash because of the privacy features it could offer. But Szabo, May, and some of the other Cypherpunks that had joined the movement from the Extropian community in particular, were also motivated by monetary reform. And they were especially interested in Hayek's ideas around free banking, as also outlined by Max More in the digital cash edition of *Extropy*.

In addition, Szabo had studied the work of George Selgin—whose book *The Theory of Free Banking* had been reviewed in that same magazine—and that of Selgin's colleague Lawrence H. White, who himself had contributed an article to the magazine. With Hayek having passed away just before the formation of the Cypherpunk movement, Szabo thought that the cofounders of the Hayek-inspired modern free banking school could perhaps help inform the design of an electronic cash system.

By the mid-1990s, he therefore decided to create a new, more topic-dedicated mailing list: the *Libtech* list. Here, free bankers like Selgin and White as well as interested Extropians and Cypherpunks had targeted discussions about banking, monetary economics, and—most importantly—digital currency designs.[206]

As two very different worlds were colliding on the Libtech list, Szabo reflected on the insights from Austrian economics from his own perspective as a computer scientist. This allowed him to see the faults of fiat currency even more clearly than before. Where Hayek had warned extensively of the ills of central banking, Szabo recognized that this was ultimately because the modern monetary system essentially suffered from a fundamental design flaw.

Central banks were TTPs.

"The problem, in a nutshell, is that our money currently depends on trust in a third party for its value," Szabo later argued. "As many inflationary and hyperinflationary episodes during the 20th century demonstrated, this is not an ideal state of affairs."[207]

By pinpointing this core weakness, Szabo in a way validated Hayek's analysis—at least for himself.

But in the same stroke, he also somewhat contested the monetary ecosystem Selgin predicted would emerge in a free-banking environment. If the problem of the modern monetary system was that everyone had to trust a central bank, free banking would just make private banks the new trusted third parties. Even if competition could keep them honest, TTPs represented a broader set of security risks—ranging from rogue employees to draconian governments—that market dynamics would not necessarily solve completely.

If and when these new trusted third parties—the banks—would betray the trust of their customers, people wouldn't just switch to their competitors, Szabo predicted. Rather, people would start calling for central bank safeguards again—that's how the modern monetary system had evolved in the first place.

Before free banking could be a viable alternative, Szabo therefore concluded, they'd have to design a trust-minimized form of electronic money from the ground up. In the same way that property rights and contract law for cyberspace had to be reinvented from scratch, so too would a digital currency have to be created by starting from first principles.

The Origins of Money

To create money, Szabo had to understand it first.

The Cypherpunk was of course not the first to study the nature of money—nor did he think that he was. He was well aware of Carl Menger's and Ludwig von Mises's accounts on the origin of money, and to a large extent shared their assessment that money stemmed from barter. But whereas Menger and Mises had developed their thesis through logic and reasoning, Szabo went looking for actual historical records, and even archeological remnants.

Szabo's quest led him deep into human prehistory, and to preindustrial civilizations like that of Native Americans. Money, he found, was even older than text: early forms of currency were already used by hunter-gatherer tribes. This ultimately led him to hypothesize that money is quite literally as old as mankind itself. As first speculated by evolutionary biologist Richard Dawkins in his seminal work *The Selfish Gene*,[208] the ability to use money could well be embedded in human DNA, and might have benefited the survival of the species.

In his later essay "Shelling Out: The Origins of Money,"[209] Szabo would explain how.

One of mankind's great advantages in mother nature's merciless struggle for survival, Szabo found, is that most members of the species are willing and able to cooperate in order to bundle their forces, or to divide labor and specialize to then share the proceeds. This has probably always been true: prehistoric hunters that successfully killed a wild boar would share the meat with their tribe members. Their fellow tribe members would return the favor some other time, perhaps by sharing the blueberries or edible fungi they gathered the next day.

This form of altruistic behavior could benefit everyone as long as all tribe members knew each other, and could roughly keep track of each other's contributions; all tribe members had a public reputation. Because freeloaders—those who never contributed anything to the tribe—could eventually be excluded from the sharing routines or even expelled from the tribe, everyone was strongly incentivized to contribute and do their part.

But this model would break down when a tribe (or more typically: a group of tribes) grew too large. Human brains can only maintain a limited number of social relationships (popularly known as "Dunbar's number," which is 150[210]), so it would become difficult to keep track of everyone's reputations if there were more people than this number. If no one can remember who shared with the others and who did not, the "public reputation system" breaks down, and freeloaders get free rein at everyone else's expense.

To avoid being taken advantage of, it would even become rational for each individual to stop sharing and become a freeloader themselves—even though everyone would be better off if everyone shared. In other words, something of a grand *prisoner's dilemma*[211] would emerge.

But Szabo explained that genes can code for strategies to find solutions for real-world game theory challenges like these. Over long periods of time, and through natural selection, the best traits—those that benefit survival of a species—would become dominant.

The ability to use money, the Cypherpunk believed, was such a trait.

For most of human history, though, this was a very different type of money than what modern societies use.

Throughout the ages and across cultures, humans wore jewelry, like necklaces, which no other animal does. The superficial explanation for this is that people simply enjoy wearing such ornaments. But Szabo understood that there was a more fundamental question hidden underneath this simple explanation—the type of question an evolutionary biologist would ask. *Why* did people evolve to enjoy wearing ornaments?

Like Dawkins, Szabo suspected that humans had over the ages developed a liking for ornaments because it offered an evolutionary benefit: it allowed them to cooperate and "share" resources at larger scales than just their own tribe.

Szabo learned, for example, that necklaces and other collectibles were traded between tribes in exchange for food, weapons, or brides. The ornaments could later be traded back, or exchanged with yet another tribe, for other resources. Instead of remembering who shared their resources, jewelry served as proto-money, and facilitated what evolutionary psychologists call *reciprocal altruism*.

It allowed tribes to adopt a level of collaboration and specialization between them, with different tribes for example hunting different types of animals in different parts of the year, ultimately benefiting them all.

Proto-Money

Not any piece of jewelry would do, however.

As he analyzed the remains of precivilized societies, Szabo found that humans across cultures gravitated toward collectables with a few very specific properties. Although archeologists had found examples of proto-money as varied as shells from a rare type of snail, to Ostrich egg shards, to mammoth teeth, it all tended to share three common features.

First, the collectibles were relatively easy to secure from accidental loss and theft. Necklaces are probably the best example in this regard: they are almost impossible to lose if worn around the neck. Alternatively, ornaments that couldn't be worn on a person's body, were typically at least easy to hide.

Second, the collectibles represented *unforgeable scarcity*. That is, they would have been costly to create or hard to find: a mammoth tooth was scarce because killing a mammoth isn't easy, while Ostrich eggs are difficult to come by.

"At first, the production of a commodity simply because it is costly seems quite wasteful," Szabo later elaborated in "Shelling Out." "However, the unforgeably costly commodity repeatedly adds value by enabling beneficial wealth transfers. More of the cost is recouped every time a transaction is made possible or made less expensive. The cost, initially a complete waste, is amortized over many transactions."

And third, it was usually fairly easy to establish that the proto-money was indeed unforgeably scarce by simple observations or measurements. The rare snail shells would have been easy to recognize as such by anyone in these tribal societies, for example, while forging them would have been impossible with the tools at their disposal.

In summary, Szabo found that the oldest forms of money were usually easy to secure and verifiably hard to obtain.

Modern fiat currencies arguably possessed none of the three qualities of proto-money. It wasn't particularly easy to secure from theft, and most people didn't even *try* to protect their own money, instead relying on third parties (banks) for safekeeping. But perhaps more importantly: fiat currency wasn't fundamentally scarce; governments and central banks could print it at will, or even type more of it into existence digitally.

Szabo recognized that the floating fiat currency system that had been the global standard for a few decades at this time was a major historic outlier. Considering that the few similar examples that he was aware of all failed miserably—some in dynastic China, two in eighteenth-century France, and the confederate dollar during the American civil war—he didn't expect the new monetary experiment to last, either. He believed that fiat currency would eventually perish.

Many Austrian economists had of course come to similar conclusions as Szabo. Those that favored a return to the gold standard in particular believed that the precious metal was the best form of money, in large part because of its unforgeable scarcity.

Szabo was not convinced that gold was the best alternative, however: although the precious metal was indeed hard to obtain, it was also difficult to secure.

"Precious metals and collectibles have an unforgeable scarcity due to the costliness of their creation. This once provided money the value of which was largely independent of any trusted third party. Precious metals have problems, however. It's too costly to assay metals repeatedly for common transactions. Thus a trusted third party (usually associated with a tax collector who accepted the coins as payment) was invoked to stamp a standard amount of the metal into a coin. Transporting large amounts of valuable metal can be a rather insecure affair, as the British found when transporting gold across a U-boat infested Atlantic to Canada during World War I to support their gold standard," Szabo wrote.

Adding:

"What's worse, you can't pay online with metal."[212]

The Cypherpunk wanted to reproduce the desirable monetary characteristics of gold in an electronic cash system instead—a digital currency with unforgeable costliness.

When Adam Back announced hashcash in 1997, this finally seemed possible.

Bit Gold

Less than a year later, in 1998, Szabo had designed his own digital currency proposal: *Bit Gold*. While he hadn't implemented Bit Gold in code—it was still only an idea—he shared a description of it on the Libtech list.

Like hashcash, Bit Gold was designed around proof of work. Because the processing power required to create proof of work essentially tied generating the currency to the cost of energy, it produced something akin to digital scarcity. Seen from Szabo's framework, proof of work represented unforgeable costliness.

Bit Gold's proof-of-work system would kick off with a "candidate string"—basically a random number. The idea was that anyone could take this string and combine it with their own nonce to produce (something similar to) a hash.[213] Per the nature of hashing, the resulting hash would be a new, seemingly random string of numbers.

The trick, as also utilized by hashcash, was that not all hashes would be considered valid within the Bit Gold protocol. Instead, a valid hash would have to start with a predetermined number of zeroes. Because of the unpredictable nature of hashing, the only way to find such a hash would be through trial and error, using a new nonce on each try.

When someone would find a valid hash, this hash would become the new candidate string. The next valid hash would have to be generated from this new candidate string and another nonce. Once a second valid hash would be found, it would in turn become the new candidate string, and so on.

The Bit Gold system would over time produce a long chain of hashes, with the most recent hash always acting as the new candidate string.

The money part, then, loosely resembled that of Hadon Nash's earlier Cypherpunks mailing list proposal to own numbers. Whoever produced a valid hash would quite literally get to "own" this hash. Ownership of hashes would be recorded in a digital ownership registry, where all the hashes would be attributed to the public keys of their owners.[214] Since the registry would only use public keys—no names—Bit Gold could be used fairly anonymously.

To "spend" a hash, then, its owner would have to sign a message specifying who the new owner is (again, referring to this person only by their public key). If the digital signature corresponds with the public key listed in the ownership registry, the transfer would be valid, and the registry would be updated to reflect the new owner of the hash. Without a valid signature, the transfer should be rejected and the hash would remain in possession of its current owner.

Proof of work would make Szabo's electronic cash verifiably hard to obtain, while public key cryptography would make it secure.

That is, of course, assuming the registry itself is secure.

The Registry

So who would maintain the registry?

Szabo understood that any single entity maintaining the registry would be a trusted third party. Although even this TTP would be unable to forge proof of work—anyone could instantly recognize the hashes as invalid—it could potentially still double-spend them, or censor transactions, or maybe even outright steal hashes from other users.

In Szabo's proposal, the ownership registry would therefore be maintained by a Bit Gold "property club." This property club consisted of "club members" (or internet servers), that would replicate the ownership registry between them, and collectively keep track of who owns what. If any of the club members would try to cheat or steal, the other club members would notice and reject this transfer, thus distributing trust between them.

Szabo proposed to implement this using the same types of distributed computing protocols he envisioned for smart contracts. Detailed in his paper "Secure Property Titles with Owner Authority," these designs were best understood as advanced voting systems: as long as most servers remained honest, they would achieve consensus over the state of the registry. If only a minority of the servers would fail or fall out of line, the system as a whole should continue to operate fine.

This wasn't perfect; the Byzantine Generals Problem had not been fully solved. Particularly nasty problems could occur if the registry were to be Sybil-attacked, a computer system attack where one malicious person would pretend to be many different participants and overwhelm the voting procedures. (The "sock puppet problem," as Szabo would later describe it.[215])

Still, Szabo believed that this could work itself out. He suggested that even in the scenario where a majority of club members would attempt to cheat, the registry would be public, so cryptographic proofs like (the lack of) valid signatures could be used to inform Bit Gold users of this misconduct, and the honest minority of registry maintainers could branch off to create a competing ownership registry. Given the choice between a provably dishonest majority registry or an honest minority registry, Szabo figured users would probably prefer the latter.

"If the rules are violated by the winning voters, the correct losers can exit the group and reform a new group, inheriting the old titles," he explained. "Users of the titles (relying parties) who wish to maintain correct titles can securely verify for themselves which splinter group has correctly followed the rules and switch to the correct group."[216]

Szabo knew that it wasn't the most elegant solution, and some important questions remained unanswered: in the case of a double-spend attack, how would users that were offline when it happened know which transaction came first? And by extension, if this double-spend would result in the creation of a competing registry because different property club members saw different transactions first, how would these users know which one is "correct"?

Still, this was in Szabo's mind a better solution than relying on a trusted third party.

Controlling Inflation

The last problem Szabo had to solve was inflation.

Besides the inability to transfer the ownership of proof of work, the other big problem with Adam Back's hashcash was that generating valid hashes would become easier over time, as computers were becoming more powerful each year. The hashes therefore couldn't function as money very well in the first place: hyperinflation (or even just the prospect of hyperinflation) would probably make such a currency a nonstarter.

Szabo figured out a solution for this as well.

Because all valid Bit Gold hashes would have served as candidate strings for the next hash, they were necessarily time-stamped, in that the order of them could not be changed. On top of that, new hashes could potentially be time-stamped separately on actual time-stamp servers to keep a record of when they were generated.

Szabo explained that these time-stamps would give a good idea of how hard it must have been to produce any Bit Gold hash: an older hash would have been harder to produce than a more recent hash.

This difference, then, should factor into the value of a hash, Szabo reasoned:

"The cost of the string is proportional to improbability of the string. We have empirical evidence that verifiably improbable documents, e.g., rare printing errors on postage stamps, become quite valuable—the more rare and the more verifiable, the more valuable."[217]

In other words, a valid "1998 hash" should be worth more than a valid "2008 hash."

To determine how much more, Szabo wanted to leverage an age-old, battle-tested solution: the market. On a special marketplace where Bit Gold hashes could be traded against each other, buyers and sellers would find a fair relative price for each of them. Perhaps a single 1998 hash would trade against ten 2008 hashes, where the exact exchange rate would presumably be guided by the declined cost of processing power throughout that decade.

But this would create yet another problem, Szabo knew: "the bits (the puzzle solutions) from one period [. . .] to the next are not fungible."[218]

The Cypherpunk understood that fungibility—where any currency unit is equal in value to any other unit of the same denomination—is a critical property of money. A shopkeeper should be able to accept a payment without having to think about the exact value of one bank note compared to another; any dollar bill should suffice. If hashes would be valued differently, it would break Bit Gold's fungibility.

To wrap it all up, Szabo came up with a solution to this problem as well: he envisioned a free banking-inspired "second layer" *on top of* Bit Gold's "base layer."[219] This second layer would consist of a special type of banks, which should be securely auditable due to the Bit Gold registry being public. These banks would collect different hashes from different time periods and, based on their relative market value, bundle them into packets of a standard value. A "1998 pack" might include just one hash, while a "2008 pack" would include ten.

These packets, finally, were to be cut up in a specific number of units, perhaps unique per bank. Alice Bank could issue 10,000 Alicebucks per bundle, whether that bundle was a 1998 pack or a 2008 pack. It's these units that would ultimately be used as the fungible money handled by regular users for daily expenses, ideally in the form of private, Chaumian eCash, while Alice Bank's users should always be able to redeem their Alicebucks for the actual hashes backing them.

"In summary," Szabo concluded his proposal, "all money mankind has ever used has been insecure in one way or another. This insecurity has been manifested in a wide variety of ways, from counterfeiting to theft, but the most pernicious of which has probably been inflation. Bit gold may provide us with a money of unprecedented security from these dangers."[220]

Nick Szabo was right—at least in theory. Whereas hashcash had introduced the concept of digital scarcity, the Bit Gold proposal showed how this might be converted into transferable electronic cash.

Chapter 12:
B-money (and BitTorrent)

SHORTLY AFTER BIT GOLD had shown how proof of work might be converted into transferable electronic cash, a somewhat similar digital currency proposal was submitted to the Cypherpunks mailing list. Its author, Wei Dai, was well known within the Cypherpunk community—though only by name.

Indeed, while privacy was the Cypherpunks' founding principle, few put it in practice like Wei Dai did. Although his involvement with the Extropians suggested that he resided in the Bay Area, Dai never showed up at the in-person Cypherpunk meetings, and for some time list subscribers weren't actually sure if they were corresponding with a man or a woman. At times, Cypherpunks even questioned whether Dai really existed, speculating that the name might be a pseudonym; some suspected it was really Nick Szabo's alter-ego.

In actuality, Wei Dai—a *he*—was a young computer scientist who'd coincidentally been a few years Szabo's junior at the University of Washington—though the two never met on campus. As an aficionado of cyberpunk books, Dai had as a student developed an interest for cryptography because he believed that it could help protect humanity against future entities like the Blight, an artificial superintelligence that served as the main antagonist in Vernor Vinge's novel *A Fire Upon the Deep*.[221]

His interest in cryptography eventually led Dai to the Cypherpunks mailing list, where he came across Tim May's many contributions. As he immersed himself in May's vision for the future of society, the young computer scientist became even more fascinated with the transformative potential of cryptography, now with a stronger emphasis on privacy and freedom from government intrusion.

Dai, who's name suggests he has Chinese heritage, eventually began engaging with the Cypherpunks mailing list himself. By the mid-1990s, Dai involved himself in discussions on a wide range of topics, varying from the economics of digital reputation systems to the application of game theory in the domain of cryptography, proposals to turn traceable payment systems into anonymous ones, and much more.

Throughout these years, Dai adopted the Cypherpunk philosophy and mission as his own.

"There has never been a government that didn't sooner or later try to reduce the freedom of its subjects and gain more control over them, and there probably never will be one," Dai at one point summarized what he believed to be the movement's binding ethos. "Therefore, instead of trying to convince our current government not to try, we'll develop the technology (e.g., remailers and ecash) that will make it impossible for the government to succeed."[222]

Cypherpunks write code.

Wei Dai, too, developed a number of tools to further the Cypherpunk cause, including an encrypted tunneling protocol (allowing for the transmission of data from one network to another), a secure file sharing system, and the Crypto++ software library (containing freely available cryptographic algorithms written in the C++ programming language). Between his coding work and his generally intelligent and insightful emails, Dai's contributions earned him a reputation as one of the most prolific and valuable Cypherpunks mailing list participants—despite his more elusive persona.

Still, it wasn't entirely outlandish that some suspected that Nick Szabo and Wei Dai were really the same person: the two had a lot in common. Besides attending the same university, and being part of both the Cypherpunk and the Extropian communities, Szabo and Dai shared a particular interest in electronic cash, and for many of the same reasons. They wanted to help realize Tim May's "Galt's Gulch in cyberspace," and both of them understood the importance of digital contracts in this context.

It was in November 1998, just after graduating from university, that Wei Dai casually announced his own electronic cash proposal, almost as an afterthought to an updated version of his anonymous communication protocol *PipeNet*, announced in the same email.[223] Published just weeks after Szabo had first described his digital currency system on the Libtech mailing list, Dai—who was also active on the Libtech list—had designed *b-money*.

"I am fascinated by Tim May's crypto-anarchy," Dai explained his motivation in the proposal. "Unlike the communities traditionally associated with the word 'anarchy', in a crypto-anarchy the government is not temporarily destroyed but permanently forbidden and permanently unnecessary. It's a community where the threat of violence is impotent because violence is impossible, and violence is impossible because its participants cannot be linked to their true names or physical locations."

To conclude:

"The protocol proposed in this article allows untraceable pseudonymous entities to cooperate with each other more efficiently, by providing them with a medium of exchange and a method of enforcing contracts. [. . .] I hope this is a step toward making crypto-anarchy a practical as well as theoretical possibility."[224]

B-money

B-money resembled Bit Gold in important ways—though it differed in others.

Like Bit Gold, b-money would essentially exist on a ledger (which Szabo had called a "registry"). This ledger would list public keys, and specify the amount of currency units attributed to each public key. To transfer the electronic cash, users would cryptographically sign a message stating how many currency units were being spent from the corresponding public key, and to which public key they were spent. If the transaction was valid (the public key had sufficient funds and the signature matched), the ledger would be updated accordingly.

Like Szabo, Dai laid a strong emphasis on the importance of contracts. B-money was designed to facilitate the effecting of contracts, and a significant chunk of the proposal was dedicated to explaining the tasks of arbitrators in dispute resolution. (Although it wasn't quite the autonomous smart contracts Szabo had originally envisioned, there were some cryptographic safeguards in place to prevent certain forms of cheating.)

Szabo had also been able to convince Wei Dai that trust-minimization was essential. *Trusted third parties are security holes*, Dai agreed, and he concluded that an electronic cash system shouldn't depend on any single entity to track user balances, facilitate transactions, or prevent double-spends.

Instead, Dai came up with two alternative solutions.

The first b-money variant was especially ambitious. In this variant, instead of a central entity, *all* users of the system would maintain individual copies of the ledger. For every new b-money transaction, each user would individually check its validity, and update their own version of the ledger if the transaction checked out. As long as everyone would stay up to date, the ledgers should remain synchronized across all users.

In theory, the great benefit of such a distributed system is that it would be impossible to corrupt. If someone would for example falsely attribute too much money to their own public keys, this simply wouldn't affect anyone else; all other ledgers would remain unchanged. If the cheater were to try to spend his spoofed cash, no one else would consider that transaction as valid. Like with Scott Stornetta and Stuart Haber's time-stamping solution, everyone would keep everyone else honest.

It made distributing the ledger across all users an ideal solution—in theory.

Unfortunately, Wei Dai knew, it wasn't going to be possible in practice: to prevent double-spends, the system required a "synchronous and unjammable anonymous broadcast channel."[225] Only if all users could be sure they received all the same transactions in the exact same order, could everyone be confident that their ledgers were synchronized, and that a payment they'd receive would be registered by everyone else as well. This seemed unworkable: double-spend transactions could be sent to different parts of the network simultaneously, while unreliable participants could simply lie about the order of transactions they received.

Or in technical terms: Wei Dai's first solution ignored the Byzantine Generals Problem.

This is why Dai came up with a second solution in the same proposal.

In this second version of the b-money system, not everyone would maintain a version of the ledger. Rather, the system would consist of two types of participants: regular users and "servers." Much like the "property club" from Szabo's Bit Gold proposal, only these servers would maintain the b-money ledgers. To make sure that a transaction went through, regular users would have to check with a random subset of the servers, and only consider a payment final if all these servers recognized it.

Of course, this did reintroduce some trust back into the system. The servers could potentially collude to block transfers, double-spend transactions, possibly steal funds, or even create money for themselves outright.

Wei Dai therefore suggested a way to keep the servers honest.

"Each server is required to deposit a certain amount of money in a special account to be used as potential fines or rewards for proof of misconduct," he proposed. "Also, each server must periodically publish and commit to its current money creation and money ownership databases. Each participant should verify that his own account balances are correct and that the sum of the account balances is not greater than the total amount of money created."

However, the b-money proposal did not go into detail on any of these solutions. Perhaps most problematically, Dai didn't explain who would get to decide if misconduct took place, if it wasn't decided by the (colluding) servers themselves, or how the fines could be enforced. In much the same way that Bit Gold had not quite provided a solution to settle disputes between servers, b-money hadn't done so either.

B-money's Monetary Policy

Like Bit Gold, b-money would be a purely digital currency. There'd be no bank or company backing the digital units with dollars or gold, and ultimately no guarantee that anyone would accept the currency for payment.

But like Szabo, Dai did not think this would be a problem.

"Think about it this way," he argued on the Cypherpunks mailing list. "In the case of commodity money, its value comes partly from the industrial/ aesthetic value of the commodity and partly from the usefulness of the commodity money as a medium of exchange. In the case of fiat money and b-money, all of its value comes from its usefulness as a medium of exchange."[226]

As opposed to Szabo, however, Dai wanted to embed his currency with a targeted monetary policy. Whereas the purchasing power of Bit Gold would have to be decided on the market, with valid proof-of-work hashes freely trading for whatever buyers and sellers were willing to settle on, b-money was explicitly designed to offer predictable purchasing power.

Like Irving Fisher and the Stable Money Association some 80 years prior, Dai proposed to peg the purchasing power of his currency to a consumer price index. He wanted the same amount of b-money units to be able to buy an equal share of this index across time. Put differently, the average price of goods and services as measured in b-money had to remain stable.

Zooming out, currency creation in b-money would work similar to Bit Gold: anyone could generate new currency units through proof of work by producing a valid hash, presumably also based on some candidate string. Whoever created the hash would get to keep it. (Or perhaps they'd be issued some equivalent in b-money units; valid proof of work could well be reflected on the ledger as 100 digital "coins.")

The key difference with Bit Gold, however, was that the difficulty of generating a valid proof of work could change.

All users of the system (b-money version 1) or the servers (b-money version 2) would continually have to determine how much a basket of goods would cost relative to the production of a valid hash. That is, if creating a hash became cheaper (due to computer hardware improvements) relative to the price index, the difficulty of producing a valid hash would have to be adjusted upwards: the hash would need to start with more zeroes.

A new hash would then only be added to the ledger if the most recent threshold was met.

As an alternative approach to achieve a similar result, which Wei Dai mentioned in the appendix of his proposal, currency creation could be managed through an auction. All users (b-money version 1) or the servers (b-money version 2) would in this case first determine an optimal increase of the money supply, after which these new b-money units would be auctioned off to whoever was willing and able to pay for it with the most proof of work.

A big benefit of these approaches was that all b-money hashes, no matter when they were created, should be worth the same: they'd be fungible. This did away with the need to architect a whole other banking layer on top of the currency's base layer, as Szabo had proposed for Bit Gold.

It was an innovative approach, but once more, much was left unspecified. For both the difficulty adjustment approach and the auction model, it remained unclear from the b-money proposal how users (or servers) would decide on the next proof-of-work difficulty, or the optimal money supply increase . . . or how disputes in this part of the process could be resolved. (Indeed, the Byzantine Generals Problem persisted throughout Dai's proposal.)

"B-money wasn't a complete practical design yet," Dai later acknowledged.[227] The proposal offered a raw outline of what an electronic cash system could look like, but several problems remained to be solved before it could function as an actual digital currency.

Dai himself, however, decided that he wasn't going to be the one to solve them.

Disillusionment

In his b-money proposal, Wei Dai still sounded optimistic about the prospects and potential of Tim May's crypto-anarchist vision. But in actuality, the elusive computer scientist had already started giving up on the Cypherpunk dream.

"I didn't continue to work on the design because I had actually grown somewhat disillusioned with cryptoanarchy by the time I finished writing up b-money," Dai later recalled. "I didn't foresee that a system like it, once implemented, could attract so much attention and use beyond a small group of hardcore cypherpunks."[228]

Dai's disillusionment was indicative of a growing sentiment within Cypherpunk quarters by the late 1990s. The internet had by now really started going mainstream, but the Cypherpunks were finding that the general public was rather indifferent about online privacy. It appeared that most people were perfectly happy to give payment processors full insight into their spending habits, and they didn't seem to mind leaving a record of other online activity either. The average internet user never even considered encrypting their emails.

Ever since the Cypherpunks gathered for the first time in Eric Hughes's unfurnished apartment, they had spent the better part of a decade turning revolutionary crypto protocols into working software—only to find out that almost no one was interested in it. Relentless privacy activism may have helped them to victory in the crypto wars, but that was turning out to have been a rather pointless exercise now that most internet users appeared perfectly comfortable giving up just about any personal data in exchange for a little bit more convenience.

Hughes himself had by this time even withdrawn from the community and mailing list almost completely—but not before he'd offered his more sober revision of the "cypherpunks write code" philosophy, characteristic for the recent disillusionment of Wei Dai, himself, and other Cypherpunks.

"Perhaps the single most important thing I've learned from cypherpunks is that code alone doesn't cut it. Not code alone, not code widely distributed, not even code widely used," Hughes wrote to the Cypherpunks mailing list. "Some measure of toleration in society for activities conducted in private is _necessary_ for long term success. Not convenient, not easier, but necessary."[229]

Hughes had come to see it as vital that the general public understood why privacy mattered. Code was still necessary as well, of course—code enabled privacy in the first place. But he now believed that in the end code was really only useful if there existed a broad public consensus that people should in fact be allowed to protect their privacy. Without such a public consensus, use of cryptography could become marginalized and perhaps outlawed, with the remaining users potentially targeted and persecuted.

"Similarly with anonymous transactions," Hughes wrote. "Unless a similar consensus exists, we will have another marginal activity. I count this a loss."[230]

The optimism and assertiveness that characterized the movement in its early days was being overtaken by a sense of despondency and abandon.

Instead, some of the more hopeful impulses for the Cypherpunk mission in the late 1990s came from relative outsiders to the community . . .

Zero-Knowledge Systems

The Canadian brothers Austin and Hamnett Hill had only been in their mid-20s when they sold TotalNet, the internet service provider they founded and turned into the third largest of their country. With some cash in hand and time to spend, the two had been on the lookout for their next project when they came across the Cypherpunks mailing list, and became enthralled with the movement's techno-libertarian ethos.

In 1997, the two brothers along with their father Hammie Hill decided to put their resources, connections, and business-savvy skills to use and founded Zero-Knowledge Systems. The new company set out to make the Cypherpunk vision reality, and earn a bit of money while doing it.

At the heart of the startup was a privacy network they called "Freedom." Freedom was based on Wei Dai's PipeNet, the anonymous communication protocol for which an updated version would be announced in the same Cypherpunks mailing list post that introduced b-money. Like PipeNet, Freedom's obfuscation techniques embedded a more advanced variation of David Chaum's original remailer protocol, but where remailers anonymized only emails, Freedom applied the mixing technology to obscure all types of internet data: emails, web browsing, text chat and more.

Freedom users could essentially "log in" to the Internet under different identities: perhaps a regular identity for professional work, a pseudonymous identity for political engagement, and another pseudonym for web sex. No one, not even Zero-Knowledge Systems, would be able to link the pseudonymous online identities to a real-world identity, or to other pseudonyms.

The startup generated some buzz throughout the Cypherpunk community and, more importantly, the Zero-Knowledge Systems founders knew how to explain to venture capitalists why they shouldn't miss out on the opportunity to invest in *the future of privacy*. Within a few years, the startup managed to raise tens of millions of dollars.

Probably better salesmen than most Cypherpunks had been, the Hills also knew how to present Zero-Knowledge Systems's ambitious goals to the general public. Good-looking print ads soon popped up in publications like *Wired, Forbes,* and *Fortune*, featuring texts like "I am not a piece of your inventory," "I am an individual and you will respect my privacy," and "On the Net, I am in control." (Particularly sharp readers could also extract a hidden message from a binary code on the pages which deciphered into "Who is John Galt?"—a famous line from Ayn Rand's *Atlas Shrugged*.)

And perhaps most important of all, Zero-Knowledge Systems managed to attract top talent in the privacy space. Some of the best-known cryptographers and computer scientists on the Cypherpunks mailing list decided to join the startup, including Ian Goldberg—who had during the Crypto Wars broken Netscape's crypto-protocol SSL and would be the company's "Chief Scientist and Head Cypherpunk"—and Adam Back. Brands Cash inventor Stefan Brands was also hired, while his electronic cash patents were bought by the startup, too.

The Hills certainly had no shortage of ambition. Freedom was the company's main project, but Zero-Knowledge Systems ultimately wanted to realize Cypherpunk ideals in a broad sense. The startup's research and development team (dubbed the "Evil Geniuses") was tasked with designing additional products, which among other things included an electronic cash scheme based on Brands's design, code-named Zorkmid; a reference to the currency unit of an early online game.

Yet, despite it all, one problem seemed to persist. Most internet users just didn't care about privacy very much.

Zero Knowledge Systems had been planning to accommodate 2.5 million Freedom users by 2000, but while its 250 employees had been hard at work to facilitate this, there were by the turn of the millennium not much more than twelve thousand active identities on the network—less than one percent of the target.

This was in part because many people had trouble installing the software, it turned out, but even those that did manage to get Freedom running found that their internet speed experienced a significant drop when they used the service. Few outside of a relatively tech-savvy core user base (mostly 25-to-35-year-old males) were willing to put up with this, and cough up Zero-Knowledge Systems's annual $50 fee to boot. At the end of the day, people simply didn't see a reason to use Freedom; the privacy benefits were invisible to them.

Or as Austin Hill put it a few years later: "everyone says they care about privacy, but people would give a DNA sample for a 'free' Big Mac."[231]

To save the company, Zero Knowledge Systems eventually changed its strategy. Instead of the general internet user, the startup would from 2001 onwards focus its efforts on established corporations, like financial institutions and telecom companies, offering them secure database and communication systems. To the upset of its small but committed user base, Freedom was discontinued.

With that, the startup largely abandoned the Cypherpunk ethos, and people like Back and Brands left soon after. When the company ultimately changed its name to Radialpoint, Zero Knowledge Systems had for all means and purposes been replaced by an entirely different IT business.

Despite a hopeful start, it represented another blow to the Cypherpunk objective.

Mojo Nation

Another positive impulse came from two previously unknown teenagers, disrupting a very different corner of cyberspace: in 1999 Shawn Fanning and Sean Parker—eighteen and nineteen years old, respectively—hurled the digital equivalent of a hand grenade right into the heart of the music industry when they launched Napster.

Napster was such a powerful idea for one specific, technical reason. Instead of relying on a central server to provide users with what they needed like most internet services up until this point had done, Napster was designed as a peer-to-peer (P2P) network. Peers (Napster users) on the Napster network operated as equals, helping each other when needed; specifically, they were sharing their own music files with one another. Since Napster itself didn't distribute any music files, Fanning and Parker thought they could sidestep copyright infringement claims, while users could still download songs for free.

But as Napster's popularity exploded, the music industry launched a successful counterattack. Fanning and Parker may not have been sharing music themselves, but artists and record labels claimed that the service was nonetheless actively enabling copyright infringement: Napster offered users a platform, it managed and stored the indexes to locate all the music files, and the service matched peers accordingly. Soon buckling under enormous legal pressure, Fanning and Parker took Napster offline by July 2001.

In the end, Napster had been a short-lived project. However, it had in its few years in the spotlight popularized P2P technology, inspiring a whole new class of innovators. Alternative file sharing services like Kazaa and eDonkey soon popped up, each of them designed to be even more decentralized than Fanning and Parker's creation was. For the next couple of years, the creators of these new protocols engaged in a high-tech, cat-and-mouse game with the record labels who tried to shut their projects down.[232]

The thirty-one-year-old Cypherpunk Jim McCoy decided he wanted to play, too. In early 2000, he had quit his job at Yahoo—"I got tired of not doing something revolutionary"[233]—and, flanked by several fellow-Cypherpunks including DigiCash alumni Bryce "Zooko" Wilcox, McCoy founded Autonomous Zone Industries.

Its name inspired by "temporary autonomous zones," a term first used in 1991 by anarchist Hakim Bey to describe nonpermanent local societies free from government, the startup would develop an ambitious open source software project called Mojo Nation. Like Napster, Mojo Nation was at its heart a P2P file sharing system. But McCoy, being a veteran Cypherpunk, had a few extra tools in his crypto toolkit to improve on Fanning and Parker's design.

As one of its most interesting innovations, all files on Mojo Nation were cut into small pieces, encrypted, and strategically copied and distributed across the network. If someone were to download a file, they'd actually download all these tiny encrypted pieces from different users across the network, to eventually puzzle them together and decrypt the complete file all at once. Because all uploaders would only need a little bit of bandwidth to share their piece, download speed could be ramped up, enabling Mojo Nation users to share bigger files than typical MP3s. In addition, it would offer more privacy: users sharing the encrypted pieces often wouldn't know what type of content they shared (or whether this content was copyright protected or not.)

Further, some of the tasks that Napster had still performed as a centralized facilitator were in Mojo Nation delegated to users. Users acting as content trackers would for example keep indexes of the files hosted on the network, while other users, acting as search agents, would offer searches through these indexes. By putting such responsibilities in the hands of users, McCoy believed that Mojo Nation wouldn't be susceptible to the types of lawsuits Napster had faced. Instead, the users themselves would be responsible if they broke the laws of their jurisdiction—but all these individual people were of course much harder to find than Fanning and Parker had been.

Making all this tick was perhaps Mojo Nation's most interesting feature: a digital currency called *Mojo*.

Mojo

Mojo was designed as an unbacked digital currency that was really only useful within the context of the file sharing network.

Specifically, Mojo had to enable a market for file sharing and other tasks. Whereas Napster users had been sharing their own files for free, Mojo Nation users could pay each other for the service, with prices to be determined through supply and demand. Someone might offer to pay 1,000 Mojo for each encrypted fraction of a file that can be puzzled together into a DVD-rip of *The Matrix*, for example; anyone who had one or several of these encrypted fractions could then accept the offer if they thought it'd be worth their time, effort, and bandwidth to upload them. The Mojo they earned could in turn be used to buy other services on the network— or perhaps exchanged for dollars on a special Mojo exchange.[234]

"The people who get paid are those who perform the services, so those agents that helped direct you to find that block [file] get paid," McCoy explained. "The distributed search agents get paid. All of the different block servers that you purchased blocks from get paid, and if the user was running through a relay server, either because they were behind a firewall or because they wanted to protect their privacy, the person passing those messages would also get a cut."[235]

McCoy's vision was for all of Mojo Nation to be guided by market processes, where one user's problem was the next user's opportunity to make some money by solving it. This would allow the Mojo Nation network to operate near-autonomously, the Cypherpunk hoped, with very little day-to-day involvement from Autonomous Zone Industries at all.

There was a notable exception to this rule, however. The Mojo currency *itself* was managed by Autonomous Zone Industries, through a special token server that kept track of account balances and prevented double-spends. Moreover, the server acted as a centralized mint: it could issue new Mojo whenever McCoy and his colleagues believed this was needed, with no technical limitation on how much of it could be created.

It eventually destroyed the currency. When some users figured out clever ways to trick others into sending them their coins, the Mojo Nation team decided to reimburse the victims with new money. This eventually led to the issuance of so many Mojo that it ultimately resulted in hyperinflation. Mojo had relied on a trusted third party—the mint—and that trust was broken.

For something like Mojo Nation to really work, it would have probably required an independent digital currency.

"[. . .] we had a hard look at MojoNation, as our primary goal was -- and to some extent remains -- a workable community currency for p2p services," computer scientist Daniel A. Nagy wrote to Jim McCoy shortly after Mojo Nation's demise, "As a reason of failure, we pinpointed hyperinflation. MN had no anti-inflation measures and in due course, mojo got inflated into oblivion." He added that "I have bought into the vision that the world desperately needs a p2p cash system. Without one, e-commerce will remain a major PITA."[236]

That said, reliance on a centralized digital currency system wasn't the only issue Mojo Nation faced. Although the software was downloaded and used by over 100,000 people,[237] multiple parts of the system proved to be very difficult to get (and keep) working. With problems ranging from network instability, to missing file fractions, to a lack of trust between peers,[238] the service was probably too ambitious for Autonomous Zone Industries's modest budget: the company ran out of money within a few years, and the negative publicity around Napster made it difficult to raise more funding.

By 2002, McCoy was left with no choice but to lay off most employees.

BitTorrent

Mojo Nation was done, but several of the startup's developers didn't want their innovative technologies to go to waste. Wilcox, for example, decided to fork (copy) the Mojo Nation code to release a version of the protocol called Mnet, while another Autonomous Zone Industries employee and Cypherpunk, the twenty-eight-year-old software developer Bram Cohen, released his own Mojo Nation-inspired file sharing solution.

He called it: *BitTorrent.*

Cohen had essentially stripped Mojo Nation down to its bare essentials. BitTorrent incorporated some of McCoy's ideas, like the chopping of files into smaller fractions. But besides that, the protocol was fairly basic: there were no embedded content trackers (indexes, called torrent files, were maintained and distributed outside of the protocol), no search agents (regular websites, again outside the protocol, could help users find specific torrent files), and no native currency.

BitTorrent did not need a native currency, because no one had to pay for files. Instead, users that downloaded the different fractions of a file would at the same time upload these fractions to other downloaders. This meant that files were technically shared altruistically, but in such a way that the burden on resources was mostly shared by those who were also benefiting from the file transfers.

With that, Cohen had designed a truly peer-to-peer and entirely distributed file sharing protocol. Where Napster's P2P network could effectively be shut down by applying legal pressure on the company behind it and even the much more ambitious Mojo Nation couldn't operate without Autonomous Zone Industries maintaining a currency system for the network, BitTorrent did not depend on any trusted third party whatsoever.

From a legal perspective, for the first time this made the users themselves fully responsible for their own file sharing activity. Not unlike email (SMTP), or even the internet itself (IP), BitTorrent was essentially just an internet protocol, and Cohen was in no way liable for how people used it— even though there's no question that copyrighted files were being shared illegally over BitTorrent on a large scale.

What's more: if Cohen would for whatever reason face legal pressure regardless, neither he nor the BitTorrent company he later founded could control the BitTorrent network on a technical level anyways. Although Cohen first created the file sharing software, it was operated by people all around the world. The network quickly became virtually impossible to censor and practically unstoppable—and not even its creator could change this.

BitTorrent would in the following years establish itself as a standard for file transfers. About a decade after Cohen's first software release, in the early 2010s, the protocol had at least fifteen million concurrent users at any time of the day,[239] and some 150 million people worldwide connected to the network in a typical month.[240] Combined, BitTorrent users were estimated to have accounted for some 25 to 30 percent of all internet traffic in the world, which was more than any other protocol at this time.[241]

With no central entity left that they could sue, music artists and record companies had little other choice but to adapt to the new reality as well. Instead of trying to remove their music from the internet, they eventually shifted their efforts to compete with file sharing services by making their songs easily available through convenient software applications (like Apple's iTunes) and, later, streaming services. Just a few years after the introduction of BitTorrent, buying a physical CD (or even owning music at all) would seem archaic.

Perhaps, this knowledge could have offered the veteran Cypherpunks in the late 1990s some optimism. Not only would one of "their" technologies take the world by storm, but even more to the point: Cohen's code revolutionized how people used, and thought about, the internet, ultimately forcing a transformation of the entire entertainment industry.

Whereas Wei Dai, Eric Hughes, and other Cypherpunks thought that electronic cash and other crypto tools could only succeed if public awareness about the importance of online privacy increased, BitTorrent would years later demonstrate that it could work both ways: a powerful enough technology could, itself, help change the prevailing culture.

Chapter 13:
RPOW

BY THE EARLY 2000s, the Cypherpunk movement had lost most of its momentum.

As some of the original Cypherpunks had grown disillusioned and stopped engaging with the Cypherpunks mailing list, overall quality on the discussion hub degraded, with many new submissions entailing little more than name-calling and shouting matches—or downright spam. While John Gilmore, the original host of the list, had in the late 1990s made attempts to introduce a moderation policy, this was starkly rejected by the likes of Tim May, who in response unsubscribed.[242] (May returned when the policy was tweaked to redirect rather than censor flames and other low-quality content, though he still wasn't happy with the changes.)

Gilmore eventually decided to stop hosting the Cypherpunks mailing list altogether, after which some of the remaining subscribers created and migrated to Usenet newsgroups, which were more distributed and could be hosted by multiple people at once.[243] Nevertheless, the demise of the movement would only accelerate. In the aftermath of the terrorist attacks of September 11, 2001, a sharp increase in digital surveillance made people more hesitant to facilitate discussions about radical privacy tools, and when the only remaining Cypherpunks server was hosted from the web address al-qaeda.net, even Tim May decided it was time to leave. This time, for good.

That didn't mean the Cypherpunk ethos was lost or forgotten completely, however. Many of the cypherpunks retained an interest in existing privacy tools like PGP, as well as new technologies such as Tor (The Onion

Router): the privacy network launched in 2002 resembled Zero-Knowledge Systems's Freedom, but didn't require a paid subscription. Tor enabled anyone to use the internet anonymously.

Many of the Cypherpunks also kept in touch through other means. Online, a good number of them eventually migrated to the more strictly moderated Cryptography mailing list, which was therefore sometimes considered the de facto successor of the Cypherpunks list. Offline, some of the Cypherpunks regularly ran into each other at cryptography conferences or hacker events.

Meanwhile, there were many more electronic currency initiatives. Around the turn of the millennium, hundreds of startups worked on online payment schemes, and many of those branded their solutions as a form of digital cash—though that often just meant that the payment systems were fast, cheap, and easy to use, while not necessarily private at all. CyberCash, for example, attracted a flurry of media coverage for its digital currency system called CyberCoin, and specialized in micropayments rather than anonymity. The same was true for Compaq's electric currency system that attracted significant attention, called Millicent.

Other initiatives that showed some potential, like n-Count (codesigned by a former DigiCash employee), Proton (a collaborative project by European banks), or Mondex (an initiative by the British NatWest bank that was later sold to Mastercard), were designed primarily around the concept of physical smart cards. Like the smart card that had been in development at David Chaum's startup, these credit card-sized pieces of hardware were to be preloaded with value representing fiat currencies, to then be used for in-person transactions. Although most of these did offer privacy features, they were primarily designed to replace physical cash rather than serve as an anonymous currency for cyberspace.

Perhaps closer to the Cypherpunk vision, Robert Hettinga—who had since 1996 been organizing the annual Financial Cryptography conferences—in 1999 founded the Internet Bearer Underwriting Corporation. After the failure of DigiCash, the Cypherpunk wanted to secure funding in order to develop a new eCash-like system, but this time optimized for low-cost transactions. He believed that strong privacy guarantees didn't just protect individuals from Big Brother, but could also reduce friction and therefore offer economic benefits.

However, none of these projects would live up to their promise. Although some of the technologies found niche use cases in specific sectors—like public transport or payphone cards—digital cash still wasn't gaining much traction with the general public, while interest and funding slowly dried up because of it.

"Quite frankly, the dot-com money has gone away," Hettinga concluded in 2001, after failing to raise enough money for his company to develop its electronic cash system. "We're also running over ground that Cyber-Cash, DigiCash and a lot of other people have burned."[244]

Instead, traditional banks and financial service providers shifted their focus to improving existing cashless payment systems (credit card and debit card transactions), while flashy new web-based payment processors like Pay-Pal were rapidly gaining market share as well—and most of them did not seem to have much concern for privacy (never mind monetary reform). The dystopian future that Chaum and many of the Cypherpunks had warned about, a future where all financial transactions can be monitored, recorded, and potentially censored, was quickly becoming reality.

Yet, not everyone was ready to give up hope . . .

Hal Finney

Born in the spring of 1956 in the small Californian town of Coalinga, Hal Finney showed an early interest in cyphers even as a young kid: in elementary school, he liked to create codes with letters and numbers for arbitrary texts he came across.

A little later, in his teenage years, Hal adopted a fascination for computers. Lucky enough, the high school he attended was quite ahead of its time: the school administration used a computer to manage and store student records years before this became commonplace. Eager to work with the machine, young Hal volunteered to help the school staff out, which landed him something of a side gig between classes.

Finney graduated from high school in 1974 at the top of his class, and was accepted into the California Institute of Technology (Caltech), one of the most prestigious and selective universities in the world. Because Caltech did not yet offer bachelor's degrees in computer science at this time, he decided to pursue a degree in engineering instead, while separately taking all the programming classes he could.

Around the same time Finney developed a deep appreciation for reason, and adopted a libertarian philosophy. He liked to engage in philosophical discussions with his fellow students at university, where a combination of thought-provoking ideas, solid argumentation, and a thoughtful approach to conversations garnered him the attention of many of his peers. Among them was Fran, the girl he'd later marry and spend the rest of his life with.

Shortly after graduating from Caltech, in 1978, Finney landed his first real programming job at the small engineering firm APh Technological Consulting. APh had just partnered with toy manufacturer Mattel to develop the operating system for their Intellivision game console, as well as some early games. In the years following, Finney worked on pioneering video games like *Space Battle* and *Star Strike* for the Intellivision, as well as *Adventures of Tron, Astroblast!* and *Space Attack* for the Atari Video Computer System.

As a generally optimistic person, Finney was convinced that the world of tomorrow would be better than that of today, and welcomed change with open arms. So when the Extropian community started forming in the late 1980s, he, too, fitted right in. The prospect of technological innovations like nanotechnology, artificial intelligence, and mind uploading excited him, and as a long-time atheist who did not believe in the afterlife, Finney had been very interested in the potential of cryonics ever since he read about the concept during his freshman year in college.

As Fran later put it: "He did not believe in God. He believed in the future."[245]

Cypherpunk Realism

When the internet became publicly available for the first time in the early 1990s, Finney had been among the very first batch of users to secure himself a connection.

As he explored the different—at this point solely text-based—corners of the brand new information superhighway, Finney quickly recognized the revolutionary potential embedded in the nascent digital domain. Humanity would for the first time be connected across the globe, regardless of geographic distances, arbitrary borders, or cultural differences, and he believed that the implications of this were world-changing.

But he soon realized there was a flip-side to communication going digital as well. Well-versed in the technical architecture of the internet, Finney knew that without safeguards, cyberspace could facilitate devastating encroachments on individual privacy; anything that anyone does online could potentially be spied on. He foresaw that the internet could actually become a threat to human liberty.

This was true for regular communication, and Finney figured that it was equally true for financial transactions.

"Dossiers could be built up which would track the spending patterns of each of us," Finney warned. "Already, when I order something over the phone or electronically using my Visa card, a record is kept of exactly how much I spent and where I spent it. As time goes on, more transactions may be done in this way, and the net result could be a great loss of privacy."[246]

The internet needed an untraceable form of money, Finney concluded—digital cash. And he was happy to discover that such a system was already in development.

"It seemed so obvious to me," Finney later recalled. "Here we are faced with the problems of loss of privacy, creeping computerization, massive databases, more centralization - and Chaum offers a completely different direction to go in, one which puts power into the hands of individuals rather than governments and corporations. The computer can be used as a tool to liberate and protect people, rather than to control them."[247]

Finney had therefore accepted an invitation from fellow Extropian Tim May, who was organizing a meeting with a group of local Bay Area hackers and cryptographers that would soon call themselves the Cypherpunks.

Shortly after, Finney found himself promoting Chaum's eCash project to his fellow Extropians, at one point authoring a seven-page explainer for the

Extropy magazine. Cryptography could protect individuals from government power, intrusion, and control, Finney wrote to the techno-libertarian crowd, as he laid out how electronic cash could benefit the Extropian cause.

And, as a true Cypherpunk, Finney wrote code. The game developer had been responsible for an early Cypherpunk success when he helped Eric Hughes develop the world's first Chaumian remailer, while it had also been Finney's idea to organize the challenge to break Netscape's export-grade (weakened) encryption standard that fellow Cypherpunk Ian Goldberg completed. It had represented a big win in the crypto wars.

But Finney's most notable contributions were probably made to PGP: after Phil Zimmermann first released the encryption tool, Finney became a major contributor to the project. The second version of the software—a great improvement over version 1—was mostly developed by him, although this was kept a bit quiet to spare Finney potential legal trouble of the kind Zimmermann was facing. A few years later, Finney would be the first employee of Zimmermann's PGP company.

Finney did not, however, subscribe to Tim May's vision of establishing a crypto-anarchist society through Cypherpunk tools.

This wasn't because he disliked the idea of removing the state from economic interactions, or because May's ideas in that regard were too radical for his taste. As an Extropian and libertarian, Finney in fact thought May's vision sounded great in principle. However, he did not believe that May's idea of achieving an anarchist society through cryptography was very realistic.

"[. . .] there is no such place as cyberspace," Finney at one point wrote to the Cypherpunks mailing list in response to one of May's disquisitions. "I am not in cyberspace now; I am in California. I am governed by the laws of California and the United States even though I am communicating with another person, whether by postal mail or electronic mail, by telephone or TCP/IP connection. What does it mean to speak of a government in cyberspace? It is the government in physical space I fear. Its agents carry physical guns which shoot real bullets. Until I am able to live in my computer and eat electrons, I don't see the relevance of cyberspace."[248]

Although individuals could use Cypherpunk tools to protect their privacy, Finney did not believe that most people could "hide" in cyberspace their whole life. Even if Cypherpunk tools could help a small, tech-savvy elite circumvent certain laws, he rejected the notion that this would fundamentally reshape civilization, because he ultimately did not believe that a libertarian society could be realized without widespread popular support.

Instead of an anarchist utopia to migrate to, Finney saw the internet more as a meeting of the minds; rather than a Galt's Gulch, he thought of cyberspace as a place to freely exchange and discuss ideas. And this, Finney believed, was the real key to achieving true liberty; the best and only way to create a free society was to convince the masses that a free society is a good idea.

"Fundamentally, I believe we will have the kind of society that most people want. If we want freedom and privacy, we must persuade others that these are worth having. There are no shortcuts. Withdrawing into technology is like pulling the blankets over your head. It feels good for a while, until reality catches up."[249]

Electronic Cash

Despite his more sober, and perhaps more realistic outlook on the potential of cryptography, Finney was always motivated to realize electronic cash, and he discussed the possibilities extensively with both Extropians and Cypherpunks on their respective mailing lists, as well as on Nick Szabo's Libtech mailing list.

On the Cypherpunks mailing list in particular, he was consistently among the most active participants in email conversations about digital currency, at times taking on a somewhat guiding role. While some of the Cypherpunks could strongly disagree on how best to approach the topic of electronic cash, Finney could seem more receptive to different ideas: rather than insisting on one solution or another, he preferred to outline the different tradeoffs that each of them implied.

Finney for example appeared mostly undecided (or, if you will, open-minded) on the topic of backing. He saw that backing electronic cash with fiat currency worked, but at times also mused about digital currencies backed by a basket of commodities, or by a synthetic average of several national currencies, or not backed at all.

Whenever a new electronic cash proposal popped up on the Cypherpunks mailing list, Finney was always eager to review it, with a special focus on their privacy features. After studying the design, he would often come back to the mailing list to explain in his own words how it worked, how this compared to previous proposals, and what he thought of the idea. Besides (usually constructive) feedback for the proposer, Finney essentially offered a public service to other Cypherpunks by helping them understand the possibilities and limitations of various approaches.

Finney also took a particular interest in the legality of electronic cash, which had in the early Cypherpunk days sent him down a rabbit hole of monetary history, where he first came across George Selgin's work on free banking. As he studied legal tender laws, tax rules, banking regulation and more, Finney shared his findings on the Cypherpunks mailing list, and began mapping out the possibilities and risks accordingly. (It was, for example, Finney who found that non-commercial experiments for eCash-like systems should be tolerated, even if they used Chaum's patented blind signature scheme.)

At the same time, Finney pushed back against some of the claims inspired by crypto-anarchy about the promise of electronic cash as well. Here, too, he was skeptical of some of the more radical predictions regarding mass tax evasion and how electronic cash would enable this.

"We are dazzled by the picture of monetary flows flashing all around the world. What I am always unable to pin down is, what exactly prevents this kind of thing from being done today?" Finney posed to the mailing list. "If you want to invest in gold, you can go down to the coin store and buy some, right? Or you can put your money into a gold-investing mutual fund and use it as a checking account. If you want yen, or marks, you can invest in those. If the point is to do so secretly, why is it easier to mail your paycheck to the digicash bank in the Bahamas than to mail it to an existing bank there?"[250]

Here, too, it wasn't that Finney found Tim May's more radical promises unappealing. He just didn't consider them very realistic. Besides the fact that most people paid their taxes directly from their paycheck anyways, at the end of the day everyone had to live in the physical world, where tax evasion would still be illegal. It was far from obvious to Finney that hiding wealth in cyberspace would benefit most people in real life.

"It seems to me that the weak point in these bypass-the-government digicash schemes is the conversion between paper cash and digital cash. That looks like the choke point where the government can still keep control," Finney concluded.[251]

Reusable Proofs of Work

By the 2000s, about a decade after Finney began advocating for electronic cash in Extropian circles, there still was no successful electronic cash system. Although an array of ideas had been discussed on the Cypherpunks mailing list, and Finney had personally reviewed many of the proposals, none of them had taken off. In some cases, like Chaum's or Hettinga's startups, this was because the product turned out to not be commercially viable—or at least that's what it had seemed like. But in other cases, like Nick Szabo's Bit Gold or Wei Dai's b-money proposals, the systems had never been implemented in the first place.

Perhaps it was because of his expectations for the potential of electronic cash had been more restrained than that of Tim May and other crypto-anarchists in the first place, or maybe it was just because of his generally optimistic character, but where many other Cypherpunks had by this time grown disillusioned, Finney wanted to give the idea another go. He decided to finally develop a proof of work-based electronic cash system—even if it had to be done in a simplified form.

In 2004, he launched *Reusable Proofs of Work*, or *RPOW* (pronounced as "arpow") for short. He invited people to try the system out, advertising the electronic cash scheme on a simple blue-and-green web page featuring an RPOW logo in comic book style. (Think of the "POW" letters marking the spot where Batman's uppercut meets some poor henchman's jaw.)

"Security researcher Nick Szabo has coined the term bit gold to refer to a similar concept of tokens which inherently represent a certain level of effort," Finney wrote on the project's website. "Nick's concept is more complex than the simple RPOW system, but his insight applies: in some ways, an RPOW token can be thought of as having the properties of a rare substance like gold. It takes effort and expense to mine and mint gold coins, making them inherently scarce."[252]

Where Bit Gold was designed around a "property club," RPOW, too, would be managed by dedicated servers. For the prototype, Finney had set up an RPOW server himself, which performed the basic operations needed to make the electronic cash system work: it issued new RPOW tokens (the currency units), and checked that tokens weren't being double-spent.

Importantly, the RPOW server would only issue new tokens if one of two conditions was met: either a valid hash had to be submitted, or an older token had to be deposited in exchange.

The first option was a straightforward proof-of-work function. If user Alice wanted an RPOW token, she would have had to connect with Finney's server (potentially over Tor for optimal privacy), take some data unique to the server and to herself, and start hashing it until she'd find a valid hash (starting with enough zeroes). She'd then send the hash to the server, which would check it for validity, and (if valid) send her a unique RPOW token in return—really just a unique string of data. The server would also store a copy of the token in a local database.

When Alice wanted to spend the RPOW token, let's say to buy an MP3 file, she'd simply send it to the intended recipient, Bob. It wouldn't technically matter for the RPOW system how she'd send it, as long as she'd be sure it made its way to Bob without anyone intercepting it. (A message to Bob encrypted with his public key would do the trick.)

When Bob would receive the RPOW token, he'd need to validate it, and make sure it hadn't been double-spent. He'd therefore immediately forward the token to the RPOW server, which would check that it was included in its internal database, and wasn't double-spent. If valid, the server would confirm this to Bob, so he could send Alice the MP3 file. The server would also mark the RPOW token as spent, deeming it invalid for future use.

Finally, the server would issue Bob a new RPOW token, and include this new token in its internal database. As such, Bob could spend this new token later on.

So let's say Bob were to spend his new RPOW token to buy access to Carol's website. As Carol received Bob's RPOW token, she'd once again send it to Finney's RPOW server. The server would confirm validity, mark it as spent in its internal database, and issue a new RPOW token to Carol, which would in turn also be added to the server's internal database.

In this way, the proof of work represented by a single valid hash (created by Alice) could effectively continue circulating indefinitely. It was, indeed, *reusable* proof of work.

Trusted Computing

The system as described so far would work pretty well—except that it requires trust in the operator of the RPOW server not to double-spend or mint RPOW tokens for himself without performing proof of work. Finney didn't want users to have to trust the operator of the RPOW server, however—even if that operator was him. Finney therefore added one more special property to the design.

For one, the RPOW server would use free and open source software. Anyone could find RPOW's source code online, and check how it worked.

And, as the system's main innovation, the RPOW server was hosted on a secure hardware component, the IBM 4758. This allowed for "trusted computing."

In short, the tamper-proof hardware contained a private key, embedded in there by IBM, that no one—not even the owner of the secure hardware component—could meddle with or extract. Using a trick called "remote attestation" the private key could then cryptographically sign the free and open source software installed on the secure hardware component. With this signature and IBM's corresponding public key, anyone could verify that the secure hardware component was indeed running the RPOW source code that Finney had published, without backdoors or tweaks.

As long as they trusted IBM not to collude with Finney to forge a signature (and assuming that the central server didn't go offline completely), RPOW users could be sure that the electronic cash system worked as advertised.

"[. . .] the RPOW system is architected with one overriding goal: to make it impossible for anyone, even the owner of the RPOW server, even the developer of the RPOW software, to be able to violate the system's rules and forge RPOW tokens," Finney explained on the RPOW website. "Without such a guarantee against forgeability, RPOW tokens would not credibly represent the work that was done to create them. Forgeable tokens would be more like paper money than bit gold."[253]

Fate of RPOW

The first RPOW release was bare-bones, but Hal Finney intended to improve the project over time. Perhaps most importantly, he planned to upgrade the system to run on several independently operated servers, so the entire RPOW system wouldn't go down if his server went offline for whatever reason.

Meanwhile, the Cypherpunk also liked to experiment and tinker with the RPOW software. He for example modified a BitTorrent client to work in conjunction with his electronic cash system; resembling the Mojo Nation concept, this allowed users to pay other users if they wanted to speed up their download. As a similarly creative application of the RPOW technology, he worked on a peer-to-peer poker application where users could play each other, and RPOW tokens were automatically transferred to the winner's digital wallet.

Finney would soon get help from a younger developer named Gregory Maxwell who took an active interest in the electronic cash system. Maxwell contributed code to the project, and considered implementing advanced spending conditions like escrow payments. He also discussed possible solutions for some of the more subtle technical challenges with Finney, like expiry times for tokens, or the relatively weak encryption securing the secure hardware component.

Unfortunately for Finney, however, Maxwell seemed to be the rare exception. As almost no one else showed an interest in the electronic cash system, RPOW was failing to take off.

This was probably at least in part because RPOW wasn't a very good form of money. Facing the same problem as Adam Back's hashcash—a problem that Szabo and Dai had tried to solve in roundabout ways—computational improvements would over time make it cheaper to generate valid hashes, suggesting that the market would eventually be flooded with RPOW tokens. The anticipation of high inflation served as a disincentive to own the RPOW currency units.

"If Moore's Law continues to hold true, the cost of creating a [proof of work] token will drop at a steady, exponential rate," Finney acknowledged on the project website. "[. . .] keep in mind that this is not money and is not intended to be a stable store of value, but rather an easy-to-exchange representation of computer effort."[254]

Indeed, instead of functioning as a widely accepted store of value or unit of account, Finney's electronic cash system was expected to be mainly useful as a means of exchange in the same types of places where hashcash could be deemed useful—for example to serve as "postage" to limit spam.

But the electronic cash system was probably also failing to take off because it couldn't overcome the bootstrapping hurdle. Money is only useful if others will accept it as payment, but with no economic incentive to hold RPOW tokens, most people had no reason to. And without anyone accepting the tokens for payment, there was also no one to spend them, meaning there was even less reason for anyone to accept them for payment in the first place . . .

"It had an issue that there was more or less nothing to use it with," Maxwell also concluded, looking back on the RPOW project years later, "which made it hard to keep attention up in it."[255]

Like eCash and hashcash before it, RPOW, too, suffered from a chicken-and-egg problem.

e-gold

Despite Hal Finney's best intentions, RPOW had by the mid-2000s ended up as yet another failed attempt at creating electronic cash.

It was at this point that some techno-libertarians had been finding some perspective in an alternative form of internet money that, with a very different design, seemed to be having more success: e-gold.

Douglas Jackson's gold-backed digital currency project was growing rapidly by the mid-2000s, and it ticked several of the boxes that Cypherpunks had wanted to see in electronic cash schemes: transactions could be made with some degree of anonymity, the system supported microtransactions down to one ten-thousandth of a gram of gold, and, of course, gold itself represented unforgeable costliness. As the e-gold technology improved, developers could even plug computer programs into the system through an application programming interface (API), facilitating solutions that resembled smart contracts.

But there was one box that e-gold didn't tick, of course. DigiCash's Cyberbucks episode had taught Cypherpunks what could happen to a digital currency if it relied on a single company, and Douglas Jackson's customers would soon learn this lesson as well. With the CEO arrested and the company's offices raided by federal agents in 2006, another internet currency scheme had failed, and Szabo's adage once again rang true: *trusted third parties are security holes.*

After more than twenty years of unrealized proposals, abandoned projects, and failed startups, there still was no electronic cash.

Meanwhile, an alternative to fiat currency was becoming more needed than ever . . .

PART III

BITCOIN

Chapter 14:
Twenty-First Century Fiat

FOR MOST OF his life, Friedrich Hayek found that his ideas had been marginalized. Bottom-up spontaneous order had to take a backseat to John Maynard Keynes's top-down state intervention in the economy. Instead of market-based interest rates, central banks had abandoned gold to make interest rate manipulation even easier. And far from denationalized, money had become a strategic tool on the global geopolitical chessboard.

Few chess players were as shrewd as US President Richard Nixon.

By effectively disbanding the Bretton Woods system, Nixon had in 1971 avoided a liquidity crisis when nations started converting their dollar reserves back into gold. But that of course wouldn't, in itself, solve the problems caused by America's deficit spending. Trust in the dollar was dwindling now that it was no longer backed by precious metal, and it started to look like the United States could lose its dominant position in the international financial system.

Nixon would find a solution against the backdrop of a worldwide oil crisis.

In 1973, oil-producing Arab nations, united in the multi-governmental Organization of the Petroleum Exporting Countries (OPEC), proclaimed an oil embargo on countries that supported Israel during the October War between the Jewish state and Egypt. Among the embargoed nations were the US, the UK, and many other Western nations. It caused a surge in the price of oil, with far-reaching negative effects on the entire world economy.

In response, newly appointed US Treasury Secretary William Simon was in 1973 sent out to visit OPEC-member Saudi Arabia. He was tasked with neutralizing oil as an economic weapon, he had to prevent the Soviet Union from establishing a firmer grip in the region while he was at it, and, to top it off, he was to find a solution for the dollar crisis; altogether, no easy task. But Simon went into the negotiations with a strong piece of leverage: the US military.

The deal that Simon was able to strike with the Saudi royal family would shape the geopolitical landscape for decades to come. In short, Saudi Arabia and other OPEC-countries would sell their oil for US dollars, exclusively; no matter which country wanted to buy petroleum, the oil-exporting nations would only accept the American currency as payment. These dollars, in turn, would in large part be used to buy US treasury notes, to finance America's spending. In return, the American military would provide aid and equipment to protect Saudi oilfields and guarantee the royal family's safety.[256]

With the deal, the United States secured demand for their dollars: anyone who wanted to purchase oil from OPEC nations, which together controlled over two-thirds of the world's reserves,[257] had to first get their hands on the American currency. Given the central importance of petroleum in the world economy, it practically ensured that the dollar remained the de facto world reserve currency. The unofficial arrangement would come to be known as the *petrodollar system*. (Soon after this arrangement was established, on December 30, 1974, private gold ownership was once again legalized in the United States.)

The petrodollar system was a great deal for the Americans—but not as great for most of the rest of the world. In order to get dollars in order to buy oil, most countries had to export goods or services to the US, or buy dollars in foreign exchange markets . . . while the US could simply print dollars, with no gold coverage ratio to worry about. If and when they did, other countries were really paying the price, as they saw the value of their dollar reserves decline.

The petrodollar system essentially instituted the Cantillon effect on a global scale, with the US government and American financial institutions at the heart of this monetary paradigm.[258]

The Hayekian Revival

Meanwhile, stagflation had thrown the field of economics in disarray, as the Keynesian assumption that inflation would counteract unemployment had been proven false. If using inflation to boost the economy was addictive, as Hayek had argued, the positive effects of the drug had now been exhausted, and society was experiencing the painful withdrawal symptoms. After a forty-year reign, Keynesianism was experiencing an existential crisis.

It was in this context that Hayek's ideas were rediscovered to form the basis for a revival of classical economic ideas.

This *neoliberal* revival began in the United Kingdom, where Margaret Thatcher in 1975 assumed leadership of the Conservative Party. Ever since reading *The Road to Serfdom* as a student in university, she'd been an adept of Hayek's work, and a strong proponent of free markets and small government. Thatcher rejected the Conservative Party's habit of compromising on these ideals in order to swing the centrist vote, and instead took a hard-line approach; at one point she even famously pulled out Hayek's book *The Constitution of Liberty* from her bag and slammed it on the table during a meeting with her party's research department. "This is what we believe!" she'd declared.[259]

It worked. Thatcher was in 1979 elected to be the first ever female prime minister of the UK. In office, the *Iron Lady* executed her plans to limit the size of government and give the free market more room by cutting taxes, removing regulatory barriers, and selling off state-owned companies in a wave of privatizations across the country. It earned her several reelections in the years to come, ultimately making Thatcher the longest-serving British prime minister of the twentieth century.

Thatcher's success in the UK served to encourage a kindred spirit in the United States. Republican candidate for the 1980 presidential election, Ronald Reagan, also ran on a platform promising a reduction of state expenditure. His campaign slogan, "We can get government off our backs, out of our pockets," resonated with the American voter. The former movie star defeated sitting President Jimmy Carter in a landslide victory.

As president, Reagan indeed sliced taxes and cut welfare programs. To further develop his economic policy, later referred to as "Reaganomics," the president also created a new Economic Policy Advisory Board, in which he installed free market-minded economists including, notably, an early admirer of Hayek named Milton Friedman.[260]

Decades earlier, in 1947, Hayek had invited Friedman—who'd just started working as an economics professor at the University of Chicago—to a ten-day conference in Switzerland. Some 60 leading free-market advocates, prominent libertarian thinkers, and other influential liberty-minded individuals had spent the ten days discussing how to preserve a free society and prevent the West from falling back to fascism or into socialism. For Hayek, the summit (which would become an annual event) represented "the rebirth of a liberal movement in Europe."[261]

Friedman had in the decades since that Switzerland trip gone on to establish himself as one of the most influential economists of the twentieth century. Like Hayek, Friedman rejected the at-the-time dominant Keynesian doctrine of state interventionism and government spending, and as his prominence grew, he in many ways became a more effective champion of Hayek's ideas on markets and the price system than even Hayek himself had been.

However, Friedman's views would in certain ways also come to deviate from Hayek's insights; his contributions to the field of economics eventually helped shape a distinct school of thought known as the *Chicago school of economics*.

The Chicago school differed from the Austrian school in a couple important ways.

One fundamental difference was the methodology of the Chicago school. Where Carl Menger had laid the foundation for the Austrian school of economics in praxeology, the method based on logic, reason, and first principles, the Chicago school opted for a more traditional empiricism, where hypotheses are formulated and tested against real-world data and statistics.

The second big difference was almost as fundamental as the first: the Chicago school disagreed with the Austrians on the topic of money.

Monetarism

Friedman was an effective champion of Hayek's ideas on markets and prices, but this did not include Hayek's perspective on the stages of production, or how interest rates and the intertemporal price system could guide the allocation of resources across time. And he certainly did not advocate Hayek's proposal to denationalize money. Instead, Friedman argued for strong government regulation of money.

Friedman, together with Economist Anna Schwartz, had conducted an empirical study of one hundred years of economic booms and busts in the United States.[262] With their research spanning from the mid-nineteenth century to the mid-twentieth, and with a special focus on the Great Depression of the 1930s, Friedman and Schwartz found that each economic contraction was preceded by a decrease in the money supply, or at least a reduction in its rate of growth.

As economists (including Hayek) had previously explained, the money supply can, most obviously, increase and decrease due to the widespread practice of fractional reserve banking. Any time someone takes out a loan at a fractional reserve bank, the bank issues new currency into circulation (as credit), which increases the (broad) money supply. Conversely, any time someone repays a loan at a fractional reserve bank, currency is taken out of circulation, decreasing the money supply.

Friedman and Schwartz explained that when the Federal Reserve had in 1928 increased interest rates, people's willingness to take out loans naturally decreased. But as old loans were repaid and money was therefore removed from circulation while not as many new loans were issued to compensate, the total money supply fell, and—as Hayek had explained as well—a deflationary debt spiral was set in motion.

But Friedman did not adopt Hayek's explanation of how interest rate manipulation had set the stage for this deflationary debt spiral, and he especially disagreed with Hayek's proposed solution to let this debt spiral run its course. Instead, he proposed a solution that was much more similar to what Irving Fisher and the stabilizers had proposed in the 1920s (but which he believed hadn't been well-executed in the 1930s).

The Chicago school economist argued that the money supply should grow at a steady and predictable rate, so the economy can grow along with it, and the aggregate price level remain stable or perhaps very slowly inflate. As long as prices were kept stable, the market could take care of the rest. *Monetarism*, as this monetary doctrine was called, became a fundamental part of the Chicago school of economics.

The proposed tools to manage the money supply were also the same as Fischer's: the consumer price index would serve as the measure of stability and interest rates could be steered to increase or decrease the money supply. If prices would fall, monetarists wanted central banks to lower interest rates, in order to stimulate borrowing, spending, and put upward pressure on prices. If prices would rise too fast, monetarists wanted central banks to increase interest rates. If prices remained stable, the amount of money in the economy would grow steadily along with the economy itself, and the interest rate was set precisely right.

Monetarists mostly disagreed with Keynesians on the role of the government in all this. They did not think that governments should leverage low interest rates to increase spending, and instead believed that government spending should be financed exclusively through fiscal policy, i.e., taxes. Although monetarists did agree that aggregate spending was vital to escape economic downturn, they maintained that the private sector could do the spending just as well, and *would* indeed do the spending if people could borrow money cheaply enough. In a way, monetarists merged ideas from both Austrians and Keynesians into a new approach.

The theory did not convince Hayek, however, for many of the same reasons that the stabilizers had never convinced him before: he believed that manipulating interest rates distorted spontaneous order across time, and he also didn't buy into the monetarist idea of stability. (He had earlier in his career argued that stable prices aren't really stable, since deflation is actually the natural state of a healthy economy, while he later in his career added that the free market should determine *what* is stable—not some top-down government committee.)

While Hayek's ideas on markets and the price system were making a comeback in the 1980s, his ideas on money were largely left behind.

Currency remained under state control, and not even Chicago's new batch of free-market economists believed that this had to change.

Savings and Loans

In 1987, President Reagan nominated Alan Greenspan, another member of his Economic Policy Advisory Board, to be the new Chairman of the Federal Reserve. Like Friedman, Greenspan was a fervent monetarist, so when the US Senate confirmed the nomination shortly after, the Chicago school monetary theory was for the first time about to be put in practice.

Barely settled into his new role, Greenspan was almost immediately faced with the worst banking crisis since 1929. In an economy with both high inflation and high interest rates to dampen the inflation, savings and loan associations were suffering. Many of these bank-like cooperative financial institutions, which issued long-term, fixed-rate loans like mortgages, were now having trouble attracting sufficient funds to honor all savers' withdrawal requests. It ultimately forced many savings and loan associations to default and file for bankruptcy.

As concerns grew among economists and policymakers that these bankruptcies could trigger a cascading effect across the American economy, Greenspan by 1989 slashed interest rates. This made it cheaper for the savings and loan associations to get some money, while anticipating and counteracting the early stages of an economic downturn at the same time.

Regardless, the Federal Savings and Loan Insurance Corporation (FSLIC) eventually had to bail the failing industry out, repaying savers a total of $125 billion. This FSLIC, as well as the Federal Deposit Insurance Corporation (FDIC), had been installed during the Great Depression to help restore the public's trust in banks: the government agencies would assure that banking customers are repaid their deposits (up to a certain limit) in the event of a bank failure. As the Federal Reserve had been failing in its role as lender of last resort during the economic crisis of the 1930s, it gave depositors a second reason not to be concerned about fractional reserve banking.

Indeed, the bailouts limited the scope of the savings and loans crisis and averted many personal dramas. But it did so at a significant cost: the $125 billion had to be paid for by the government, and therefore, ultimately, by the American taxpayer. Even those Americans that were careful and prudent with their savings had to indirectly bear some of the burden. Meanwhile, the savings and loans associations and their customers got off relatively easy.

Hayek had early in his career been concerned that central banks introduced moral hazard into the economy. Since then, the FDIC and FSLIC had made this even more explicit. During the savings and loans crisis, it became clear that financial institutions could take big risks; the US government would pick up the bill if things went south.

Dot-Com

About ten years after the savings and loans crisis, by the late 1990s, stock markets were in a frenzy.

This was in part because of a general sense of optimism across the Western world: earlier in the decade, the Soviet Union had finally crumbled. Although Ludwig von Mises had passed away in 1973, his economic calculation problem finally seemed vindicated. As the folly of central planning finally appeared to have been confirmed, former Soviet countries embraced free-market economics.

On top of that, the United States was engulfed by exorbitant tech-euphoria, most clearly reflected on the Nasdaq stock exchange. With Silicon Valley giants like Netscape going public at multibillion dollar valuations, technology stocks across the board soared; even internet startups with little more to show for than a domain name were in some cases valued at tens if not hundreds of millions of dollars. The internet was the future, and everyone wanted a piece of it.

But students of Hayek's work had reason to suspect that there was something else at play, too. Greenspan's Federal Reserve had in the wake of the savings and loans crisis dropped interest rates to their lowest levels since the 1960s. Just like in the 1920s, money was cheap, and people were happy to borrow and invest in the stock market. Artificially low interest rates were spurring the economic boom.

And, these students of Hayek would have known, economic reality would sooner or later have to catch up. Indeed, it eventually did. When, just before the turn of the millennium, Greenspan decided to hike interest rates, the dot-com bubble popped, and the Nasdaq came crashing down. The frenzy was over.

Had he still been alive, Hayek would probably have argued that the best way forward would be to bite the bullet and let the market return to normal. The economy would have to go through a painful recession as unprofitable businesses failed, and resources could slowly be reallocated to more sustainable endeavors.

But Greenspan had a different idea. The monetarist was set on preventing a deflationary debt spiral, so he once again decided to lower interest rates. Dropping them well below the 1990s' levels this time, credit was by the early 2000s even cheaper than it had been during the run-up of the dot-com bubble.

On the surface, it seemed to work. Over the next couple of years, the stock market was slowly recovering. For many economic commentators, it served as confirmation that monetarism worked as intended. Greenspan had maneuvered the American economy through the dot-com crash with minimal damage, even earning him a new nickname—"the Maestro."

One sector in particular was by the mid-2000s experiencing nothing short of a full-blown economic boom: the housing market.

Too Big to Fail

This boom in the housing market was not a great concern for Greenspan in light of monetary stability. Although some derivative prices, like the cost of renting and maintenance, were taken into account, home prices themselves were not actually included in the CPI; they had been removed from the index in 1983. Real estate has since then largely been categorized as a form of investment, which was particularly convenient as politicians at the time wanted to bring the inflation numbers down.[263]

Regardless, the boom could to a large extent be explained by Greenspan's policy. Low interest rates had by the early 2000s sent mortgage rates to new lows, and the American housing market was surging as a direct result. The price of a new home increased year after year, as everyone seemed to want to make use of the opportunity to get in cheap.

And there was also another, hidden reason for this boom. Financial institutions had, especially since the late 1980s, been using complex types of mortgage-backed securities called *collateralized debt obligations*. This allowed them to chop up and resell mortgage debts; instead of the bank that issued it, mortgage debts were increasingly owned by investors, which included other financial institutions like banks, insurance companies, and pension funds.

The problem, however, was that any mortgage debt could be repackaged and masqueraded as a virtually risk-free asset. As such, some mortgage-issuing financial institutions were happy to issue new mortgages to just about anyone who applied for one: checks on income, job security, or creditworthiness were largely thrown out of the window. The risks inherent to these mortgages were obscured in order to be resold.

But the risks couldn't remain obscured forever. By the mid-2000s, Federal Reserve chairman Greenspan started jacking interest rates up again, and his successor in 2006, Ben Bernanke, followed his lead. Once more, for those who studied Hayek's work, what happened next wouldn't come as a surprise.

As borrowing became more expensive, the housing market began drying up, while at the same time more and more Americans started defaulting on the mortgages that had been given to them so freely. As housing prices in the United States began to fall, those who had invested in the mortgage-backed securities were finding that they were nowhere near as safe as advertised, in turn leaving some of them strapped for money to honor their own debts.

As defaults began spreading through the US financial sector like a contagion, affecting bigger and bigger firms, the scope of the crisis was becoming increasingly evident. When financial giant Lehman Brothers in September of 2008 became the largest company to file for bankruptcy in the history of the United States, finance professionals, policy makers, and anyone else who was paying attention knew that further escalation could well result in a full-blown economic collapse.

By the time it looked like major insurance firm AIG could be next in line to cave, the Fed, backed by a new emergency law, took a truly unprecedented step. The central bank declared the insurer "too big to fail," and, along with the US Treasury, bailed it out with an injection of $68 billion (plus another $112 billion in guarantees).

It heralded in a new policy era, both in the US and abroad as the crisis spread internationally. In the following weeks, the Federal Reserve once more coordinated with the US Treasury to let it purchase $405 billion worth of troubled assets, while on the other side of the Atlantic, the Chancellor of the UK's Treasury, Alistair Darling, rolled out an emergency measure in the form of a bank rescue plan worth $230 billion (£137 billion), and similar measures were taken in other European countries.[264]

An immediate financial collapse was averted, but only because large swaths of the financial sector were saved by public institutions and the creation of massive amounts of new money out of thin air; moral hazard was now on full display.

A New World

Government interventions wouldn't stay limited to bailouts, either.

The Federal Reserve had in the midst of a crisis once again lowered interest rates with the intention to avoid deflation and get the economy back on track, this time dropping them to nearly zero percent: borrowing money became almost free. But it seemed to have little effect.

In November 2008, therefore, the Federal Reserve announced a large-scale asset purchasing program dubbed *Quantitative Easing* (QE). The Fed would buy up another $600 billion' worth of mortgage-backed securities with freshly created dollars, and shortly after expanded this to also buy up bank debt and government debt. The central bank soon owned over $2 trillion' worth of these three assets, nearly tripling the total value of its balance sheet.

QE lets central banks take risky assets off the market, but the main goal of the programs is to increase the money supply and counter deflation when the conventional tools aren't accomplishing the job. In other words, QE can help spur inflation when interest rates have been dropped to zero (or close), by desperately spending trillions into the economy directly; an example that was soon followed by other central banks around the world.

And it *was* desperate. According to Bernanke's own leading theory on money and interest, QE shouldn't even work to boost inflation if zero percent interest rates didn't do that already. Yet, it did seem to work, at least a bit. As the Fed chairman quipped: "The problem with QE is that it works well in practice, but not in theory."[265]

Still, with the introduction of QE, central banks were stepping onto almost entirely untrodden terrain. No one in charge of these purchasing programs knew exactly what the effects would be, or how long it would take for such effects to play out. Indeed, the 2008 financial crisis and its aftermath ushered in a new and uncertain world of money and finance.

Originally established to act as a lender of last resort about a century earlier, the Federal Reserve had been manipulating interest rates for almost as long. Now, it also started picking winners and losers in the market with bailouts, and even began allocating resources throughout asset markets via QE. The central bank's mandate had over time expanded to include tasks that could equally well describe the types of duties more commonly attributed to Soviet-style central planners.

Meanwhile, the crisis—like the crisis of the 1930s—provided an environment where Keynesian ideas could make a comeback: a group of economists known as the "New Keynesians"[266] urged governments around the globe to increase deficit spending in order to stimulate national economies. When IMF Managing Director Dominique Strauss-Kahn in 2008 endorsed this "Keynesian resurgence," world leaders, including US President George W. Bush and British Prime Minister Gordon Brown, agreed to support the plans. Financial stimulus packages were soon rolled out all across the world.

For most of his life, Hayek found that his ideas were marginalized. Hayek had critiqued the role of central banks as early as the 1920s, and he'd warned since the 1930s that Keynesian measures did little more than prolong unsustainable economic booms. Yet, things seemed to only get worse over time. Money had evolved into a geopolitical chess piece for nationalists, a power tool for economic planners at central banks, and, most of all, a source of economic turmoil—which in turn facilitated the resurgence of Keynesian doctrine.

The monetary system was by the early twenty-first century about as far removed from Hayek's ideal as it could have possibly been, and a solution was not in sight.

Not, unless you happened to subscribe to a niche technology mailing list in a nearly forgotten corner of the internet . . .

Chapter 15:
The White Paper

THE FINANCIAL MARKETS were already rumbling when in the summer of 2008 Adam Back received an email from someone going by the name "Satoshi Nakamoto." Nakamoto explained that he had designed a digital cash scheme based on the proof-of-work system that Back first introduced in hashcash over a decade earlier. The email included a link to a draft white paper, titled "Electronic Cash Without a Trusted Third Party." Nakamoto was interested in feedback.

Back had never heard the name Satoshi Nakamoto before and, having been involved with the Cypherpunk movement since the mid-1990s, he'd seen one too many failed attempts at creating digital currency to have high expectations for the new proposal in his inbox. Still, Nakamoto had piqued the British Cypherpunk's interest enough for him to read the paper, and he'd noticed some similarities with Wei Dai's b-money proposal. Back pointed this out to Nakamoto in his reply, but left it at that.

Wei Dai soon heard from Satoshi Nakamoto as well.

"I was very interested to read your b-money page," Nakamoto's email read. "I'm getting ready to release a paper that expands on your ideas into a complete working system."[267]

Nakamoto went on to ask when the b-money design was first published: he wanted to refer to Dai's electronic cash proposal in the final version of his white paper. This email, too, included a link to the draft.

Dai—who like Back did not know a Satoshi Nakamoto—replied with links to a web archive with the original b-money email and the relevant discussions on the Cypherpunks mailing list from ten years earlier. "Thanks for letting me know about your paper," Dai added. "I'll take a look at it and let you know if I have any comments or questions."[268]

Dai never did follow up. By this time, he had given up hope that Cypherpunk-inspired digital cash systems could attract enough users to make a meaningful difference in the world, and didn't pay much attention to Nakamoto's design. He preferred to focus his time on decision theory and other approaches to AI safety (the original reason he got interested in cryptography).

Nakamoto, meanwhile, appeared to have gotten the information he needed. As the financial crisis of 2008 was fully coming to a head in the following weeks and months, Nakamoto retreated back into obscurity.

Until October 31. This time, all subscribers to the Cryptography mailing list received an email from Satoshi Nakamoto. With the Cryptography mailing list serving as the de facto successor of the Cypherpunks list, many of the original Cypherpunks were now introduced to the new digital currency proposal. "Bitcoin P2P e-cash paper," the subject announced.[269]

Indeed, Nakamoto's electronic cash project now had a name: *Bitcoin*.

"I've been working on a new electronic cash system that's fully peer-to-peer, with no trusted third party," Nakamoto's email read, before summing up the main properties:

- *Double-spending is prevented with a peer-to-peer network.*

- *No mint or other trusted parties.*

- *Participants can be anonymous.*

- *New coins are made from Hashcash style proof-of-work.*

- *The proof-of-work for new coin generation also powers the network to prevent double-spending.*

Included was a link to the updated version of the white paper.[270] "Bitcoin: A Peer-to-Peer Electronic Cash System," the title now read. In just nine pages (including a page for external references), Nakamoto outlined the core mechanics of his proposed digital currency scheme. It made for a compact, yet very effective description of—as the paper's introduction described it—"an electronic payment system based on cryptographic proof instead of trust."

The Block Chain

The system Satoshi Nakamoto described in his white paper indeed resembled b-money—now included as the first of eight references—in several ways.

Like in Wei Dai's electronic cash design, Bitcoin's currency units (also called *bitcoin,* but typically written with a lowercase b) would be unbacked, while bitcoin ownership would be attributed to public keys. Transactions, then, would essentially be cryptographically signed messages specifying that the coins attributed to these public keys are transferred to some other public keys. Bitcoin ownership would therefore be cryptographically guaranteed; funds could only be moved with valid signatures.

Because of this, and also like b-money, Bitcoin users wouldn't need to reveal their real names to use the system; they could send and receive money semi-anonymously, revealing *only* their public keys. To avoid that a public key becomes associated with their true identity, Nakamoto suggested that users generate a new key pair for each incoming transaction. This would go a long way to protect users' privacy—though Nakamoto acknowledged in his white paper that it wouldn't be quite perfect.

"Some linking is still unavoidable with multi-input transactions, which necessarily reveal that their inputs were owned by the same owner," he wrote. "The risk is that if the owner of a key is revealed, linking could reveal other transactions that belonged to the same owner."

But perhaps most interestingly, Nakamoto designed Bitcoin in line with the most ambitious variation of b-money, with all users maintaining a ledger to track currency ownership within the system. Every node (each peer on the network) would see all new transactions, check their validity, and update their ledgers accordingly—while invalid transactions (including double-spends) would be rejected.

Ten years earlier, Dai had concluded that such a distributed approach wasn't practical. Absent a synchronous and unjammable anonymous broadcast channel, different parts of the network could see different transactions first, so double-spend transactions would essentially split the network, where different nodes maintain conflicting ownership ledgers. With potentially dishonest participants out to sow discord, and without anyone in charge to decide which version of the ledger is the one true state of the network, Dai saw no way to resolve such splits. Indeed, it was a perfect example of the Byzantine Generals Problem.

Now, Satoshi Nakamoto believed he had solved the Byzantine Generals problem.

In designing this system, Nakamoto seemed to have taken inspiration from Scott Stornetta and Stuart Haber: three out of the next four references in the white paper pointed to Stornetta and Haber's trustless time-stamping papers (including the one they coauthored with Dave Bayer), while the fourth referred to a time-stamping proposal by Belgian researchers who leaned heavily on Stornetta and Haber's work. In a separate reference, Nakamoto also credited Ralph Merkle's foundational paper that first described Merkle Trees.

It was a natural fit. Wei Dai's idea to distribute the ledger of ownership across all users was philosophically very close to Haber and Stornetta's concept of sharing copies of the backbone record of a time-stamping protocol. In both cases, every participant would verify the important information themselves, so they'd be sure that no one could have cheated. Everyone would keep everyone honest.

In Stornetta and Haber's most advanced proposal, users hashed documents together in a big Merkle Tree, for the Merkle Root—the tree's final hash—to be included in the next Merkle Tree. It resulted in a mathematically provable chronological order of Merkle Trees, and therefore also a chronological order of documents embedded in the Merkle Trees. As long as the users of the system maintained their own backbone records, they could always prove that a particular document was included before another document, and at what time.

Nakamoto's electronic cash system was designed in a very similar way: the documents from Haber and Stornetta's time-stamping solutions were in Bitcoin essentially replaced by transactions. As transactions would be sent over Bitcoin's peer-to-peer network, users would, with some regularity, hash them together into a Merkle Tree. Such a batch of transactions would make up the bulk of what was called a "block." If two or more conflicting transactions circulated on the network, only one of them could be included in a block, and importantly: only transactions that were included in a block would be considered confirmed.

And, much like in Haber and Stornetta's backbone records, each new Bitcoin block would also contain the hash of the previous block, called the "block hash." This would make it impossible to edit an older block and still have it mathematically fit in the chain of all blocks, as this would necessarily change the entire chain since that block, which all users would therefore notice.

Indeed, the contents of Bitcoin blocks, their chronological order, and therefore the order of all transactions in them, would in effect be cryptographically sealed.

Nakamoto called this chain of blocks: the *block chain*.

Mining

Because a Bitcoin block would only be considered valid if it didn't include conflicting transactions, the block chain offered the beginning of a solution to the double-spend problem. Even if different users would see *transactions* in a different order, their ownership records would still be in consensus as long as they all received the *blocks* in the same order. In the event of a double-spend attempt, only the transaction that was included in a block would be used to update all ledgers.

Still, this didn't quite solve the double-spend problem entirely. After all, if different users create different blocks (potentially with conflicting transactions in these different blocks), and the different blocks are sent to different parts of the network simultaneously, the exact same problem would resurface: the network would split.

And since each next block would include the previous block hash, this would even mean that different parts of the network would end up creating entirely different, incompatible block chains, over time probably causing different users to update their ownership records differently, and permanently fall out of consensus. Users on the different parts of the network would be unable to transact with each other.

Nakamoto knew that all Bitcoin users would have to converge on the same block chain—even if that meant that some users had to occasionally abandon the blocks they received first in case of a conflict. But with potentially dishonest participants and no one in charge, determining which block chain to settle on was—again—a great example of the Byzantine Generals Problem.

This is where Adam Back's proof-of-work system came in, with his original hashcash proposal representing the next reference in the Bitcoin white paper. Proof of work had by then already formed the basis of several Cypherpunk digital currency designs, of course, including b-money as well as Bit Gold and RPOW. But where these designs had typically used the proof of work hashes *themselves* as a form of money, Nakamoto, in what was one of his key insights, had figured out an ingenious new use for it.

Proof of work would be used as a consensus mechanism.

Besides a batch of transactions and the previous block hash, Bitcoin blocks would include a third ingredient: a nonce. This random number would be hashed along with the rest of the contents of a block to generate the block hash. The proof-of-work trick, then, was that not every block would be considered valid. Only blocks with a block hash starting with some predetermined number of zeroes would be accepted by the network of users.

Just like producing hashcash, the only way to find a valid block would be through trial and error, a process that Satoshi Nakamoto would later call "mining." Mining users (or "miners") would need to randomly try including many different nonces in a block they wanted to construct, until one of them would result in the generation of a valid block hash. A valid block—which could not be edited by anyone after it was produced, since that would also change the block hash—would then be sent across the network, where each user would update their ownership records with the transactions in this block.

Miners, meanwhile, would switch their mining efforts to include the new block hash in a potential next block, which would in turn require its own valid block hash. Similar to how Bit Gold users (and presumably b-money users) would produce a cryptographic chain of hashes to create currency, with each valid hash serving as the candidate string for the next, Bitcoin miners would produce a cryptographic chain of block hashes.

And crucially: the length of this chain would serve as the tie-breaker in case of a conflict.

In the event that two conflicting blocks would circulate over the Bitcoin network, every user would initially accept the block they received first, and miners would include its block hash in the next block they'd try to mine. In a sense, the Bitcoin network would, indeed, split. But this split would be temporary. As soon as one side of the split mines the next block quicker than the other side of the split, and their version of the block chain grows longer than the alternative, Bitcoin users and miners from both sides of the split would settle on this longest chain, abandoning the shorter chain and thus resolving the split.

To overcome the Byzantine Generals Problem, Satoshi Nakamoto cleverly repurposed proof of work as a decentralized tie-breaker to reach consensus. Exactly because anyone can produce proof of work, and because anyone can easily check its validity without needing to trust anyone else, it was perfectly compatible with Bitcoin's leaderless design.

"The network is robust in its unstructured simplicity," Nakamoto concluded his white paper. "Nodes work all at once with little coordination."

Coin Issuance

If Bitcoin users were to produce proof of work—mine blocks—they needed an incentive.

Miners would therefore be awarded bitcoin currency units if they mine a valid block, Nakamoto explained in his white paper. This *block reward* would consist in part of transaction fees, paid by other users for including their transaction in a new block. But the biggest part of the block reward would initially consist of brand new coins.

This elegantly solved two problems at once: besides providing an incentive to mine (thus allowing the network to reach consensus on the state of the ledger), it was also a way to bring new currency into circulation without a central issuer. Moreover, it would do so in a particularly smart way: although proof of work could be used to earn new currency, the amount of bitcoin to come into circulation with each new block was actually fixed. No matter how much energy it had cost to produce a valid block, the number of new coins rewarded per block would remain the same.

Furthermore—and this was arguably Nakamoto's most important original innovation, not borrowed from previous digital cash schemes—a *difficulty adjustment algorithm* would ensure that new blocks would be mined at a somewhat consistent pace. If too many blocks would be produced too quickly, as indicated by the time-stamps included in each new block, all nodes on the network would automatically start requiring new blocks to include more proof of work. (That is, it would require more processing power to find a valid block hash, as new hashes would require more leading zeroes.) While if blocks would on average be found too slowly, all nodes would start accepting new blocks that included less proof of work (fewer leading zeroes).

With blocks mined at a fairly steady rate, and each block issuing a fixed amount of new coins, the rate of currency creation would be predictable—no matter the amount of hash power attributed to the network. Where systems like hashcash and RPOW would have experienced a hyperinflation as the cost to produce a valid hash kept dropping over time due to hardware improvements, Bitcoin was designed to stick to a preprogrammed issuance schedule.

By decoupling the amount of proof of work and the rate of currency creation, Nakamoto had solved the inflation problem, allowing Bitcoin issuance to more closely resemble that of a precious metal.

"The steady addition of a constant amount of new coins is analogous to gold miners expending resources to add gold to circulation," the Bitcoin white paper explained. "In our case, it is CPU time and electricity that is expended."

Positive Incentives

Furthermore, Nakamoto believed that Bitcoin's coin issuance model would discourage potential attackers.

Most obviously, dishonest participants couldn't easily double-spend transactions, since only one of the conflicting transactions could be included in the block chain.

The only way to pull off a double-spend attack, then, would be for the attacker to have one of his transactions included in a block and accepted as payment by the recipient, to then mine a conflicting block with the conflicting transaction himself, and continue mining on this alternative block chain until it overtakes the original chain in length. If he'd indeed manage to create the longest chain (with the double-spend transaction in it), all Bitcoin users would switch to this alternative chain, and everyone would update their ledgers accordingly. The original transaction would be revoked, and the double-spend would've succeeded.

However, as long as the attacker would not have more processing power than the rest of the whole rest of the network combined, the probability that he'd overtake the honest chain would shrink exponentially for each block he'd fall behind, Nakamoto explained. The honest chain would almost certainly grow in length faster. He backed up his explanation with the eighth and last reference in the white paper, and also the oldest: the 1957 handbook *An Introduction to Probability Theory and Its Applications*, by mathematician William Feller.

To avoid being double-spent on, the simple solution would therefore be to wait until a few more blocks have been mined on top of the block that includes an incoming transaction, before considering the payment final, Nakamoto wrote. Each new block would represent an additional confirmation of the transaction in question, and with just a handful of confirmations it would in most cases be exceedingly unlikely that an attacker could ever catch up. And since an attacker would have to expend computational resources to even try, attempting an attack would usually not be worth it in the first place.

That said, waiting for more confirmations would not help if an attacker did, in fact, have more processing power than the rest of the network combined. In that scenario, the attacker could eventually always catch up and generate the longest chain, enabling him to double-spend at will.

Even if that were to be the case, though, the attacker couldn't perform his attack for free; he'd still have to produce the proof of work needed to create valid blocks.

By extension, Nakamoto speculated that the block rewards awarded by the Bitcoin protocol could in themselves compel a potential attacker not to double-spend:

"The incentive may help encourage nodes to stay honest. If a greedy attacker is able to assemble more CPU power than all the honest nodes, he would have to choose between using it to defraud people by stealing back his payments, or using it to generate new coins. He ought to find it more profitable to play by the rules, such rules that favour him with more new coins than everyone else combined, than to undermine the system and the validity of his own wealth."

Even in the worst case, Bitcoin's incentives probably aligned for everyone to act honestly.

Peer-To-Peer

Bitcoin was, as Nakamoto's email announcement had promised, designed to be a truly peer-to-peer system.

All users would be equals on the network, helping each other to keep the system running by creating and forwarding transactions and blocks, and with no special privileges or trusted entities whatsoever. There'd be no DigiCash company to go bankrupt, no Bit Gold property club to decide who owns what, nor even a trustless RPOW server to shut down. Much like BitTorrent, Bitcoin was essentially designed to be a new internet protocol that anyone could use, but no one would control.

To realize this, Satoshi Nakamoto had to solve some of the most persistent problems decentralized electronic cash designs had struggled with: he overcame the Byzantine Generals Problem to prevent double-spends without any central party, and figured out how to limit inflation in a proof-of-work system despite continuous hardware improvements. And, with the exception of the time-stamp-based difficulty adjustment algorithm, he'd achieved this without requiring any major breakthrough technologies. Nakamoto had taken different tools from the electronic cash and cryptography toolboxes that had been invented at least a decade earlier, and pieced them together in a nifty way.

On top of that, his timing was impeccable, too. Just as central banks across the world were deploying unprecedented interventions across the financial system in desperate attempts to prevent a full-blown economic collapse, Satoshi Nakamoto proposed a new type of money that could operate without financial institutions altogether—a digital currency system based entirely on math.

Yet, most of the initial responses to Bitcoin's public announcement failed to recognize or appreciate the significance of this breakthrough . . .

Scalability

The first reply to Nakamoto's announcement came about a day later, from James A. Donald, a Cypherpunk who happened to be in the late stages of designing a digital cash system himself.

"We very, very much need such a system, but the way I understand your proposal, it does not seem to scale to the required size," Donald wrote. "To detect and reject a double spending event in a timely manner, one must have most past transactions of the coins in the transaction, which, naively implemented, requires each peer to have most past transactions, or most past transactions that occurred recently. If hundreds of millions of people are doing transactions, that is a lot of bandwidth - each must know all, or a substantial part thereof."[271]

Indeed, Nakamoto's design did require that users keep track of all transactions on the Bitcoin network, in order to update their local versions of the ownership ledger. They would have to know exactly which coins had been spent and which hadn't, to be sure that a coin they received as payment wasn't already spent to someone else. If the Bitcoin network would grow large enough, this could become infeasible for most regular users.

It was a problem Satoshi Nakamoto had considered. In his white paper, he offered a two-step solution called "Simplified Payment Verification" (SPV). First, to minimize the amount of disk space needed to run Bitcoin on a regular computer, older blocks could be removed from users' computers, so they'd only have to store the block hashes. And second, by using Merkle proofs, users could check with these block hashes that transactions to them are included in the block chain—largely ignoring all other transactions. Running a fully validating network node "would be left more and more to specialists with server farms of specialized hardware," Nakamoto wrote in reply to Donald on the mailing list.[272]

But unfortunately this solution didn't entirely solve the problem, as Nakamoto did also acknowledge in the white paper, while introducing new issues of its own. SPV abandoned the security model where everyone keeps everyone honest, because instead only dedicated miners would verify that the rules of the system were being followed at all times.

Donald, in response to Nakamoto on the mailing list, warned that if only a small subset of Bitcoin users could muster sufficient resources to be a miner, it could make these miners a target and point of leverage for regulators.

In a long and detailed follow-up email, he described how states would capture financial networks step-by-step, to ultimately control the money issuing entity: "as for example the Federal reserve act of 1913, the goal always being to wind up the network into a single too big to fail entity, and they have been getting progressively bigger, more serious, and more disastrous."

Bitcoin, Donald predicted, would be subject to the same type of pressure.

"If a small number of entities are issuing new coins, this is more resistant to state attack [than] with a single issuer, but the government regularly attacks financial networks, with the financial collapse ensuing from the most recent attack still under way as I write this," he argued.

To keep the system decentralized, and ensure that most users could process all transactions on the network, the Cypherpunk instead suggested that Bitcoin could benefit from a payment layer for low-value transactions, so only large transactions would need to be processed by all users and stored in the block chain.

"I think we need to concern ourselves with minimizing the data and bandwidth required by money issuers - for small coins, the protocol seems wasteful. It would be nice to have the full protocol for big coins, and some shortcut for small coins wherein people trust account based money for small amounts till they get wrapped up into big coins," he wrote. "The smaller the data storage and bandwidth required for money issuers, the more resistant the system is [to] the kind of government attacks on financial networks that we have recently seen."[273]

Nakamoto did not comment on Donald's payment layer suggestion specifically, but he did make sure to address the possible state-level attacks Bitcoin could ultimately face. Whereas the mysterious author of the new white paper had through his writings conveyed a rather scientific, matter-of-factly approach to the topic, Nakamoto now unequivocally confirmed the driving motivation behind the system's decentralized design.

"Yes, but we can win a major battle in the arms race and gain a new territory of freedom for several years," he wrote. "Governments are good at cutting off the heads of [. . .] centrally controlled networks like Napster, but pure P2P networks like Gnutella and Tor seem to be holding their own."[274]

Concerns and Confusion

The first response Nakamoto received—James. A. Donald's scaling concerns—did have some merit; scaling Bitcoin up to serve millions or even billions of users was going to be a big challenge indeed. But much of the feedback that followed after that was more of a mixed bag, with commenters in some cases clearly confused about Bitcoin's design.

Ray Dillinger, a computer scientist and Cypherpunk who'd been one of the first contributors to the Cryptography mailing list, for example dismissed Bitcoin because of its inflation rate of 35 percent—even though no inflation schedule was mentioned in the white paper. He wrongly assumed that the issuance of new coins would increase along with computer hardware performance over the years, as had been the case for a system like RPOW.[275]

As a potential solution to the inflation problem, Dillinger in a later email suggested that Bitcoin should have a difficulty adjustment algorithm—apparently not realizing that this was already part of Nakamoto's design.[276]

Meanwhile, Donald argued that Nakamoto's difficulty adjustment algorithm could not work at all. He seemingly believed that this would remove the incentive to mine new blocks altogether—though his email did not explain why.[277]

Both Dillinger and Donald did agree, however, that Bitcoin's proof-of-work consensus mechanism was not robust or fast enough. They disliked the idea that transactions could be reversible in the event that the block chain is overtaken by a longer rival chain, and didn't consider waiting for more block confirmations to be a satisfactory solution.

"How does anybody know when a transaction has become irrevocable?" Dillinger asked, rhetorically. "Is 'a few' blocks three? Thirty? A hundred?"[278]

Whatever the "correct" number would be, it wouldn't work, he predicted: neither consumers nor merchants would be willing to wait "an hour" for transactions to clear.

Donald shared that assumption: "We want spenders to have certainty that their transaction is valid at the time it takes a spend to flood the network, not at the time it takes for branch races to be resolved."[279]

John Levine, another computer scientist who had frequented the Cypherpunks mailing list before migrating to the Cryptography mailing list, cast doubt on Bitcoin's consensus model as well, but for a different reason. Levine predicted that the proof-of-work consensus model would not be very secure against attackers.

"Bad guys routinely control zombie farms of 100,000 machines or more. People I know who run a blacklist of spam sending zombies tell me they often see a million new zombies a day," Levine wrote. "This is the same reason that hashcash can't work on today's Internet—the good guys have vastly less computational firepower than the bad guys."[280]

Yet, not everyone on the Cryptography mailing list was ready to dismiss Bitcoin as a flawed design.

Optimism

On November 7, about a week since Nakamoto publicly shared his white paper, a strikingly more optimistic response found its way to the list as well.

"Bitcoin seems to be a very promising idea," Hal Finney opened his email, before accurately pinpointing the two main innovations compared to previous electronic cash schemes.

"I like the idea of basing security on the assumption that the CPU power of honest participants outweighs that of the attacker," he wrote. "I also do think that there is potential value in a form of unforgeable token whose production rate is predictable and can't be influenced by corrupt parties. This would be more analogous to gold than to fiat currencies. Nick Szabo wrote many years ago about what he called 'bit gold' and this could be an implementation of that concept."[281]

Like Donald, Finney was also quick to suggest that Bitcoin could benefit from a lightweight payment solution on top of its protocol. Besides better scalability, the electronic cash veteran pointed out that this could provide more and even stronger privacy features.

"There have also been proposals for building light-weight anonymous payment schemes on top of heavy-weight non-anonymous systems, so Bitcoin could be leveraged to allow for anonymity even beyond the mechanisms discussed in the paper," he wrote.[282]

Another couple of days later, in a separate email, Finney identified that one source of confusion in the various responses on the mailing list had been that Bitcoin was really two different ideas rolled into one proposal. Bitcoin, he explained, was first of all an attempt to create a globally consistent but decentralized database, which, in turn, was used to realize an electronic cash system. Where different subscribers to the mailing list were more focused on one of these aspects or the other, and emphasized that the aspect they focused on was solved somewhat imperfectly, Bitcoin's true ingenuity was that it did both, and did so in a way that they complimented each other.

"Solving the global, massively decentralized database problem is arguably the harder part," Finney wrote. "The use of proof-of-work as a tool for this purpose is a novel idea well worth further review IMO."

His own email included some of this review. As he considered the security of the system, he figured that users could keep the network running even if it was simply to support it as a socially useful project, not unlike the types of internet projects where people volunteer computational resources to help medical research or analyze radio signals in search for signs of extraterrestrial life. "In this case it seems to me that simple altruism can suffice to keep the network running properly," Finney concluded.[283]

Nakamoto agreed.

"It's very attractive to the libertarian viewpoint if we can explain it properly," Bitcoin's inventor answered. "I'm better with code than with words though."[284]

The Pseudonym

The predominantly skeptical responses to the Bitcoin white paper on the Cryptography mailing list could probably in part be explained because the name of the paper's author, Satoshi Nakamoto, carried no reputational weight.

No Satoshi Nakamoto had been active on the Cryptography mailing list, the Cypherpunk mailing list, or any other relevant mailing list, and no one by that name had ever shown up to a Cypherpunks meeting. Satoshi Nakamoto hadn't proposed any digital cash schemes before, and he hadn't published other cryptography or computer science papers of note either. For all means and purposes, Satoshi Nakamoto was a nobody in Cypherpunk and crypto circles, and any time a nobody had announced a new electronic cash system, it hadn't amounted to much.

However, the inventor of Bitcoin may have had more experience in the field than he let on. Although most subscribers to the Cryptography mailing list probably presumed that they were contacted by a Japanese man, or at least a man from Japanese descent, "Satoshi Nakamoto" was in actuality almost certainly a pseudonym. Whoever was behind the moniker may well have been one or several of the prominent contributors to the Cryptography mailing list, or the Cypherpunk list before it.

Then again, he, she, or they may have been just as new and inexperienced in the electronic cash domain as their pseudonym suggested.

Whatever the truth may have been, the entity only known as Satoshi Nakamoto didn't seem particularly bothered by the skeptical responses. Although his white paper was a very succinct overview of the Bitcoin protocol, he acknowledged that he'd left out many functional details. He therefore patiently addressed most of the concerns and confusion about his proposal, and took the time to re-explain whatever parts of the design were perhaps unclear.

And even though he hadn't included every detail in the white paper, he *had* thought about most of them. In one of his email responses, Nakamoto clarified to have gone about designing Bitcoin "backwards": he'd actually written most of the Bitcoin code even before drafting the white paper.[285]

Indeed, Bitcoin wasn't just a proposal, like Bit Gold and b-money had been. Satoshi Nakamoto had already spent two years implementing the idea in code. After a little more than two weeks of back-and-forth with the handful of respondents, he offered to send the main files to Cryptography mailing list subscribers on request. The full release, he promised, would follow soon.

For list administrator Perry Metzger—another early Cypherpunk—this made it a good time to issue a Bitcoin break.

"I'd like to call an end to the bitcoin e-cash discussion for now — a lot of discussion is happening that would be better accomplished by people writing papers at the moment rather than rehashing things back and forth," Metzger wrote. "Maybe later on when Satoshi (or someone else) writes something detailed up and posts it we could have another round of this."[286]

Chapter 16:
The Release

"LAW, LANGUAGE, MONEY: the three paradigms of spontaneously occurring institutions. Now fortunately, law and language have been allowed to develop. Money has originated in original form, but as soon as it was there in its most primitive form, it was frozen. Governments said it must not develop any further. And what we have had since that development, were matters of government inventions, mostly wrong, mostly abuses of money, and I have come to the position of asking, has monetary policy ever done any good? I don't think it has. I think it has done only harm. That's why I am now pleading for what I've called denationalization of money."[287]

In one of his last recorded interviews, conducted in 1984 at the University of Freiburg, an elderly Friedrich Hayek was still championing radical monetary reform. The economist remained convinced that fiat currency and central banks' interest rate policies perverted the economy, and that money was ultimately best left to the free market.

However, in the eight years since the publication of *Denationalisation of Money*, the Austrian had become even less hopeful that sitting governments would be willing to change laws to allow for currency competition. He reckoned they benefited too much from the status quo.

"I still believe that my original plan is right, but I'm afraid I have come to the conclusion that politically, it is completely utopian," Hayek soberly explained. "Governments will *never* allow [it], and even bankers do not understand the idea, because bankers have all grown up in a system in which they are so completely dependent on central banks, government institutions, as lenders of last resort."[288]

Yet, the now eighty-four-year-old economist still cherished hope that money could be fixed. It just required a different approach than the type of civil movement he described in his book. Since governments wouldn't lift the restrictions that were preventing free market currency competition, he suggested, people would need to be creative, and find a way around these restrictions.

Instead of trying to convince governments to give up their de facto money monopoly, the people would have to, *by some sly, roundabout way, introduce something they can't stop.*

When almost twenty-five years later, on January 8, 2009, Satoshi Nakamoto reappeared on the Cryptography mailing list to launch a completely trustless and fully peer-to-peer electronic cash system, he leveraged decades of research in privacy technology, decentralized network architecture, and digital currency systems to do precisely that.

Satoshi Nakamoto introduced something governments can't stop.

The Codebase

Bitcoin v.0.1 released, read Nakamoto's email header this time.[289]

Those Cryptography mailing list subscribers who opened the email found Satoshi Nakamoto's two-sentence description of the newly released project:

"Announcing the first release of Bitcoin, a new electronic cash system that uses a peer-to-peer network to prevent double-spending. It's completely decentralized with no server or central authority."

Besides the short description, the email included a download link for the software, the link to the project's website—bitcoin.org—and several paragraphs with additional information, disclaimers ("the software is still alpha and experimental") and basic instructions for how to use it.

A little over two months since he'd submitted his white paper to the Cryptography mailing list, Satoshi Nakamoto put the first version of the Bitcoin software out there. The program—Bitcoin version 0.1—was ready to be downloaded and used: key pairs could be generated, transactions could be transmitted, and blocks could be mined.

The software release also revealed important new information about the project.

The first thing worth noting—though not at all a big surprise—was that Satoshi Nakamoto released Bitcoin as free and open source software. Anyone was free to copy, use, share, and change the code; published under the MIT license, even proprietary projects could integrate Nakamoto's work. (This makes the MIT license more permissible than Richard Stallman's GPL license, which grants this freedom only to other free software projects.)

It was crucial that Bitcoin was free and open source software, because the codebase necessarily had to be auditable: for the system to be truly trustless, users would have to be able to verify that it worked as advertised. This was arguably even more important for Bitcoin than it was for many other software projects, since the code quite literally represented money. In line with Stallman's free software philosophy, people shouldn't have to trust Satoshi Nakamoto not to include coin-stealing malware or a secret money-printing backdoor.

More generally, Nakamoto's free and open source code—written in the programming language C++ and years later described by Bitcoin's first full-time developer as "brilliant but sloppy"[290]—for the first time fully detailed the inner workings of the electronic cash system.

Transactions for example turned out to use "Script," a new programming language for Bitcoin inspired by Forth, which was itself designed in the 1960s to operate radio telescopes. Having somewhat tweaked Forth's functionality, Script could be used to write basic smart contracts on Bitcoin. Coins could be stored so that they could only be moved if certain programmable conditions were met. (A basic example of which was multisignature, or *multisig*, where not one, but several cryptographic signatures were required to spend coins.)

The signature scheme embedded in Bitcoin was the Elliptic Curve Digital Signature Algorithm (ECDSA), which—as the name suggests—leveraged mathematically generated elliptic curves to calculate key pairs. Invented in 1985, some eight years after RSA, elliptic curve cryptography offered the same level of security as Rivest, Shamir, and Adlemen's solution, but required much smaller key sizes, and had over the years become a widely used alternative.

At the same time, Nakamoto had added some features to make Bitcoin a bit more user friendly. While payments were for example technically still made to public keys, users could encode their public key (or the hash of their public key) in a Bitcoin *address*. When receiving funds, only these addresses were typically shared with other users.

The Bitcoin codebase also revealed many of the more-or-less arbitrary parameters that Nakamoto picked. As he'd already hinted at on the Cryptography mailing list earlier, a new block should be found on average every ten minutes. Clusters of 2,016 blocks would then be used to adjust the mining difficulty: if the 2,016 blocks were found in less than two weeks, Bitcoin's difficulty would be adjusted upwards proportionally, and if it took more than two weeks to find the 2,016 blocks, the proof-of-work difficulty would adjust downwards.

And, to actually get the Bitcoin network started, the codebase also included the very first block: the "Genesis Block." This first block indeed had to be embedded in the release itself; the block chain needed a jumping-off point. As an interesting detail, however, the block reward in this Genesis Block was effectively worthless: the protocol rules didn't allow these particular coins to be spent under any condition. In Bitcoin, new coins can only be earned through competitive mining, and Nakamoto apparently refused to accept a one-block head start for himself. If he wanted bitcoin, even he, the creator of the system, had to earn them— just like everyone else.

Further emphasizing his explicit refusal to enjoy some unfair advantage over other Bitcoin users, Nakamoto also included proof that he hadn't been mining privately in the weeks or months prior to making the code publicly available. He'd embedded a headline from the January 3 front page of English newspaper *The Times* in the Genesis Block, establishing that this Genesis Block could not have been created before that date—which in turn meant that any subsequent block must have been mined later than that as well.[291]

As an extra touch, the specific headline for this purpose did not appear to be picked at random, either:

The Times 03/Jan/2009 Chancellor on brink of second bailout for banks

The world of money and finance had become a mess. With Bitcoin, Satoshi Nakamoto was proposing an alternative.

Twenty-one Million

The most interesting newly revealed property of all, however, was Bitcoin's "monetary policy."

The white paper had described how Bitcoin could, thanks to the fixed block rewards and the difficulty adjustment algorithm, support a predictable issuance schedule. But this document had not yet outlined what this schedule would actually look like.

It now turned out that Bitcoin's code was programmed to halve the amount of new coins awarded per block after every 210,000 mined blocks, or about once every four years. Specifically, over the first four years, miners would earn 50 new coins per block, but in the four years after that they'd only earn 25 new coins per block. Then 12.5 in the next four years, 6.25 in the four after that, and so on.

Nakamoto announced in his email:

> *Total circulation will be 21,000,000 coins. It'll be distributed to network nodes when they make blocks, with the amount cut in half every 4 years.*
>
> *first 4 years: 10,500,000 coins*
>
> *next 4 years: 5,250,000 coins*

next 4 years: 2,625,000 coins

next 4 years: 1,312,500 coins

etc...

When that runs out, the system can support transac-tion fees if needed.

Twenty-one million coins.[292] Bitcoin was designed to have a fixed supply.

The implications of this were probably more significant than many Cryptography mailing list subscribers had immediately realized.

Just a couple years earlier, Hal Finney's RPOW project had failed to take off in part because people had no economic incentive (even negative economic incentive) to hold RPOW tokens, which meant that virtually no one was prepared to accept them for payment in the first place. With almost no places to spend them the tokens were practically without merit, and therefore worthless, which meant they couldn't really be used as money. Like eCash and hashcash even earlier, RPOW suffered from a chicken-and-egg problem that it hadn't been able to overcome.

Bitcoin, too, had to bootstrap itself from zero. When Nakamoto first released his code, bitcoin of course wasn't accepted as payment anywhere, and these coins had no monetary value.

Yet, it was precisely Hal Finney who realized that the incentives aligned a bit differently this time around.

On January 10, two days after Bitcoin's release, Finney was the first person on the Cryptography mailing list to respond to the announcement email. After congratulating Nakamoto with the release and promising to try it out, the electronic cash veteran quickly turned his attention to Bitcoin's fixed supply.

"One immediate problem with any new currency is how to value it," he wrote. "Even ignoring the practical problem that virtually no one will accept it at first, there is still a difficulty in coming up with a reasonable argument in favor of a particular non-zero value for the coins."

But Finney, who was well versed in the domain of statistics and probability, believed that Bitcoin's fixed supply could offer the solution. It enabled people to make basic estimations about the potential future value of the coins.

"As an amusing thought experiment, imagine that Bitcoin is successful and becomes the dominant payment system in use throughout the world. Then the total value of the currency should be equal to the total value of all the wealth in the world. Current estimates of total worldwide household wealth that I have found range from $100 trillion to $300 trillion. With 20 million coins, that gives each coin a value of about $10 million," he calculated.

"So the possibility of generating coins today with a few cents of compute time may be quite a good bet, with a payoff of something like 100 million to 1! Even if the odds of Bitcoin succeeding to this degree are slim, are they really 100 million to one against? Something to think about. . ."[293]

It was something to think about, indeed. Finney's estimates were rough, of course; it was just some back-of-a-napkin math. But as long as the odds of Bitcoin succeeding in the future weren't zero, it could indeed be rational to get a hold of some coins for cheap.

If other people, then, followed the same reasoning, it should immediately drive up demand for the coins, roughly up to the point where the market estimated that the risk/reward ratio would still be worth it. The potential future value of a bitcoin, and the estimated odds of this future becoming a reality, would in effect have to be reflected in the market price *today*.

And once a market price for the coins is established—that is, *any* non-zero market price—they could actually start to be used as a form of money as well, probably starting in places without any alternatives.

"[. . .] like reward points, donation tokens, currency for a game or micropayments for adult sites," Nakamoto suggested in a follow-up mail.[294]

This should, in turn, drive up demand even more. Overcoming the classic chicken-and-egg problem that previous digital cash projects had suffered from, bitcoin could in fact benefit from a *positive* feedback loop!

In a way, Finney had flipped Ludwig von Mises's regression theorem on its head: rather than deriving the value of a currency from its purchasing power in the *past*, the cypherpunk suggested that a currency's value can initially be derived from its expected purchasing power in the *future*.

"It might make sense just to get some in case it catches on," Satoshi Nakamoto agreed. "If enough people think the same way, that becomes a self fulfilling prophecy."[295]

Hayek's Ideal

Overcoming the chicken-and-egg problem wasn't the only potential benefit of the twenty-one-million limit, however. Nor was it even necessarily the biggest benefit, especially on a greater timescale. If Friedrich Hayek's analysis of monetary economics early in his career was correct, *Bitcoin could help fix the economy.*

As an unbacked currency that operated without a central bank, bitcoin was an entirely homogeneous form of money. Anyone could control their own coins, and there were no reserve ratios to worry about. And, since bitcoin existed on the internet, it was borderless as well. Anyone with an internet connection, anywhere in the world, could download the software and start sending and receiving transactions to anyone else.

This combination—a homogenous, borderless type of money with a fixed supply—is what Hayek once described as *neutral money.*

Back when he first wrote about this, Hayek had considered neutral money an unattainable ideal, a perfect currency that couldn't actually be realized. Most importantly, he did not believe there was any international authority that could be trusted to issue such a currency. The economist thought that, on a very fundamental level, nations could not depend on one another to honor the fixed supply. And he was probably right. Under extreme enough circumstances (like war), those in control of the money printer would always find themselves tempted to abuse this privilege, irrespective of prior arrangements, conventions, or treaties.

But bitcoin was not issued by any such international authority, and there was no money printer to be in control of; Satoshi Nakamoto had designed the system so no trusted third party was required at all. Bitcoin did not require monetary arrangements, conventions, or treaties in the first place, so there were also no arrangements, conventions, or treaties to break down. At least in theory, Bitcoin realized what Hayek thought impossible.

It meant that if bitcoin had any chance to become the global currency, the potential—as outlined by Hayek in the 1920s and '30s—would be tremendous.

For starters, Bitcoin could make an end to monetary nationalism. If Nakamoto's electronic cash was widely adopted in international trade, aggregate price changes between countries could finally provide accurate signals to the market, allowing the best allocation of resources across borders, regardless of nationalities. By extension, Bitcoin would also facilitate international trade in a much more straightforward manner, where only the buyer and seller and (the prices of) their respective products are affected—not the price levels across their entire countries.

Moreover, Bitcoin could put an end to currency wars. If the whole world uses the same, neutral money, competitive devaluations and the economic misery that comes from them would be a thing of the past.

And Bitcoin could make an end to the Cantillon effect, too. Especially when all twenty-one million coins would be in circulation, no one would benefit from spending new money into circulation, skewing the allocation of resources in their favor. But even when new coins are still being mined, this shouldn't really benefit any individual, group, or industry in particular. Anyone would be free to mine, and because of this (and the difficulty adjustment algorithm), open competition should drive profit margins towards zero: the proof of work it would cost to mine a block would come to approximate the value of the block reward.

But maybe even more impactful than that, Bitcoin could for the first time ever cleanly enable the intertemporal price system. By extension, interest rates would—at last—reflect the aggregate time preferences throughout society, which would in turn inform producers what stage of production they should invest in, facilitating the efficient allocation of resources over time. By resisting artificial interest rate policies, Bitcoin could make an end to centrally managed monetary policy and, per the Austrian business cycle, the associated economic booms and busts.

And finally, thanks to its fixed money supply, changing production costs would be accurately reflected in changing prices. If production costs were to fall, so would prices; this was the type of deflation that Hayek considered natural and healthy.

In about 32,000 lines of code, Satoshi Nakamoto embedded the potential to displace the stabilizers' monetary dogma that had influenced the dominant Keynesian and Monetarist monetary theories for almost a century.

. . . *if* it would be widely adopted.

The Last Point of Centralization

On January 8, 2009, Bitcoin started out with one user: the creator of the electronic cash scheme himself. And although at least a couple hundred people had probably heard of the project after Nakamoto's announcement on the Cryptography mailing list, the low engagement to his email and the—once again—generally skeptical responses, suggest that in the early days only a handful of them probably gave the software a spin (with Hal Finney famously receiving the first-ever transaction on January 12, from Nakamoto).

Nevertheless, the seed was planted. With a fixed currency supply, semi-anonymity, censorship resistant payments, basic smart contract capabilities, and relatively fast and cheap global transactions embedded in its DNA, Bitcoin was ready to be adopted by anyone who believed they could benefit from it.

And one thing was clear: if Bitcoin would attract users, they'd come on their own accord. Bitcoin was a currency that people used if and when they chose to use it—not because anyone forced them to. Whereas using fiat currency was mandated by law—it's the money that had to be used to pay taxes, if nothing else—sending and receiving bitcoin would be entirely voluntary.

Eventually, users did indeed come. Despite a very slow first year, Bitcoin began to gain some real traction throughout 2010. Transaction volume slowly picked up, new developers were finding the project, and a small online community was forming on an internet forum dedicated to the electronic cash project.

That's when Satoshi Nakamoto removed the last significant point of centralization from the project: himself.

The pseudonymous creator of Bitcoin had initially taken a leading role in continued software development, and held a large sway over the direction of the free and open source project. But as the digital currency started to grow in popularity, Nakamoto had slowly been stepping back. Eventually, by the end of 2010, he stopped responding to messages completely, and removed his contact information from the bitcoin.org website.

Technically, Nakamoto's disappearance was inconsequential. The mysterious developer did not actually control Bitcoin: it existed as a peer-to-peer network operated by users around the world.. But in practice, the project's creator had enjoyed the natural authority to dictate code changes.

By extension, Satoshi Nakamoto could decide the rules of the system, and he indeed rolled out some changes to these rules during his tenure as lead developer. He removed functionality from Script that he believed could be dangerous, for example, while adding certain restrictions to the protocol to limit resource requirements and ensure smooth operation.[296]

In the early days, this type of leadership was probably necessary. Bitcoin was a small project with experimental software, and it was helpful to roll out critical fixes quickly and unilaterally. But down the line, Nakamoto's influence may have become a liability: as the project leader, he could become a target for regulators, blackmailers, or various forms of corruption. Alternatively, he could lose his mind and bring Bitcoin in jeopardy simply through his own whims.

With Nakamoto gone, no one had a similar level of natural authority over the project. By the end of 2010, Bitcoin became truly decentralized.

The Bitcoin Project

Today, Bitcoin's code is maintained and developed by an open community of volunteer programmers from around the world. Whether motivated for ideological reasons, out of interest for the technology, because they're sponsored by a company with a vested interest in the project, or for some other reason, they take it upon themselves to keep Bitcoin up to date and improve it in whatever way they can.

Part of this work consists of simply updating the software. Anyone with the right skillset can improve the existing codebase, contribute new code, or review the work of others. The more developers do this, Linus's Law prescribes, the better Bitcoin's software quality should be: *given enough eyeballs, all bugs are shallow.*

In addition to that, Bitcoin can be upgraded by adding new features to the protocol, which can in turn help the system overcome some of its original limitations in domains like scalability and privacy. Script can for example be expanded to offer new spending conditions, enabling more types of smart contracts, and even facilitating entirely new payment layers on top of the base protocol much like those hinted at by James A. Donald and Hal Finney in their initial responses to Nakamoto's white paper.[297]

This does not mean that anyone can make any change to Bitcoin's code and deploy it across the network at will. As a collaborative effort, the development community has to generally agree with a change to the original codebase (now called "Bitcoin Core"), and this is even more true when changes affect the Bitcoin protocol rules. Without broad consensus, a change will usually not be made.

That said, since Bitcoin consists of free and open source software, any developer can make a fork (copy) of this codebase, and make changes in this new version of the software. They are also free to run this software, and free to distribute it to others. However, no developer—whether they contribute to Bitcoin Core or a fork—has the power to impose their software on users.

Indeed, users—not developers—ultimately decide which code they want to use. They can always decide against adopting a change by refusing to download and run a new software release, and instead continue to use the Bitcoin software they were already using, while the opposite is also true: users can adopt a new version of the software (or any fork) that includes a change. In Bitcoin, no one is in charge . . . and everyone is in charge.

The Bitcoin ecosystem has over the years indeed seen the introduction of various new software versions. Some of these are complete reimplementations of the Bitcoin protocol, with all new code. Others are forks of Bitcoin Core with some fairly minor tweaks to better fit personal preferences. Yet others are specialized clients that focus on a specific task, like mining. And there are even versions of the software that intentionally deviate from Bitcoin's existing protocol rules.

Yet, this hasn't led to chaos. Most users wouldn't want to adopt changes that negatively affect the value of their coins, like code that introduces currency inflation beyond the twenty-one-million limit, or a version of the software that could fall out of consensus with the rest of the network. Rather, users, acting in their best self-interest, tend to adopt only valuable changes; upgrades that make the protocol more robust, nodes more efficient, and the network more reliable.

In the more than ten years since Satoshi Nakamoto left, developers and users have self-organized to organically settle on a highly reliable Bitcoin protocol: new blocks are found roughly every ten minutes, block chain splits are rare and brief, and double-spends are nonexistent, while the number of use cases, overall transaction volume as well as bitcoin's market value have grown spectacularly.

In a world with top-down, centrally managed fiat currencies and all their troubles, Bitcoin represents a potent expression of spontaneous order.

Acknowledgments

I could not have written this book without the help I received from so many people.

First of all, a big thank you to David Bailey, who offered me the time and opportunity to work on this book while at *Bitcoin Magazine*.

Next, I need to thank my editors Pete Rizzo, who was patient enough to read the very sloppy early drafts and help structure the story, and Joakim Book, who made the text look good, caught some mistakes that no one else saw, and helped me get it all over the finish line.

I'm also very grateful for the support I received from other *Bitcoin Magazine* colleagues, in particular Ellen Sullivan and Christian Keroles.

I was very lucky that a number of people featured in the book itself were available for interviews and/or feedback, including (in alphabetical order) Adam Back, David Chaum, Douglas Jackson, Gregory Maxwell, Martin Hellman, Nick Szabo, Richard Stallman, Scott Stornetta, Tom Morrow, Wei Dai, and Whitfield Diffie. Thank you!

Special thanks go out to domain experts who were gracious enough to proofread early chapter drafts, most notably Adam Gibson, Bryan Bishop, Eduard de Jong, Jan Burgers, Tony Klausing, Vijay Boyapati, and Wolf von Laer.

For various reasons, I'd also like to thank Austin Hill, Andreas Antonopoulos, Ferdinando Ametrano, Jurjen Bos, LENA, Marcel van der Peijl, Tuur Demeester, and Wouter Habraken.

In May of 2023, I "open sourced" this book, that is, I published the text on Google Docs as an open invitation for anyone to read it and make suggestions. Throughout the following months a range of people indeed offered contributions, some small, some big. These are: 0x3phemeral-soul, Antoine Poinsot, Ben Murdock, Bitcoin Graffiti, Fractal Encrypt, Giacomo Zucco, Haarman Haarman, Info Scholarium, Jake Franklin, Jake Thomas, Jan-Paul Franken, Joao Bordalo, Jonathan Bier, John Doe, Leonhard Weese, Ludovic Lars, Marc Bonenberger, Mengu Gulmen, Muhammad Saqib Arfeen, Nadir Khan, Nick Nell, Pieter Meulenhoff, Richard Hogan, Thomas Farstrike, Will Wohler, and Zionfuo.

Finally, I'd like to thank my family and friends (especially Frederique Mol) for their support over the years, as well as anyone who helped me on my Bitcoin journey since 2013.

And of course, thank you Satoshi Nakamoto, whoever you may be.

Sorry to anyone I forgot.

Free Ross.

About the Author

Aaron van Wirdum studied Journalism at the University of Applied Sciences Utrecht and Politics and Society in Historical Perspective at Utrecht University, where he adopted a focus on the historic influence of new technologies on societal structures. He discovered Bitcoin in 2013, and has been writing about the world's first successful electronic cash project ever since. For most of these years, this was for *Bitcoin Magazine*: first as journalist, then as technical editor, and finally as editor-in-chief of the print edition. *The Genesis Book* is his first book.

Bibliography

American Banker. "Digicash Sends Signal by Hiring Visa Veteran." *American Banker*. May 6, 1997. https://www.americanbanker.com/news/digicash-sends-signal-by-hiring-visa-veteran.

Back, Adam. "[ANNOUNCE] hash cash postage implementation." Originally sent to the Cypherpunks mailing list. March 28, 1997. Accessed via: https://cypherpunks.venona.com/date/1997/03/msg00774.html.

Back, Adam. "cypherpunks digicash bank?" Originally sent to the Cypherpunks mailing list. October 7, 1995. Accessed via: https://cypherpunks.venona.com/date/1995/10/msg00690.html.

Back, Adam. "digital cc transactions, digital checks vs real digital cash." Originally sent to the Cypherpunks mailing list. May 2, 1997. Accessed via: https://cypherpunks.venona.com/date/1997/05/msg00104.html.

Back, Adam. "distributed virtual bank." Originally sent to the Cypherpunks mailing list. August 27, 1997. Accessed via: https://cypherpunks.venona.com/date/1997/08/msg01289.html.

Back, Adam. "no government regulation of the net (was Re: bulk postage fine)." Originally sent to the Cypherpunks mailing list. August 3, 1997. Accessed via: https://cypherpunks.venona.com/date/1997/08/msg00087.html.

Back, Adam. "Re: 'why privacy' revisited." Originally sent to the Cypherpunks mailing list. March 22, 1997. Available via: https://cypherpunks.venona.com/date/1997/03/msg00586.html.

Back, Adam. "Re: bulk postage fine (was Re: non-censorous spam control)." Originally sent to the Cypherpunks mailing list. August 3, 1997. Accessed via: https://cypherpunks.venona.com/date/1997/08/msg00070.html.

Back, Adam. "Re: Bypassing the Digicash Patents." Originally sent to the Cypherpunks mailing list. April 30, 1997. Accessed via: https://cypherpunks.venona.com/date/1997/04/msg00822.html.

Back, Adam. "Re: cypherpunks digicash bank?" Originally sent to the Cypherpunks mailing list. October 8, 1995. Accessed via: https://cypherpunks.venona.com/date/1995/10/msg00734.html.

Back, Adam. "Re: Remailer problem solution?" March 23, 1997. Accessed via: https://cypherpunks.venona.com/date/1997/03/msg00631.html.

Back, Adam. "The Bitcoin Game #59: Dr. Adam Back." Interview by Rob Mitchell. *The Bitcoin Game*, YouTube. October 25, 2018. https://youtu.be/xxYsRjanphA?si=XVdLXPWGUk6oVPXg&t=647 47:59.

Barnes, Douglas. "Re: cypherpunks digicash bank?" Originally sent to the Cypherpunks mailing list. October 8, 1995. Accessed via: https://cypherpunks.venona.com/date/1995/10/msg00731.html.

Bayer, Dave, Stuart Haber, and Scott W. Stornetta. "Improving the Efficiency and Reliability of Digital Time-Stamping." Conference Paper, Sequences II: Methods in Communication, Security, and Computer Science (1993): 329–34. https://www.math.columbia.edu/~bayer/papers/Timestamp_BHS93.pdf.

BitTorrent. "BitTorrent and μTorrent Software Surpass 150 Million User Milestone; Announce New Consumer Electronics Partnerships." BitTorrent.com. January 9, 2012. Accessed via https://web.archive.org/web/20140326102305/http://www.bittorrent.com/intl/es/company/about/ces_2012_150m_users.

Black Unicorn. "DigiCash Announcement." Originally sent to the Cypherpunks mailing list. May 10, 1994. Accessed via: https://cypherpunks.venona.com/date/1994/05/msg00616.html.

Blaug, Mark. *Economic Theory in Retrospect*. 4th edition. Cambridge: Cambridge University Press, 1985.

Brafman, Ori and Rod A. Beckstrom. *The Starfish and the Spider: The Unstoppable Power of Leaderless Organizations*. New York: Portfolio, 2006.

Brimmer, Andrew F. "Remembering William McChesney Martin Jr.," Federal Reserve Bank of Minneapolis. September 1, 1998. https://www.minneapolisfed.org/article/1998/remembering-william-mcchesney-martin-jr.

Brunton, Finn. *Digital Cash: The Unknown History of the Anarchists, Utopians, and Technologists Who Built Cryptocurrency*. Princeton, NJ: Princeton University Press, 2019.

Butler, Eamonn. *Hayek: His Contribution to the Political and Economic Thought of Our Time*. New York: Universe Books, 2010.

Caldwell, Bruce and Hansjoerg Klausinger. *Hayek: A Life, 1899–1950*. Chicago: University of Chicago Press, 2022.

Casey, Michael J. "Bitcoin Foundation's Andresen on Working With Satoshi Nakamoto." *The Wall Street Journal*. March 6, 2014. https://www.wsj.com/articles/BL-MBB-17626.

Cave, Damien. "The Mojo solution." *Salon*. October 9, 2000. https://www.salon.com/2000/10/09/mojo_nation/.

Chaum, David. "Achieving Electronic Privacy." *Scientific American* 267, no. 2 (August 1992): 96–101. https://www.jstor.org/stable/24939181.

Chaum, David. "Blind Signatures for Untraceable Payments," *Advances in Cryptology: Proceedings of Crypto* 82: 199–203. https://link.springer.com/chapter/10.1007/978-1-4757-0602-4_18.

Chaum, David. "Security Without Identification: Transaction Systems to Make Big Brother Obsolete." Communications of the ACM 28, no. 10 (October 1985): 1030–1044. https://dl.acm.org/doi/10.1145/4372.4373.

Chaum, David. "Untraceable Electronic Mail, Return Addresses, and Digital Pseudonyms," *Communications of the ACM* 24, 2 (February 1981): 84–90. https://dl.acm.org/doi/10.1145/358549.358563.

Dai, Wei. "Law vs Technology." Originally sent to the Cypherpunks mailing list. February 10, 1995. Accessed via: https://cypherpunks.venona.com/date/1995/02/msg00508.html.

Dai, Wei. "PipeNet 1.1 and b-money," originally sent to the Cypherpunks mailing list, November 26, 1998, accessed via: https://cypherpunks.venona.com/date/1998/11/msg00941.html.

Dai, Wei. "Re: alternative b-money creation." Originally sent to the Cypherpunks mailing list. December 11, 1998. Accessed via: https://cypherpunks.venona.com/date/1998/12/msg00448.html.

Dai, Wei. "Work on Security Instead of Friendliness?" *GreaterWrong*, July 21, 2012, https://www.greaterwrong.com/posts/m8FjhuELdg7iv6boW/work-on-security-instead-of-friendliness.

Dai, Wei. Comment in the discussion thread "AALWA: Ask any LessWronger anything." *LessWrong*. 2014. https://www.lesswrong.com/posts/YdfpDyRpNyypivgdu/aalwa-ask-any-lesswronger-anything.

Dai, Wei. Untitled b-money description. 1998. Accessed via https://web.archive.org/web/20090415130807/https://www.weidai.com/bmoney.txt.

Dawkins, Richard. *The Selfish Gene*. Oxford: Oxford University Press, 2016.

de Jong, Eduard. "Electronic Money: From Cryptography and Smart Cards to Bitcoin and Beyond," *Fraunhofer SmartCard Workshop* 2017 (2017): 1–10.

Diffie, Whitfield and Martin E. Hellman. "Multiuser Cryptographic Techniques." *AFIPS '76: Proceedings of the June 7-10, 1976, national computer conference and exposition* (June 1976): 109–112. https://dl.acm.org/doi/10.1145/1499799.1499815.

Diffie, Whitfield and Martin E. Hellman. "New Directions in Cryptography," *IEEE Transactions On Information Theory* vol. IT-22, no. 6 (November 1976): 644–654. https://ieeexplore.ieee.org/document/1055638.

DigiCash, "Bank Austria and Den norske Bank to Issue ecash™ the Electronic Cash for the Internet." DigiCash. April 14, 1997. Accessed via https://web.archive.org/web/19970605025912/http://www.digicash.com:80/publish/ec_pres8.html.

DigiCash. "Advance Bank First to Provide DigiCash's ecash™ System in Australia." DigiCash. October, 1996. Accessed via https://web.archive.org/web/19961102121407/https://www.digicash.com/publish/ec_pres6.html.

DigiCash. "DigiCash's Ecash™ to be Issued by Deutsche Bank." DigiCash. May 7, 1996. Accessed via https://web.archive.org/web/19961102121355/https://www.digicash.com/publish/ec_pres5.html.

Dillinger, Ray. "Bitcoin P2P e-cash paper," originally sent to the Cryptography mailing list, November 6, 2008. Accessed via: https://www.metzdowd.com/pipermail/cryptography/2008-November/014822.html.

Dillinger, Ray. "Bitcoin P2P e-cash paper," originally sent to the Cryptography mailing list, November 14, 2008, Accessed via: https://www.metzdowd.com/pipermail/cryptography/2008-November/014857.html.

Dillinger, Ray. "Bitcoin P2P e-cash paper." Originally sent to the Cryptography mailing list. November 15, 2008. Accessed via: https://www.metzdowd.com/pipermail/cryptography/2008-November/014859.html.

Dimsdale, Nicholas. "British Monetary Policy and the Exchange Rate 1920-1938." *Oxford Economic Papers* 33, New Series (Jul. 1981): 307–49. https://www.jstor.org/stable/2662793.

Donald, James A. "Bitcoin P2P e-cash paper," originally sent to the Cryptography mailing list. November 9, 2008. Accessed via: https://www.metzdowd.com/pipermail/cryptography/2008-November/014837.html.

Donald, James A. "Bitcoin P2P e-cash paper." Originally sent to the Cryptography mailing list. November 2, 2008. Accessed via: https://www.metzdowd.com/pipermail/cryptography/2008-November/014814.html.

Donald, James A. "Bitcoin P2P e-cash paper." Originally sent to the Cryptography mailing list. November 3, 2008. Accessed via: https://www.metzdowd.com/pipermail/cryptography/2008-November/014819.html.

Donald, James A. "Bitcoin P2P e-cash paper." Originally sent to the Cryptography mailing list. November 9, 2008. Accessed via: https://www.metzdowd.com/pipermail/cryptography/2008-November/014841.html.

Drexler, K. Eric. *Engines of Creation*. New York: Doubleday, 1986.

Dwork, Cynthia and Moni Naor, "Pricing via Processing or Combatting Junk Mail," *Advances in Cryptology—Crypto '92* (1992): 139–147. https://dl.acm.org/doi/10.5555/646757.705669.

Economist, The. "Why Don't Rising House Prices Count Towards Inflation?" *The Economist*. July 29, 2021. https://www.economist.com/the-economist-explains/2021/07/29/why-dont-rising-house-prices-count-towards-inflation.

e-gold. "e-gold News." December 1999, accessed via https://web.archive.org/web/20001209053900fw /http://www.e-gold.com/news.html.

e-gold. "e-gold® Welcomes US Government Review of its Status as a Privately Issued Currency." January 20, 2006. Accessed via https://web.archive.org/web/20060304203618if /http://www.e-gold.com:80/letter2.html.

e-gold. "Transcript of sentence before the honorable Rosemary M. Collyer United States District Judge." 114. November 20, 2008. https://legalupdate.e-gold.com/2008/11/transcript-of-sentence-before-the-honorable-rosemary-m-collyer-united-states-district-judge.html.

Energy Exploration & Exploitation. "World Oil Reserves 1948–2001: Annual Statistics and Analysis." *Energy Exploration & Exploitation* 19, no. 2 & 3 (2001). https://journals.sagepub.com/doi/pdf/10.1260/0144598011492561

Federal Reserve Economic Data. "Consumer Price Index for All Urban Consumers (CPIAUCSL)." Available via https://fred.stlouisfed.org/series/CPIAUCSL.

Finney, Hal. "Bitcoin P2P e-cash paper." Originally sent to the Cryptography mailing list. November 7, 2008. Accessed via: https://www.metzdowd.com/pipermail/cryptography/2008-November/014827.html.

Finney, Hal. "Bitcoin P2P e-cash paper." Originally sent to the Cryptography mailing list. November 13, 2008. Accessed via: https://www.metzdowd.com/pipermail/cryptography/2008-November/014848.html.

Finney, Hal. "Bitcoin v0.1 released." Originally sent to the Cryptography mailing list. January 10, 2009. Accessed via: https://www.metzdowd.com/pipermail/cryptography/2009-January/015004.html

Finney, Hal. "Chaum on the wrong foot?" Originally sent to the Cypherpunks mailing list. August 22, 1993. Available via https://cypherpunks.venona.com/date/1993/08/msg00652.html.

Finney, Hal. "Digital Gold, a bearer instrument?" Originally sent to the Cypherpunks mailing list. August 26, 1993. Accessed via: https://cypherpunks.venona.com/date/1993/08/msg00788.html.

Finney, Hal. "POLI: Politics vs Technology." Originally sent to the Cypherpunks mailing list. January 2, 1994. Accessed via: https://cypherpunks.venona.com/date/1994/01/msg00014.html.

Finney, Hal. "Protecting Privacy with Electronic Cash." *Extropy* 10 (Winter/Spring 1993): 8–14. https://archive.org/details/extropy-10.

Finney, Hal. "Re: Re: re: re: digital cash." Originally sent to the Cypherpunks mailing list. March 16, 1994. Accessed via: https://cypherpunks.venona.com/date/1994/03/msg00694.html.

Finney, Hal. "Re: Voluntary Governments?" Originally sent to the Cypherpunks mailing list. August 4, 1994. Accessed via: https://cypherpunks.venona.com/date/1994/08/msg00239.html.

Finney, Hal. "Reusable Proofs of Work." RPOW website index page. Accessed via: https://web.archive.org/web/20090217090451/http://rpow.net/index.html.

Finney, Hal. "RPOW FAQs." RPOW website FAQ page. Accessed via https://web.archive.org/web/20090217090439/http://rpow.net/faqs.html#inflation.

Finney, Hal. "RPOW Theory," RPOW website theory page. Accessed via https://web.archive.org/web/20040815154951/http://rpow.net/theory.html.

Finney, Hal. "Why remailers..." Originally sent to the Cypherpunks mailing list. November 15, 1992. accessed via: https://cypherpunks.venona.com/date/1992/11/msg00108.html.

Finney, Hal. "Re: Physical to digital cash, and back again." Originally sent to the Cypherpunks mailing list, August 19, 1993. Accessed via: https://cypherpunks.venona.com/date/1993/08/msg00581.html.

Fisher, Irving. *The Purchasing Power of Money*. New York: The Macmillan Company, 1920.

Forste, Eric Watt. "The Theory of Free Banking (George A. Selgin)," *Extropy* 15 (2nd–3d Quarter 1995): 51–53. https://archive.org/details/extropy-15/Extropy-15/.

Frauenfelder, Mark. "Homeless Cypherpunks Turn to Usenet." *Wired*. February 17, 1997. https://www.wired.com/1997/02/homeless-cypherpunks-turn-to-usenet/.

Friedman, Milton and Anna Schwartz, *A Monetary History of the United States*. Princeton, NJ: Princeton University Press, 1963.

Gladstein, Alex. "Uncovering The Hidden Costs of the Petrodollar." *Bitcoin Magazine*. April 28, 2021. https://bitcoinmagazine.com/culture/the-hidden-costs-of-the-petrodollar.

GNU Operating System, "What is Free Software?" 1996. https://www.gnu.org/philosophy/free-sw.html.

GNU Operating System. "The GNU Manifesto." 1985, https://www.gnu.org/gnu/manifesto.html.en.

Graeber, David. *Debt: The First 5,000 Years*. New York: Melville House, 2011.

Graetz, Michael J. and Olivia Briffault. "A 'Barbarous Relic': The French, Gold, and the Demise of Bretton Woods." In *The Bretton Woods Agreements*, edited by Naomi Lamoreaux and Ian Shapiro, 121–142. New Haven: Yale University Press, 2019.

Grant, Mark. "Introduction to Digital Cash." *Extropy* 15 (2nd–3d Quarter 1995): 14–16. https://archive.org/details/extropy-15/Extropy-15/.

Haber, Stuart and Scott W. Stornetta, "How to Time-Stamp a Digital Document." *Journal of Cryptology* 3 (1991): 99–111.

Haber, Stuart and Scott W. Stornetta, "Secure Names for Bit-strings." CCS '97: Proceedings of the 4th ACM Conference on Computer and Communications Security, (April 1997): 28–35. https://dl.acm.org/doi/10.1145/266420.266430.

Hayek, Friedrich A. "Can We Still Avoid Inflation?" in *The Austrian Theory of the Trade Cycle and Other Essays*, edited by Richard M. Ebeling, 93–110. New York: Center for Libertarian Studies, 1978.

Hayek, Friedrich A. "F. A. Hayek on Monetary Policy, the Gold Standard, Deficits, Inflation, and John Maynard Keynes." Interview by James U. Blanchard III. Re-uploaded by Libertarianism.org on April 19, 2015. https://youtu.be/EYhEDxFwFRU 26:27.

Hayek, Friedrich A. "Intertemporal Price Equilibrium and Movements in the Value of Money," in *The Collected Works of F.A. Hayek, Good Money: part I*, edited by Stephen Kresge, 186–227. Indianapolis, IN: Liberty Fund, 2009.

Hayek, Friedrich A. "Monetary Nationalism and International Stability," in *The Collected Works of F.A. Hayek, Good Money: part II*, edited by Stephen Kresge, 37–105. Indianapolis, IN: Liberty Fund, 2009.

Hayek, Friedrich A. "Monetary Policy in the United States after the Recovery from the Crisis of 1920," in *The Collected Works of F.A. Hayek, Good Money: part I*, edited by Stephen Kresge, 71–152. Indianapolis, IN: Liberty Fund, 2009.

Hayek, Friedrich A. "The Gold Problem," in *The Collected Works of F.A. Hayek, Good Money: part I*, edited by Stephen Kresge, 169–85. Indianapolis, IN: Liberty Fund, 2009.

Hayek, Friedrich A. "The Use of Knowledge in Society." *American Economic Review* XXXV, no. 4 (1945): 519–530. https://www.jstor.org/stable/1809376.

Hayek, Friedrich A. *Choice in Currency: A Way to Stop Inflation*. London: The Institute of Economic Affairs, 1976.

Hayek, Friedrich A. *Denationalisation of Money: The Argument Refined*. London: The Institute of Economic Affairs, 1990.

Hayek. Friedrich A. *Denationalisation of Money*. London: The Institute of Economic Affairs, 1976.

Hayek. Friedrich A. *Prices and Production*. New York: Augustus M. Kelly, Publishers, 1967.

Hettinga, Robert. "Re: Bypassing the Digicash Patents." Originally sent to the Cypherpunks mailing list, April 29, 1997. Accessed via: https://cypherpunks.venona.com/date/1997/04/msg00811.html.

Hettinga, Robert. "Re: digital cc transactions, digital checks vs real digital cash." Originally sent to the Cypherpunks mailing list. May 3, 1997. Accessed via: https://cypherpunks.venona.com/date/1997/05/msg00147.html.

Hill, Austin. Draft document from 2005 shared with author, March 30, 2022.

House of Representatives, "Deleting Commercial Pornography Sites From the Internet: The U.S. Financial Industry's Efforts to Combat This Problem." Hearing Before the Subcommittee on Oversight and Investigations of the Committee on Energy and Commerce, One-Hundred-Ninth Congress, Second Session. September 21, 2006. https://www.govinfo.gov/content/pkg/CHRG-109hhrg31467/html/CHRG-109hhrg31467.htm.

Hughes, Eric. "A Cypherpunk's Manifesto." Originally sent to the Cypherpunks mailing list. March 17, 1993. Available via https://cypherpunks.venona.com/date/1993/03/msg00392.html.

Hughes, Eric. "Kid Gloves or Megaphones." Originally sent to the Cypherpunks mailing list. March 14, 1996. Accessed via: https://cypherpunks.venona.com/date/1996/03/msg00932.html.

Hughes, Eric. "No digital coins (was: Chaum on the wrong foot?)." Originally sent to the Cypherpunks mailing list. August 24, 1993. Accessed via: https://cypherpunks.venona.com/date/1993/08/msg00690.html.

Keynes, John Maynard. *A Tract on Monetary Reform*. London: Macmillan and Co, 1923.

Keynes, John Maynard. *The General Theory of Employment, Interest and Money* (London: Palgrave Macmillan, 1936).

Kresge, Stephen. *The Collected Works of F.A. Hayek, Good Money: part I.* Indianapolis, IN: Liberty Fund, 2009.

Kutler, Jeffrey. "Credit Suisse, Digicash in E-Commerce Test." *American Banker.* June 16, 1998. https://www.americanbanker.com/news/credit-suisse-digicash-in-e-commerce-test.

Lamport, Leslie, Robert Shostak, and Marshall Pease. "The Byzantine Generals Problem," *ACM Transactions on Programming Languages and Systems* (July 1982): 382–401. https://dl.acm.org/doi/10.1145/357172.357176.

Lavoie, Don, Howard Baetjer, and William Tulloh. "High-Tech Hayekians: Some Possible Research Topics in the Economics of Computation." *Market Process* 8 (Spring 1990): 119–146.

Law, Laurie, Susan Sabett, and Jerry Solinas. "How To Make a Mint: The Cryptography of Anonymous Electronic Cash." National Security Agency Office of Information Security Research and Technology, Cryptology Division. June 18, 1996. https://groups.csail.mit.edu/mac/classes/6.805/articles/money/nsamint/nsamint.htm.

Levine, John. "Bitcoin P2P e-cash paper." Originally sent to the Cryptography mailing list. November 3, 2008. Accessed via: https://www.metzdowd.com/pipermail/cryptography/2008-November/014817.html.

Levy, Steven. "E-Money (That's What I Want)." *Wired.* December 1, 1994. https://www.wired.com/1994/12/emoney/.

Levy, Steven. *Crypto: How the Code Rebels Beat the Government–Saving Privacy in the Digital Age.* New York: Viking, 2001.

Levy, Steven. *Hackers: Heroes of the Computer Revolution.* Sebastopol, CA: O'Reilly, 2010.

Lewis, Peter H. "Attention Internet Shoppers: E-Cash Is Here." *The New York Times.* October 19, 1994. https://www.nytimes.com/1994/10/19/business/attention-internet-shoppers-e-cash-is-here.html.

Lindenfors, Patrick, Andreas Wartel, and Johan Lind, "'Dunbar's Number' Deconstructed." *Biology Letters.* May 5, 2021. https://royalsocietypublishing.org/doi/10.1098/rsbl.2021.0158.

Martin, Douglas. "Futurist Known as FM-2030 Is Dead at 69." *The New York Times.* July 11, 2000. https://www.nytimes.com/2000/07/11/us/futurist-known-as-fm-2030-is-dead-at-69.html.

Mason, Edward S. and Robert E. Asher, *The World Bank Since Bretton Woods: The Origins, Policies, Operations and Impact of the International Bank for Reconstruction.* Washington, DC: Brookings Institution, 1973.

Maxwell, Gregory. IRC message to author, August 13, 2020.

May Tim. "What backs up digital money?" Originally sent to the Cypherpunks mailing list. March 27, 1996. Accessed via: https://cypherpunks.venona.com/date/1996/03/msg01576.html.

May, Tim. "'Stopping Crime' Necessarily Means Invasiveness." Originally sent to the Cypherpunks mailing list. October 17, 1996. Accessed via: https://cypherpunks.venona.com/date/1996/10/msg01269.html.

May, Tim. "'Who shall speak for us?'" Originally sent to the Cypherpunks mailing list. September 29, 1995. Available via https://cypherpunks.venona.com/date/1995/09/msg02189.html.

May, Tim. "Crypto Activism and Respectability." Originally sent to the Cypherpunks mailing list. April 21, 1993. Accessed via: https://cypherpunks.venona.com/date/1993/04/msg00400.html.

May, Tim. "Crypto Anarchy, the Government, and the National Information Infrastructure." Originally sent to the Cypherpunks mailing list. November 29, 1993, accessed via: https://cypherpunks.venona.com/date/1993/11/msg01106.html.

May, Tim. "Cyberspace, Crypto Anarchy, and Pushing Limits." Originally sent to the Cypherpunks mailing list. April 3, 1994. Accessed via https://cypherpunks.venona.com/date/1994/04/msg00096.html.

May, Tim. "Degrees of Freedom." Originally sent to the Cypherpunks mailing list. February 8, 1996. Available via https://cypherpunks.venona.com/date/1996/02/msg00637.html.

May, Tim. "DigiCash can use whatever currencies are valued" Originally sent to the Cypherpunks mailing list. May 4, 1994. Accessed via: https://cypherpunks.venona.com/date/1994/05/msg00243.html.

May, Tim. "Hayek (was: Cato Institute conference on Net-regulation)." Originally sent to the Cypherpunks mailing list. August 27, 1996. Accessed via http://cypherpunks.venona.com/date/1996/08/msg02102.html.

May, Tim. "Libertaria in Cyberspace." Originally sent to the Cypherpunks mailing list. August 9, 1993. Accessed via https://cypherpunks.venona.com/date/1993/08/msg00168.html.

May, Tim. "My Departure, Moderation, and «Ownership of the List." Originally sent to the Cypherpunks mailing list. February 2, 1997. Accessed via: https://cypherpunks.venona.com/date/1997/02/msg02898.html.

May, Tim. "Opportunities in Cyberspace." Originally sent to the Cypherpunks mailing list. September 8, 1993. Accessed via: https://cypherpunks.venona.com/date/1993/09/msg00140.html.

May, Tim. "Re: alternative b-money creation." Originally sent to the Cypherpunks mailing list. December 11, 1998. Accessed via: https://cypherpunks.venona.com/date/1998/12/msg00455.html.

May, Tim. "Re: Hettinga's e$yllogism." Originally sent to the Cypherpunks mailing list. June 28, 1997. Accessed via: https://cypherpunks.venona.com/date/1997/06/msg01637.html.

May, Tim. "Re: More on digital postage." Originally sent to the Cypherpunks mailing list. February 15, 1997. Accessed via: https://cypherpunks.venona.com/date/1997/02/msg02295.html.

May, Tim. "Re: Stalling the crypto legislation for 2-3 more years." Originally sent to the Cypherpunks mailing list. July 23, 1994. Accessed via: https://cypherpunks.venona.com/date/1994/07/msg01245.html.

May, Tim. "Re: The War on Some Money [long]." Originally sent to the Cypherpunks mailing list. December 21, 1995. Accessed via https://cypherpunks.venona.com/date/1995/12/msg01044.html.

May, Tim. "Scenario for a Ban on Cash Transactions." Originally sent to the Cypherpunks mailing list. November 24, 1992. Accessed via: https://cypherpunks.venona.com/date/1992/11/msg00211.html.

May, Tim. "Software Patents are Freezing Evolution of Products." Originally sent to the Cypherpunks mailing list. October 7, 1995. accessed via: https://cypherpunks.venona.com/date/1995/10/msg00685.html.

May, Tim. "The Crypto Anarchist Manifesto" Originally sent to the Cypherpunks mailing list, November 22, 1992. Available via https://cypherpunks.venona.com/date/1992/11/msg00204.html.

May, Tim. "The Cyphernomicon." Originally distributed through the Cypherpunks mailing list. September 10, 1994. Available via https://nakamotoinstitute.org/static/docs/cyphernomicon.txt.

May, Tim. "Untraceable Digital Cash, Information Markets, and BlackNet ('Governmental and Social Implications of Digital Money' panel at CFP '97)." The Computers Freedom & Privacy Conference (1997). Accessed via https://web.archive.org/web/20130501134401/https://osaka.law.miami.edu/~froomkin/articles/tcmay.htm.

May, Tim. "Untraceable Payments, Extortion, and Other Bad Things." Originally sent to the Cypherpunks mailing list. December 21, 1996. Accessed via: https://cypherpunks.venona.com/date/1996/12/msg01468.html.

McCloskey, Deirdre N. *How to be Human*– *Though an Economist*. Ann Arbor: The University of Michigan Press, 2000.

McCullagh, Declan. "Digging Those Digicash Blues." *Wired*. June 14, 2001. https://www.wired.com/2001/06/digging-those-digicash-blues/.

Menger, Carl. *Untersuchungen über die Methode der Sozialwissenschaften und der Politischen Oekonomie insbesondere*. Leipzig: Dunker und Humblot, 1883.

Merkle, Ralph C. "A Certified Signature." *Advances in Cryptology—CRYPTO '89: Proceedings* (1989): 218–238. https://link.springer.com/chapter/10.1007/0-387-34805-0_21.

Metzger, Perry E. "ADMIN: end of bitcoin discussion for now." Originally sent to the Cryptography mailing list. November 17, 2008. Accessed via: https://www.metzdowd.com/pipermail/cryptography/2008-November/014867.html.

Metzger, Perry E. "Re: Virtual Cash." Originally sent to the Cypherpunks mailing list. May 3, 1994. Accessed via: https://cypherpunks.venona.com/date/1994/05/msg00131.html.

Mor, Federico. "Bank Rescues of 2007-09: Outcomes and Cost." House of Commons Research Briefing. October 8, 2018. Available via: https://commonslibrary.parliament.uk/research-briefings/sn05748/.

More, Max. "Hayek's Denationalisation of Money." *Extropy* 15 (2nd–3d Quarter 1995): 19–20. https://archive.org/details/extropy-15/Extropy-15/.

More, Max. "The Extropian Principles: A Transhumanist Declaration." maxmore.com, accessed via https://web.archive.org/web/20090130143449/https://www.maxmore.com/extprn3.htm.

More, Max. "Transhumanism: Towards a Futurist Philosophy." maxmore.com, accessed via https://web.archive.org/web/20051029125153/http://www.maxmore.com/transhum.htm.

Nagy, Daniel A. comments in response to "The Mojo Nation Story—Part 2." *Financial Cryptography*. October 12, 2005. https://www.financialcryptography.com/mt/archives/000572.html

Nakamoto, Satoshi. "Bitcoin: A Peer-to-Peer Electronic Cash System." 2008. Available via: https://bitcoin.org/bitcoin.pdf

Nakamoto, Satoshi and Wei Dai. "Wei Dai/Satoshi Nakamoto 2009 Bitcoin emails." gwern.net. Last modified September 14, 2017. https://gwern.net/doc/bitcoin/2008-nakamoto.

Nakamoto, Satoshi. "Bitcoin P2P e-cash paper." Originally sent to the Cryptography mailing list. October 31, 2008. Accessed via: https://www.metzdowd.com/pipermail/cryptography/2008-October/014810.html.

Nakamoto, Satoshi. "Bitcoin P2P e-cash paper." Originally sent to the Cryptography mailing list. November 2, 2008. Accessed via: https://www.metzdowd.com/pipermail/cryptography/2008-November/014815.html.

Nakamoto, Satoshi. "Bitcoin P2P e-cash paper." Originally sent to the Cryptography mailing list. November 6, 2008. Accessed via: https://www.metzdowd.com/pipermail/cryptography/2008-November/014823.html.

Nakamoto, Satoshi. "Bitcoin P2P e-cash paper." Originally sent to the Cryptography mailing list. November 14, 2008. Accessed via: https://www.metzdowd.com/pipermail/cryptography/2008-November/014853.html.

Nakamoto, Satoshi. "Bitcoin P2P e-cash paper." Originally sent to the Cryptography mailing list. November 8, 2008. Accessed via: https://www.metzdowd.com/pipermail/cryptography/2008-November/014832.html.

Nakamoto, Satoshi. "Bitcoin v0.1 released." Originally sent to the Cryptography mailing list. January 8, 2009. Accessed via: https://www.mail-archive.com/cryptography@metzdowd.com/msg10142.html.

Nakamoto, Satoshi. "Bitcoin v0.1 released." Originally sent to the Cryptography mailing list. January 16, 2009. Accessed via: https://www.metzdowd.com/pipermail/cryptography/2009-January/015014.html.

Nakamoto, Satoshi. "Bitcoin v0.1 released." Originally sent to the Cryptography mailing list. January 16, 2009. Accessed via: https://www.metzdowd.com/pipermail/cryptography/2009-January/015014.html.

Nash, Hadon. "Digital Gold," Originally sent to the Cypherpunks mailing list. August 24, 1993. Accessed via: https://cypherpunks.venona.com/date/1993/08/msg00698.html.

Next! Magazine. "Hoe DigiCash alles verknalde." *Next!* January 1999. Accessed via https://web.archive.org/web/19990427142412/https://www.nextmagazine.nl/ecash.htm.

Nixon, Richard. "Address to the Nation Outlining a New Economic Policy: 'The Challenge of Peace'." August 15, 1971. Available via *The American Presidency Project*. https://www.presidency.ucsb.edu/documents/address-the-nation-outlining-new-economic-policy-the-challenge-peace

Officer, Lawrence H. "Exchange Rates Between the United States Dollar and Forty-one Currencies," *MeasuringWorth*, 2023. https://www.measuringworth.com/datasets/exchangeglobal/.

Patel, Rupal and Jack Meaning. *Can't We Just Print More Money? Economics in Ten Simple Questions.* The Bank of England. London: Cornerstone Press, 2022.

Pitta, Julie. "Requiem for a Bright Idea," *Forbes.* November 1, 1999. https://www.forbes.com/forbes/1999/1101/6411390a.html.

Pr0duct Cypher. "Magic Money Digicash System." Originally sent to the Cypherpunks mailing list. February 4, 1994. Accessed via: https://cypherpunks.venona.com/date/1994/02/msg00247.html.

Purdy, George B. "A High Security Log-in Procedure." *Communications of the ACM* 17, no. 8 (August 1974): 442–445.

Quinn, Michelle. "The Cypherpunks Who Cracked Netscape," San Francisco Chronicle. September 20, 1995. https://people.eecs.berkeley.edu/~daw/press/iang/ian1.html.

Raymond. Eric S. *The Cathedral & The Bazaar: Musings on Linux and Open Source by an Accidental Revolutionary*. Sebastopol, CA: O'Reilly, 2001.

Regis, Ed. "Meet the Extropians." Wired. October 1, 1994. https://www.wired.com/1994/10/extropians/.

Richardson, Gary and Tim Sablik. "Banking Panics of the Gilded Age: 1863–1913." *Federal Reserve History*. December 4, 2015. https://www.federalreservehistory.org/essays/banking-panics-of-the-gilded-age.

Rickards, James. *Currency Wars: The Making of the Next Global Crisis*. New York: Portfolio 2012.

Roosevelt, Franklin D. "Relating to the Hoarding, Export, and Earmarking of Gold Coin, Bullion, or Currency and to Transactions in Foreign Exchange." August 28, 1993. Available via *The American Presidency Project*. https://www.presidency.ucsb.edu/documents/executive-order-6260-relating-the-hoarding-export-and-earmarking-gold-coin-bullion-or.

Salin, Phil. "Costs and Computers." *Release 1.0* (November 25, 1991): 5–18. https://www.yumpu.com/en/document/read/17286753/25-november-1991-cdnoreillycom.

Salin, Phil. "The Ecology of Decisions, or 'An Inquiry into the Nature and Causes of the Wealth of Kitchens'." *Market Process* 8 (Spring 1990): 91–114.

Schulze, Hendrik and Klaus Mochalski. "Internet Study 2008/2009." *Ipoque*. 2009. https://sites.cs.ucsb.edu/~almeroth/classes/W10.290F/papers/ipoque-internet-study-08-09.pdf

Selgin, George. "The New Deal and Recovery, Part 15: The Keynesian Myth." Cato Institute. March 16, 2022. https://www.cato.org/blog/new-deal-recovery-part-15-keynesian-myth.

Stallman, Richard. "Free Software Is Even More Important Now." gnu.org, https://www.gnu.org/philosophy/free-software-even-more-important.en.html.

Stallman, Richard. "Free Unix!" September 27, 1983, https://www.gnu.org/gnu/initial-announcement.en.html.

Stallman, Richard. "Richard Stallman: High School Misfit, Symbol of Free Software, MacArthur-Certified Genius." Interview by Michael Gross, mgross.com, 1999. https://www.mgross.com/writing/books/my-generation/bonus-chapters/

richard-stallman-high-school-misfit-symbol-of-free-software-macarthur-certified-genius/.

Stallman, Richard. "RMS Berättar." Linköping University, http://www.lysator.liu.se/history/garb/txt/87-2-rms.txt.

Stallman, Richard. "Talking to the Mailman." Interview by Rob Lucas, *New Left Review*, Sept–Oct 2018. https://newleftreview.org/issues/ii113/articles/richard-stallman-talking-to-the-mailman.

Stornetta, Scott. "The Missing Link between Satoshi & Bitcoin: Cypherpunk Scott Stornetta." Interview by Naomi Brockwell. NBTV, with Naomi Brockwell. YouTube, September 6, 2018, https://youtu.be/fYr-keVOQ18, 57:08.

Szabo, Nick. (@NickSzabo4), "Some of the most important books I've read." *X*. January 31, 2016. https://twitter.com/NickSzabo4/status/693682157525401601.

Szabo, Nick. "Bit Gold Markets." *Unenumerated*. December 27, 2008. https://unenumerated.blogspot.com/2008/04/bit-gold-markets.html.

Szabo, Nick. "Bit Gold." *Unenumerated*. December 27, 2008. https://unenumerated.blogspot.com/2005/12/bit-gold.html.

Szabo, Nick. "Bit Gold: Towards Trust-Independent Digital Money." 1999. Accessed via https://web.archive.org/web/20140406003811/http://szabo.best.vwh.net/bitgold.html.

Szabo, Nick. "Nick Szabo on Cypherpunks, Money and Bitcoin." Interview by Peter McCormack, *What Bitcoin Did*, November 1, 2019, https://www.whatbitcoindid.com/podcast/nick-szabo-on-cypherpunks-money-and-bitcoin 1:39:37.

Szabo, Nick. "Nick Szabo—The Quiet Master of Cryptocurrency | Co-Hosted by Naval Ravikant." Interview by Tim Ferriss, *The Tim Ferriss Show*. YouTube. August 12, 2017. https://youtu.be/3FA3UjA0igY 2:34:27.

Szabo, Nick. "Re: Crypto + Economics + AI = Digital Money Economies." Originally sent to the Cypherpunks mailing list. September 19, 1995. Accessed via: https://cypherpunks.venona.com/date/1995/09/msg01303.html.

Szabo, Nick. "Re: Crypto + Economics + AI = Digital Money Economies." Originally sent to the Cypherpunks mailing list. September 19, 1995. Accessed via: https://cypherpunks.venona.com/date/1995/09/msg01303.html.

Szabo, Nick. "Secure Property Titles with Owner Authority." Satoshi Nakamoto Institute (1998). https://nakamotoinstitute.org/secure-property-titles/.

Szabo, Nick. "Shelling Out: The Origins of Money." Satoshi Nakamoto Institute (2002). https://nakamotoinstitute.org/shelling-out/.

Szabo, Nick. "Smart Contracts: Building Blocks for Digital Free Markets." *Extropy* 16 (1st Quarter of 1996): 50–64. https://archive.org/details/extropy-16.

Szabo, Nick. "Trusted Third Parties are Security Holes." Satoshi Nakamoto Institute (2001), https://nakamotoinstitute.org/trusted-third-parties/.

Szabo, Nick. "Why Cryptocurrency? Governments Abuse Their Power—Nick Szabo Interview Part 1." Interview by Zulu Republic. *Zulu Republic*, YouTube. October 25, 2018. https://youtu.be/LZw4LNLYUgc?si=_FilNeaFnWxpvv9U 1:02.

Szabo, Nick. Personal correspondence, email to author, July 10, 2018.

US Department of Justice. "Digital Currency Business E-Gold Pleads Guilty to Money Laundering and Illegal Money Transmitting Charges." July 21, 2008. https://www.justice.gov/archive/opa/pr/2008/July/08-crm-635.html.

US Department of the Treasury. "Troubled Asset Relief Program (TARP)" Available via: https://home.treasury.gov/data/troubled-asset-relief-program.

von Mises, Ludwig. *Economic Calculation in the Socialist Commonwealth.* Auburn, AL: Ludwig von Mises Institute, 2012.

von Mises, Ludwig. *Human Action: A Treatise on Economics, The Scholar's Edition* (Auburn, AL: Ludwig von Mises Institute, 1998).

von Mises, Ludwig. *The Historical Setting of the Austrian School of Economics.* New Rochelle, NY: Arlington House, 1969.

von Mises, Ludwig. *The Theory of Money and Credit*, translated by J.E. Batson. New Haven, CT: Yale University Press, 1953.

Wang, Liang. "BitTorrent Mainline DHT Measurement." MLDHT. 2013. Accessed via: https://www.cl.cam.ac.uk/~lw525/MLDHT/.

Wapshott, Nicholas. *Keynes Hayek: The Clash That Defined Modern Economics.* New York: Norton, 2011.

Watercutter, Angela. "Why Free Software Is More Important Now Than Ever Before." *Wired*. September 20, 2013. https://www.wired.com/2013/09/why-free-software-is-more-important-now-than-ever-before/.

Weinstock, Nicole. "Member Profile: Hal Finney." *Cryonics* 40, issue 2 (2nd Quarter 2019): 3–9. https://cryonicsarchive.org/docs/cryonics-magazine-2019-02.pdf.

White, Lawrence H. "Thoughts on the Economics of 'Digital Currency'." *Extropy* 15 (2nd–3d Quarter 1995): 16–19. https://archive.org/details/extropy-15/Extropy-15/.

White, Lawrence H. "The Troubling Suppression of Competition from Alternative Monies: The Cases of the Liberty Dollar and e-gold." *Cato Journal* 34, no. 2 (2014): 281–301. https://www.cato.org/sites/cato.org/files/serials/files/cato-journal/2014/5/cato-journal-v34n2-5.pdf.

Wilcox-O'Hearn, Bryce. "Experiences Deploying A Large-Scale Emergent Network." *Peer-to-Peer Systems* (2002): 104–110. https://dl.acm.org/doi/10.5555/646334.687811.

Wong, Andrea. "The Untold Story Behind Saudi Arabia's 41-Year U.S. Debt Secret." *Bloomberg*. May 31, 2016. https://www.bloomberg.com/news/features/2016-05-30/the-untold-story-behind-saudi-arabia-s-41-year-u-s-debt-secret#xj4y7vzkg.

Other Works Consulted

Ammous, Saifedean. *The Bitcoin Standard: The Decentralized Alternative to Central Banking*. Hoboken, NJ.: Wiley, 2018.

Assange, Julian. *Cypherpunks: Freedom and the Future of the Internet*. OR Books, 2012.

Back, Adam. "Adam Back Reflects on the Cypherpunk Movement, Inventing Hashcash, Satoshi & Bitcoin." Interview by Cedric Youngelman. *The Bitcoin Matrix* 114, YouTube. July 11, 2022. https://youtu.be/uCavLyzQMbk 1:06:35.

Back, Adam. "Hashcash — A Denial of Service Counter-Measure." cypherspace.org. August 1, 2002. Available via: https://archive.li/W7QWn.

Back, Adam. "Hashcash information and documentation." http://www.hashcash.org/.

Back, Adam. "who is this annoying Adam Back guy?," *Bitcoin Forum*, June 4, 2013, https://bitcointalk.org/index.php?topic=225463.0.

Back, Adam. "Why Dr Adam Back So Legendary." Interview by Trace Mayer. *Bitcoin Knowledge Podcast*, YouTube. September 7, 2015. https://youtu.be/0VboMe_2fnc.

Backhouse, Roger E. "Austrian Economics and the Mainstream: View From the Boundary." *The Quarterly Journal of Austrian Economics* 3, no. 2 (Summer 2000): 31–43.

Barta, Silas and Robert B. Murphy. *Understanding Bitcoin: The Liberty Lover's Guide to the Mechanics and Economics of Crypto-Currencies.* 2017.

Birch, David and Neil McEvoy. "Downloadsamoney." *Demos Quarterly* 8 (1996): 85–94.

Board of Governors of the Federal Reserve System. "Arthur F. Burns." Federal Reserve Bank of St. Louis. https://www.federalreservehistory.org/people/arthur-f-burns.

Brands, Stefan. "An Efficient Off-line Electronic Cash System Based On The Representation Problem." *Computer Science/Department of Algorithmics and Architecture*, Report CS-R9323 (1993). https://ir.cwi.nl/pub/5303.

Chaum, David and Adam Back. "Why Bitcoin Now: David Chaum and Adam Back Reflect on the Crypto Wars." Interview by Laura Shin. *Unchained Podcast* 186, YouTube. August 18, 2020. https://youtu.be/ZVZxRMAeIdo.

Chaum, David and Stefan Brands. "'Minting' Electronic Cash." *IEEE Spectrum*. January 4 1999. https://spectrum.ieee.org/minting-electronic-cash.

Chaum, David, Amos Fiat, and Moni Naor. "Untraceable Electronic Cash." *Crypto 1988: Advances in Cryptology* (1988), 319–27.

Chaum, David. "The Dining Cryptographers Problem: Unconditional Sender and Recipient Untraceability." *Journal of Cryptology* 1 (1988): 65–75. https://link.springer.com/article/10.1007/BF00206326.

Coulouris, George, Jean Dolllimore, and Tim Kindberg. "Low-Value electronic transactions: the Millicent protocol." *Distributed Systems*, ed. 3 (2001): 303–306. https://www.cdk5.net/security/Ed3/Millicent.pdf.

De Jong, Eduard, Nathaniel Tkacz, and Pablo Velasco. "'Live As Friends and Count as Enemies': On Digital Cash and the Media of Payment." *Moneylab Reader* (2015): 258–267. https://www.academia.edu/31349137/ You Will Live as Friends and Count as Enemies On Digital Cash and the Media of Payment.

Diffie, Whitfield. "Interview with Whitfield Diffie on the Development of Public Key Cryptography." Interview by Franco Furger. January 16, 2002. https://www.itas.kit.edu/pub/m/2002/wedi02a.htm.

Drexler, K. Eric. "Molecular engineering: An approach to the Development of General Capabilities for Molecular Manipulation." *Proceedings of the National Academy of Sciences* 78, no. 9 (September 1981): 5275–5278.

Ebeling, Richard M. *The Austrian Theory of the Trade Cycle*. Auburn, AL.:Ludwig von Mises Institute, 1996.

Epstein, Jim. "Cypherpunks Write Code Series." *ReasonTV*, YouTube. October 7-28, 2020. https://www.youtube.com/playlist?list=PLBuns9Evn1w-T2RwqMhUnTZbTTe-M-g42.

Epstein, Jim. "How Will Bitcoin Lead to More Freedom?" *Reason*. October 10, 2020. https://reason.com/2020/10/16/how-will-bitcoin-lead-to-more-freedom/.

Finney, Hal. "Bitcoin and me (Hal Finney)." *Bitcoin Forum*. March 19, 2013. https://bitcointalk.org/index.php?topic=155054.0.

Finney, Hal. "Hal Finney interview." Interview by Scott Stilphen. *Atari Compendium*, https://www.ataricompendium.com/archives/interviews/hal_finney/interview_hal_finney.html.

George Edward Durell Foundation. *Money and Banking: The American Experience*. George Mason University Press, 1995.

Gibson, William. *Neuromancer*. New York: Ace, 1984.

Greenberg, Andy. "Nakamoto's Neighbor: My Hunt For Bitcoin's Creator Led To a Paralyzed Crypto Genius." *Forbes*. March 25, 2014. https://www.forbes.com/sites/andygreenberg/2014/03/25/satoshi-nakamotos-neighbor-the-bitcoin-ghostwriter-who-wasnt/?sh=38f8f8854a37.

Greenberg, Andy. *This Machine Kills Secrets: How WikiLeakers, Hacktivists and Cypherpunks Aim to Free the World's Information*. London: Virgin Books, 2012.

Grigg, Ian. "A Quick History of Cryptocurrencies BBTC — Before Bitcoin." *Bitcoin Magazine*. April 16, 2014. https://bitcoinmagazine.com/business/quick-history-cryptocurrencies-bbtc-bitcoin-1397682630.

Hayek, Friedrich A. "A Free-Market Monetary System." Lecture delivered at the Gold and Monetary Conference, New Orleans. November 10, 1977. Republished by the Mises Institute, https://mises.org/library/free-market-monetary-system.

Hayek, Friedrich A. *Choice in Currency: A Way to Stop Inflation*. London: The Institute of Economic Affairs, 1976.

Hayek, Friedrich A. *A Tiger by the Tail: The Keynesian Legacy of Inflation*, edited by Sudha R. Shenoy. The Institute of Economic Affairs and the Ludwig von Mises Institute, 2009.

Hellman, Dorothie and Martin Hellman. *A New Map for Relationships: Creating True Love at Home & Peace on the Planet*. New Map Publishing, 2016.

Jackson, Douglas. "The Story of egold." Interview by Dustin. *Did You Know Crypto* 72. February 9, 2020. https://didyouknowcrypto.com/ep72/.

Kawamoto, Dawn. "Compaq to license digital cash technology." *CNET*. January 2, 2002. https://www.cnet.com/tech/tech-industry/compaq-to-license-digital-cash-technology/.

Koblitz, Neal. "Elliptic Curve Cryptosystems," *Mathematics of Computation* 48, no. 177 (January 1987): 203–9. https://www.ams.org/journals/mcom/1987-48-177/S0025-5718-1987-0866109-5/S0025-5718-1987-0866109-5.pdf.

Kreling, Tom. "Douglas Jackson bedacht de eerste digitale valuta en werd veroordeeld voor witwassen." *de Volkskrant*. January 13, 2018. https://www.volkskrant.nl/economie/douglas-jackson-bedacht-de-eerste-digitale-valuta-en-werd-veroordeeld-voor-witwassen~b6ea3bcd/.

Lopp, Jameson. "Bitcoin and the Rise of the Cypherpunks." CoinDesk. April 9, 2016. https://www.coindesk.com/markets/2016/04/09/bitcoin-and-the-rise-of-the-cypherpunks/.

Lynch, Daniel C. and Leslie Lundquist. *Digital Money: The New Era of Internet Commerce*. Hoboken, NJ.: Wiley, 1996.

Massias, H., X. Serret Avila, and J.-J. Quisquater. "Design of a Secure Timestamping Service With Minimal Trust Requirement." 20th Symposium in Information Theory in the Benelux. May 1999. Available via Satoshi Nakamoto Institute: https://nakamotoinstitute.org/static/docs/secure-timestamping-service.pdf.

Maxwell, Gregory. "SF Bitcoin Devs Seminar: Greg Maxwell." *SF Bitcoin Developers*, YouTube. April 29, 2015. https://youtu.be/Gs9lJTRZCDc 1:23:12.

Merkle, Ralph C. "A Digital Signature Based on a Conventional Encryption Function" *Crypto 1987: Advances in Cryptology* (1987): 369–378. https://people.eecs.berkeley.edu/~raluca/cs261-f15/readings/merkle.pdf.

Miller, Victor S. "Use of Elliptic Curves in Cryptography." Crypto 1985: *Advances in Cryptology* (1985): 417–26. https://dl.acm.org/doi/10.5555/646751.704566.

Möller, Niels, "Ncash — An Experimental Digital Cash System" (1998). https://www.lysator.liu.se/~nisse/NCash/.

More, Max and Natasha Vita-More. "Max More & Natasha Vita-More on the History of Transhumanism w/ Like Robert Mason." Interview by Luke Robert Mason. *Luke Robert Mason*, YouTube. May 28, 2020. https://youtu.be/ffEDNLRq6y8 1:23:58.

More, Max. "Max More — Transhumanism and the Singularity." *Science, Technology & the Future*. YouTube. January 4, 2012. https://youtu.be/1xIQgBXw9-o 20:43.

Narayanan, Arvind and Jeremy Clark. "Bitcoin's Academic Pedigree: The concept of cryptocurrencies is built from forgotten ideas in research literature." *Queue* 15, no. 4 (July–August 2017): 20–49. https://dl.acm.org/doi/10.1145/3134434.3136559.

Okamoto, Tatsuaki and Kazuo Ohta. "Universal Electronic Cash." *Crypto 1991: Advances in Cryptology* (1991): 324–337. https://dl.acm.org/doi/abs/10.5555/646756.705374.

Orwell, George. *Nineteen Eighty-Four*. London: Penguin Books, 2003.

Pein, Corey. "Everybody Freeze!" *The Baffler*. March 2016. https://thebaffler.com/salvos/everybody-freeze-pein.

Phillips, A. W. "The Relationship Between Unemployment and the rate of Change of Money Wage Rates in the United Kingdom, 1861–1957." *Economica* 25: 283–99. https://www.jstor.org/stable/2550759.

Popper, Nathaniel. *Digital Gold: The Untold Story of Bitcoin*. New York: Penguin Books, 2016.

Pritzker, Yan, *Inventing Bitcoin: The Technology Behind the First Truly Scarce and Decentralized Money Explained*. 2019.

Rivest, Ronald, Adi Shamir, and Leonard Adleman. "A Method for Obtaining Digital Signatures and Public-Key Cryptosystems." *Communications of the ACM* 21, no. 2 (1978): 120–126. https://web.williams.edu/Mathematics/lg5/302/RSA.pdf.

Rothbard, Murray N. "The End of Socialism and the Calculation Debate Revisited." *The Review of Austrian Economics* 5, no. 2 (1991): 51–76.

Rothbard, Murray N. *The Mystery of Banking*. Auburn, AL.:Ludwig von Mises Institute, 2008.

Rothbard, Murray N. *What Has Government Done to Our Money?* Auburn, AL.: Ludwig von Mises Institute, 2010.

Salerno, Joseph T. "Hayek on the Business Cycle." *Mises Daily*. October 8, 2008, https://mises.org/library/hayek-business-cycle.

Schneier, Bruce. *Applied Cryptography, Second Edition: Protocols, Algorithms, and Source Code in C*. London: John Wiley & Sons, Inc. 1996.

Selgin, George A. *The Theory of Free Banking: Money Supply Under Competitive Note. Issue*. Totowa, NJ.: Rowman & Littlefield Publishers, 1988.

Skidelsky, Robert. *Keynes: The Return of the Master*. London: PublicAffairs, 2010.

Stephenson, Neal. *Snow Crash*. New York: Bantham Books, 1993.

Szabo, Nick, Adam Back and David Chaum. "The Godfathers of Bitcoin: Nick Szabo, Adam Back and David Chaum." Interview by John Riggins. *Bitcoin in Asia* 29, YouTube. November 16, 2020, https://youtu.be/D5LpgX-pkUM 43:33.

Szabo, Nick. "Bitcoin, what took ye so long?" *Unenumerated*. May 28, 2011. https://unenumerated.blogspot.com/2011/05/bitcoin-what-took-ye-so-long.html.

UK Parliament. "Small Change: Britain and the Gold Standard." UK Parliament. https://www.parliament.uk/business/publications/research/olympic-britain/the-economy/small-change/.

US Office of the Historian. "Nixon and the End of the Bretton Woods System, 1971–1973." https://history.state.gov/milestones/1969-1976/nixon-shock.

Vigna, Paul and Casey, Michael J. *Cryptocurrency: The Future of Money?* London: Vintage, 2016.

Vinge, Vernor. *A Fire Upon the Deep*. New York: Tor Books, 1992.

Vinge, Vernor. *True Names: and the Opening of the Cyberspace Frontier*. London: Penguin Books, 2016.

von Böhm-Bawerk, Eugen. *Capital and Interest: A Critical History of Economic Theory*. Translated by William Smart. London: Macmillan and Co., 1890.

Wayner, Peter. *Digital Cash: Commerce on the Net*. London: Academic Press Limited, 1996.

White, Lawrence H., "Banking without a Central Bank: Scotland before 1844 as a 'Free Banking' system." In *Unregulated Banking: Chaos or Order?* Edited by F. Capie and G.E. Wood, 37–71. London: Palgrave Macmillan, 1991.

General

Extropy magazines 1–17 (1988-1996).

eCash news archives on Chaum.com, https://chaum.com/ecash/.

Cypherpunks mailing list archives, 1992–2000. Available via https://cypherpunks.venona.com/.

Cryptography mailing list archives, October 2008–January 2009. Available via https://www.metzdowd.com/pipermail/cryptography/.

Endnotes

1   Lawrence H. White, "The Troubling Suppression of Competition from Alternative Monies: The Cases of the Liberty Dollar and e-gold," *Cato Journal*, 34, No. 2 (2014): 281–301.

2   House of Representatives, "Deleting Commercial Pornography Sites From the Internet: The U.S. Financial Industry's Efforts to Combat This Problem," Hearing Before the Subcommittee on Oversight and Investigations of the Committee on Energy and Commerce, One Hundred Ninth Congress, Second Session, September 21, 2006, https://www.govinfo.gov/content/pkg/CHRG-109hhrg31467/html/CHRG-109hhrg31467.htm.

3   White, "Troubling Suppression," 289.

4   e-gold, "e-gold News," December 1999, accessed via https://web.archive.org/web/20001209053900fw_/http://www.e-gold.com/news.html.

5   e-gold, "e-gold® Welcomes US Government Review of its Status as a Privately Issued Currency," January 20, 2006, accessed via https://web.archive.org/web/20060304203618if_/http://www.e-gold.com:80/letter2.html.

6   US Department of Justice, "Digital Currency Business E-Gold Pleads Guilty to Money Laundering and Illegal Money Transmitting Charges," July 21, 2008, https://www.justice.gov/archive/opa/pr/2008/July/08-crm-635.html.

7   e-gold "Transcript of sentence before the honorable Rosemary M. Collyer United States District Judge," 114, November 20, 2008, https://legalupdate.e-gold.com/2008/11/transcript-of-sentence-before-the-honorable-rosemary-m-collyer-united-states-district-judge.html

8   Deirdre N. McCloskey, *How to be Human*– *Though an Economist* (Ann Arbor: The University of Michigan Press, 2000), 33.

9   Lawrence H. Officer, "Exchange Rates Between the United States Dollar and Forty-one Currencies," *MeasuringWorth*, 2023.

10   Eamonn Butler, *Hayek: His Contribution to the Political and Economic Thought of Our Time* (New York: Universe Books, 2010).

11   Bruce Caldwell and Hansjoerg Klausinger, *Hayek: A Life, 1899–1950* (Chicago: University of Chicago Press, 2022), Chs. 6–9.

12   Ludwig von Mises, *The Historical Setting of the Austrian School of Economics* (New Rochelle, NY: Arlington House, 1969), 12.

13   Mises, *Historical Setting*, 12–13, 19–20.

14   Ludwig von Mises, *Human Action: A Treatise on Economics, The Scholar's Edition* (Auburn, AL: Ludwig von Mises Institute, 1998), 21, 38–54.

15   Carl Menger, *Untersuchungen über die Methode der Sozialwissenschaften und der Politischen Oekonomie insbesondere* (Leipzig: Dunker und Humblot, 1883).

16   Mises, *Historical Setting*, 3–19.

17   Ludwig von Mises, *Economic Calculation in the Socialist Commonwealth* (Auburn, AL: Ludwig von Mises Institute, 2012).

18   Although this argument has indeed been made in the context of consumer goods (as it has been in this text), a more precise articulation of this argument—as fleshed out over subsequent economic debates—is that this applies especially to capital goods.

19   Mises, *Economic Calculation*, 18.

20   Friedrich A. Hayek, *Prices and Production* (New York: Augustus M. Kelly, Publishers, 1967).

21   Friedrich A. Hayek, "The Use of Knowledge in Society," *American Economic Review*. XXXV, No. 4 (1945): 526–27.

22   If person A deposits $100 into the bank, and the bank loans out $90 of this $100 to person B, person A will still think he or she has $100 while person B will have $90, for a total of $190. What's more, if person B deposits the $90 in the bank again (or perhaps a different bank), and the bank loans out $81 of these $90 to person C, three people will think they own a combined $271. This can go on and on, seemingly bringing more and more money into circulation. This concept is referred to as the "money multiplier." And in actuality, the money multiplier can be even more aggressive than this conventional fractional reserve example suggests, because banks don't need to first receive deposits before they can issue loans; they can issue loans simply by creating it as credit in customers' bank accounts.

23   Gary Richardson and Tim Sablik, "Banking Panics of the Gilded Age: 1863–1913," Federal Reserve History, December 4, 2015, https://www. federalreservehistory.org/essays/banking-panics-of-the-gilded-age.

24   Friedrich A. Hayek, "Monetary Policy in the United States after the Recovery from the Crisis of 1920," in *The Collected Works of F.A. Hayek, Good Money: part I*, ed. Stephen Kresge (Indianapolis, IN: Liberty Fund, 2009), 145.

25   Hayek, "Monetary Policy," 146.

26   Stephen Kresge, *The Collected Works of F.A. Hayek, Good Money: part I* (Indianapolis, IN: Liberty Fund, 2009), 13.

27   Most expansively (though not exclusively) outlined in John Maynard Keynes, *The General Theory of Employment, Interest and Money* (London: Palgrave Macmillan, 1936).

28   George Selgin, "The New Deal and Recovery, Part 15: The Keynesian Myth," Cato Institute, March 16, 2022, https://www.cato.org/blog/ new-deal-recovery-part-15-keynesian-myth.

29   Friedrich A. Hayek, "The Gold Problem," in *The Collected Works of F.A. Hayek, Good Money: part I*, ed. Stephen Kresge (Indianapolis, IN: Liberty Fund, 2009), 184.

30   Richard Stallman, "Richard Stallman: High School Misfit, Symbol of Free Software, MacArthur-Certified Genius." Interview by Michael Gross, mgross.com, 1999, https://www.mgross.com/writing/books/ my-generation/bonus-chapters/richard-stallman-high-school-misfit-symbol-of-free-software-macarthur-certified-genius/.

31   This section (as well as some other parts of this chapter) is largely based on Steven Levy, *Hackers: Heroes of the Computer Revolution* (Sebastopol, CA: O'Reilly, 2010).

32   Richard Stallman, "Talking to the Mailman," Interview by Rob Lucas, *New Left Review*, Sept–Oct 2018, https://newleftreview.org/issues/ii113/ articles/richard-stallman-talking-to-the-mailman.

33   Richard Stallman, "RMS Berättar," Linköping University, http://www. lysator.liu.se/history/garb/txt/87-2-rms.txt.

34   Stallman, "Talking to the Mailman."

35   Levy, *Hackers*, 448.

36   Levy, *Hackers*, 472.

37   Stallman, "High School Misfit."

38   Stallman, "RMS Berättar."

39   Steven Levy, *Hackers*, 441–42.

40   Angela Watercutter, "Why Free Software Is More Important Now Than Ever Before," *Wired*, September 20, 2013, https://www.wired.com/2013/09/why-free-software-is-more-important-now-than-ever-before/.

41   For the sake of accuracy, it should be noted that this part of the argument technically only came to prominence when Stallman launched the GNU project a year-or-so later; it hadn't yet been part of his original motivation to start the project in the first place. This minor anachronism was left in the text for the purpose of readability.

42   Richard Stallman, "Free Software Is Even More Important Now," gnu.org, https://www.gnu.org/philosophy/free-software-even-more-important.en.html.

43   GNU Operating System, "What is Free Software?" https://www.gnu.org/philosophy/free-sw.html.

44   Actually, freedom 0 was only explicitly added in the 1990s; before that, Stallman thought that it was an automatic legal consequence of the original three freedoms.

45   GNO Operating System, "What is Free Software?"

46   Richard Stallman, "Free Unix!" September 27, 1983, https://www.gnu.org/gnu/initial-announcement.en.html.

47   GNU Operating System, "The GNU Manifesto," 1985, https://www.gnu.org/gnu/manifesto.html.en.

48   To emphasize the project's heavy reliance on GNU, some (including Richard Stallman) prefer to call it "GNU/Linux."

49   Eric S. Raymond, *The Cathedral & The Bazaar: Musings on Linux and Open Source by an Accidental Revolutionary* (Sebastopol, CA: O'Reilly, 2001).

50   Richard Stallman is not a fan of this terminology either. If a term to include both sides of the schism must be used, he prefers "Free/Libre and Open Source Software" because it more clearly conveys that the "free" part is about "freedom."

51   Raymond, *The Cathedral & The Bazaar*, 52.

52 Raymond, *The Cathedral & The Bazaar*, 52.

53 Raymond, *The Cathedral & The Bazaar*, 52.

54 Ludwig von Mises, *The Theory of Money and Credit*, trans. J.E. Batson (New Haven, CT: Yale University Press, 1953).

55 This is sometimes considered "intrinsic value," which is a common expression in economics to signify that a good has economic use value apart from its monetary role. Austrians generally reject the idea that products actually have intrinsic value at all, however: value is always subjective.

56 More recent archeological research published in David Graeber's *Debt: The First 5,000 Years* (New York: Melville House, 2011), suggests that there was never a pure barter economy as described in the regression theorem. Instead, the oldest human civilizations used debt as their first currency. However, debt only works as currency in high-trust, reputation-based environments. In low-trust environments, gold was often the currency of choice, and it's entirely feasible that the precious metal garnered this status over time through a process resembling what is described in the regression theorem.

57 Nicholas Dimsdale, "British Monetary Policy and the Exchange Rate 1920-1938," *Oxford Economic Papers* 33, New Series (Jul. 1981): 307–49.

58 Irving Fisher, *The Purchasing Power of Money* (New York: The Macmillan Company, 1920).

59 John Maynard Keynes, *A Tract on Monetary Reform* (London: Macmillan and Co, 1923), 173.

60 Friedrich A. Hayek, "Intertemporal Price Equilibrium and Movements in the Value of Money," in *The Collected Works of F.A. Hayek, Good Money: part I*, ed. Stephen Kresge (Indianapolis, IN: Liberty Fund, 2009), 195.

61 Hayek, "Intertemporal Price Equilibrium," 207.

62 Hayek, "Intertemporal Price Equilibrium," 190.

63 Hayek, "Intertemporal Price Equilibrium," 214.

64 Keynes, *Tract*, 164.

65 Friedrich A. Hayek, "Monetary Nationalism and International Stability," in *The Collected Works of F.A. Hayek, Good Money: part II*, ed. Stephen Kresge (Indianapolis, IN: Liberty Fund, 2009): 55.

66   Hayek, "Monetary Nationalism," 55–56.

67   Hayek, "Intertemporal Price Equilibrium," 212.

68   Hayek, "Intertemporal Price Equilibrium," 217.

69   Hayek, "Monetary Nationalism," 87.

70   Nicholas Wapshott, *Keynes Hayek: The Clash That Defined Modern Economics* (New York: Norton, 2011): 159.

71   Franklin D. Roosevelt, "Relating to the Hoarding, Export, and Earmarking of Gold Coin, Bullion, or Currency and to Transactions in Foreign Exchange," August 28, 1993, available via *The American Presidency Project*.

72   James Rickards, *Currency Wars: The Making of the Next Global Crisis* (New York: Portfolio 2012), 56–77.

73   Much of this chapter is based on Steven Levy's *Crypto: How the Code Rebels Beat the Government–Saving Privacy in the Digital Age* (New York: Viking, 2001).

74   Whitfield Diffie and Martin E. Hellman, "Multiuser Cryptographic Techniques," *AFIPS '76: Proceedings of the June 7-10, 1976, national computer conference and exposition* (June 1976): 109–112.

75   Levy, *Crypto*, 76.

76   Whitfield Diffie and Martin E. Hellman, "New Directions in Cryptography," *IEEE Transactions On Information Theory*, vol. IT-22, no. 6 (November 1976): 644.

77   Steven Levy, "E-Money (That's What I Want)," *Wired*, December 1, 1994, https://www.wired.com/1994/12/emoney/.

78   David Chaum, "Untraceable Electronic Mail, Return Addresses, and Digital Pseudonyms," *Communications of the ACM* 24, 2 (February 1981): 84–90.

79   Edward S. Mason and Robert E. Asher, *The World Bank Since Bretton Woods: The Origins, Policies, Operations and Impact of the International Bank for Reconstruction* (Washington, DC: Brookings Institution, 1973), 29.

80   Andrew F. Brimmer, "Remembering William McChesney Martin Jr.," Federal Reserve Bank of Minneapolis, September 1, 1998, https://www.minneapolisfed.org/article/1998/remembering-william-mcchesney-martin-jr.

81 Wapshott, *Keynes Hayek*, 242.

82 Wapshott, *Keynes Hayek,* 242.

83 Richard Nixon, "Address to the Nation Outlining a New Economic Policy: 'The Challenge of Peace'," August 15, 1971.

84 Michael J. Graetz and Olivia Briffault, "A 'Barbarous Relic': The French, Gold, and the Demise of Bretton Woods," in *The Bretton Woods Agreements*, eds. Naomi Lamoreaux and Ian Shapiro (New Haven: Yale University Press, 2019): 121–142.

85 Federal Reserve Economic Data, "Consumer Price Index for All Urban Consumers," available via https://fred.stlouisfed.org/series/CPIAUCSL.

86 Friedrich A. Hayek, "Can We Still Avoid Inflation?" in *The Austrian Theory of the Trade Cycle and Other Essays*, ed. Richard M. Ebeling (New York: Center for Libertarian Studies, 1978): 101.

87 Mark Blaug, *Economic Theory in Retrospect*, 4th edition (Cambridge: Cambridge University Press, 1985), 20–23.

88 Hayek, *Prices and Production*, 203.

89 Hayek, "Can We Still Avoid Inflation?" 108.

90 Friedrich A. Hayek, *Denationalisation of Money* (London: The Institute of Economic Affairs, 1976), 89.

91 Hayek, *Denationalisation of Money*, 91.

92 Friedrich A. Hayek, *Denationalisation of Money: The Argument Refined* (London: The Institute of Economic Affairs, 1990), 13.

93 Republished in Friedrich A. Hayek, *Choice in Currency: A Way to Stop Inflation* (London: The Institute of Economic Affairs, 1976).

94 Hayek, *The Argument Refined*, 78.

95 Hayek, *The Argument Refined*, 83.

96 Hayek, *The Argument Refined*, 109.

97 Hayek, *The Argument Refined*, 77.

98 Hayek, *The Argument Refined*, 133.

99 Hayek, *The Argument Refined*, 93.

100 Hayek, *The Argument Refined*, 134.

101 David Chaum, "Security Without Identification: Transaction Systems to Make Big Brother Obsolete," *Communications of the ACM* 28, no. 10 (October 1985): 1030–1044.

102 David Chaum, "Achieving Electronic Privacy," *Scientific American* 267, 2 (August 1992): 96–101.

103 David Chaum, "Blind Signatures for Untraceable Payments," *Advances in Cryptology: Proceedings of Crypto 82* (Boston: Springer, 1983): 199–203.

104 Chaum would later also propose a solution where double-spending could de-anonymize the perpetrator, somewhat limiting the need to immediately check each incoming payment against the bank's records since the perpetrator of a double-spend attack can be identified.

105 As a nifty extra detail, the system also embeds a type of fraud prevention check—albeit one that comes at the expense of privacy if and when users would opt to use it. If Carol would falsely claim that she'd never been paid, Bob could choose to reveal the nonce to Alice Bank, proving that he created the digital dollars that Carol deposited, proving that he paid them to her.

106 That said, there are some other, perhaps more drastic measures that Alice Bank could have taken. Besides refusing to issue digital dollars to Bob in the first place, she could have also blocked *all* electronic cash payments. Similarly, she could block particular users from accepting payments; even if payments can't be traced, some users can still be excluded from participation in the system.

107 It can (and has) been argued that Chaum did use a rather loose definition of "cash," as cash typically has more distinguishing properties. Chaum's form of digital cash for example offered limited person-to-person transferability—a feature that physical cash does have, as it can freely be passed around. Regardless, Chaum invented a form of digital money that at least offered a similar level of privacy as physical cash, which was his main objective.

108 David Chaum, "Security Without Identification."

109 In the end, the toll project was not adopted: the idea proved to be too controversial in the Netherlands. However, the technology would later be licensed under the name "DyniCash" to a Dallas-based company that specialized in microwave-frequency communication for trains.

110 Peter H. Lewis, "Attention Internet Shoppers: E-Cash Is Here," *The New York Times*, October 19, 1994, https://www.nytimes.com/1994/10/19/business/attention-internet-shoppers-e-cash-is-here.html.

111 DigiCash, "Bank Austria and Den norske Bank to Issue ecash™ the Electronic Cash for the Internet," DigiCash, April 14, 1997, accessed via https://web.archive.org/web/19970605025912/http://www.digicash.com:80/publish/ec_pres8.html.

112 DigiCash, "Advance Bank First to Provide DigiCash's ecash™ System in Australia," DigiCash, October, 1996, accessed via https://web.archive.org/web/19961102121407/https://www.digicash.com/publish/ec_pres6.html.

113 DigiCash, "DigiCash's Ecash™ to be Issued by Deutsche Bank," DigiCash, May 7, 1996, accessed via https://web.archive.org/web/19961102121355/https://www.digicash.com/publish/ec_pres5.html.

114 Jeffrey Kutler, "Credit Suisse, Digicash in E-Commerce Test," *American Banker*, June 16, 1998, https://www.americanbanker.com/news/credit-suisse-digicash-in-e-commerce-test.

115 Next! Magazine "Hoe DigiCash alles verknalde," *Next!*, January 1999, accessed via https://web.archive.org/web/19990427142412/https://www.nextmagazine.nl/ecash.htm.

116 American Banker, "Digicash Sends Signal by Hiring Visa Veteran," *American Banker*, May 6, 1997, https://www.americanbanker.com/news/digicash-sends-signal-by-hiring-visa-veteran.

117 Julie Pitta, "Requiem for a Bright Idea," *Forbes*, November 1, 1999, https://www.forbes.com/forbes/1999/1101/6411390a.html.

118 Hash functions were first proposed by University of Illinois at Urbana–Champaign mathematician George B. Purdy in his paper "A High Security Log-in Procedure," *Communications of the ACM* 17, no. 8 (August 1974): 442–445.

119 Scott Stornetta, "The Missing Link between Satoshi & Bitcoin: Cypherpunk Scott Stornetta," interview by Naomi Brockwell, *NBTV, with Naomi Brockwell*, YouTube, September 6, 2018, https://youtu.be/fYr-keVOQ18.

120 Stuart Haber and Scott W. Stornetta, "How to Time-Stamp a Digital Document," *Journal of Cryptology* 3 (1991): 99–111.

121 Ralph C. Merkle, "A Certified Signature," *Advances in Cryptology— CRYPTO '89: Proceedings* (1989): 218–238. (Although the article was only published in 1989, Markle wrote the paper in 1979.)

122 Dave Bayer, Stuart Haber and Scott W. Stornetta, "Improving the Efficiency and Reliability of Digital Time-Stamping," Conference Paper, Sequences II: Methods in Communication, Security, and Computer Science (1993): 329–34.

123 Stuart Haber and Scott W. Stornetta, "Secure Names for Bit-strings," CCS '97: Proceedings of the 4th ACM Conference on Computer and Communications Security, (April 1997): 28–35.

124 Ed Regis, "Meet the Extropians," *Wired*, October 1, 1994, https://www. wired.com/1994/10/extropians/.

125 Douglas Martin, "Futurist Known as FM-2030 Is Dead at 69," *The New York Times*, July 11, 2000, https://www.nytimes.com/2000/07/11/us/ futurist-known-as-fm-2030-is-dead-at-69.html.

126 K. Eric Drexler, *Engines of Creation* (New York: Doubleday, 1986), 146.

127 Max More, "Transhumanism: Towards a Futurist Philosophy," maxmore.com, accessed via https://web.archive.org/web/20051029125153/ http://www.maxmore.com/transhum.htm.

128 Max More, "The Extropian Principles: A Transhumanist Declaration," maxmore.com, accessed via https://web.archive.org/ web/20090130143449/https://www.maxmore.com/extprn3.htm.

129 The American Food and Drug Administration (FDA) was a particularly restrictive example; the federal agency made tinkering with and trying out new types of drugs and medicine all but impossible.

130 More, "Extropian Principles."

131 Much of this section is based on Finn Brunton's *Digital Cash: The Unknown History of the Anarchists, Utopians, and Technologists Who Built Cryptocurrency* (Princeton, NJ: Princeton University Press, 2019), 118–134.

132 Max More, "Transhumanism."

133 Don Lavoie, Howard Baetjer, and William Tulloh, "High-Tech Hayekians: Some Possible Research Topics in the Economics of Computation," *Market Process* 8 (Spring 1990): 119–146.

134 E.g., Phil Salin, "Costs and Computers," *Release 1.0* (November 25, 1991): 5–18; Phil Salin, "The Ecology of Decisions, or 'An Inquiry into

the Nature and Causes of the Wealth of Kitchens'," *Market Process* 8 (Spring 1990): 91–114.

135 Facilities include Alcor and the Cryonics Institute (both in the US), Kriorus (Russia), Tomorrow Bio (Germany), and Yinfeng Biological Group (China).

136 Hal Finney, "Protecting Privacy with Electronic Cash," *Extropy* 10 (Winter/Spring 1993): 14.

137 Mark Grant, "Introduction to Digital Cash," *Extropy* 15 (2nd–3d Quarter 1995): 15.

138 Eric Watt Forste, "The Theory of Free Banking (George A. Selgin)," *Extropy* 15 (2nd–3d Quarter 1995): 53.

139 Lawrence H. White, "Thoughts on the Economics of 'Digital Currency'." *Extropy* 15 (2nd–3d Quarter 1995): 18.

140 Max More, "Hayek's Denationalisation of Money," *Extropy* 15 (2nd–3d Quarter 1995): 20.

141 More, "Hayek's Denationalisation of Money," 20.

142 Tim May, "Untraceable Digital Cash, Information Markets, and Black-Net ('Governmental and Social Implications of Digital Money' panel at CFP '97)," The Computers Freedom & Privacy Conference (1997), accessed via https://web.archive.org/web/20130501134401/https://osaka.law.miami.edu/~froomkin/articles/tcmay.htm.

143 Tim May, "The Cyphernomicon," originally distributed through the Cypherpunks mailing list, September 10, 1994, available via https://nakamotoinstitute.org/static/docs/cyphernomicon.txt.

144 Hal Finney, "Chaum on the wrong foot?" originally sent to the Cypherpunks mailing list, August 22, 1993 available via https://cypherpunks.venona.com/date/1993/08/msg00652.html.

145 Eric Hughes, "A Cypherpunk's Manifesto," originally sent to the Cypherpunks mailing list, March 17, 1993, available via https://cypherpunks.venona.com/date/1993/03/msg00392.html.

146 Tim May, "Degrees of Freedom," originally sent to the Cypherpunks mailing list, February 8, 1996, available via https://cypherpunks.venona.com/date/1996/02/msg00637.html.

147 Tim May, "'Who shall speak for us?'," originally sent to the Cypherpunks mailing list, Available via https://cypherpunks.venona.com/date/1995/09/msg02189.html.

148 The title and text was a bit of a parody of Karl Marx's and Friedrich Engels's *Communist Manifesto*, while the term crypto-anarchy is something of a pun referring to crypto-fascism, the secret support for fascism.

149 Tim May, "The Crypto Anarchist Manifesto," originally sent to the Cypherpunks mailing list, November 22, 1992, available via https://cypherpunks.venona.com/date/1992/11/msg00204.html.

150 Tim May, "Libertaria in Cyberspace," originally sent to the Cypherpunks mailing list, August 9, 1993, accessed via https://cypherpunks.venona.com/date/1993/08/msg00168.html.

151 Tim May, "Cyberspace, Crypto Anarchy, and Pushing Limits," originally sent to the Cypherpunks mailing list, April 3, 1994, accessed via https://cypherpunks.venona.com/date/1994/04/msg00096.html.

152 Tim May, "Hayek (was: Cato Institute conference on Net-regulation)," originally sent to the Cypherpunks mailing list, August 27, 1996, Accessed via http://cypherpunks.venona.com/date/1996/08/msg02102.html. As a funny aside, Tim May concluded a different email with a compliment to one of his fellow Cypherpunks: "I just want to end on a positive note before leaving for the holidays (the birthday of my savior, F. Hayek, of course)." See: Tim May, "Re: The War on Some Money [long]," originally sent to the Cypherpunks mailing list, December 21, 1995, accessed via https://cypherpunks.venona.com/date/1995/12/msg01044.html.

153 Tim May, "'Stopping Crime' Necessarily Means Invasiveness," originally sent to the Cypherpunks mailing list, October 17, 1996, accessed via: https://cypherpunks.venona.com/date/1996/10/msg01269.html.

154 Eric Hughes, "No digital coins (was: Chaum on the wrong foot?)," originally sent to the Cypherpunks mailing list, August 24, 1993, accessed via: https://cypherpunks.venona.com/date/1993/08/msg00690.html.

155 Tim May, "Crypto Activism and Respectability," originally sent to the Cypherpunks mailing list, April 21, 1993, accessed via: https://cypherpunks.venona.com/date/1993/04/msg00400.html.

156 Tim May, "Opportunities in Cyberspace," originally sent to the Cypherpunks mailing list, September 8, 1993, accessed via: https://cypherpunks.venona.com/date/1993/09/msg00140.html.

157 Michelle Quinn, "The Cypherpunks Who Cracked Netscape," *San Francisco Chronicle,* September 20, 1995, https://people.eecs.berkeley.edu/~daw/press/iang/ian1.html.

158 Tim May, "Re: Stalling the crypto legislation for 2-3 more years," originally sent to the Cypherpunks mailing list, July 23, 1994, accessed via: https://cypherpunks.venona.com/date/1994/07/msg01245.html.

159 Tim May, "Scenario for a Ban on Cash Transactions," originally sent to the Cypherpunks mailing list, November 24, 1992, accessed via: https://cypherpunks.venona.com/date/1992/11/msg00211.html.

160 Tim May, "Scenario for a Ban."

161 Tim May, "Crypto Anarchy, the Government, and the National Information Infrastructure," originally sent to the Cypherpunks mailing list, November 29, 1993, accessed via: https://cypherpunks.venona.com/date/1993/11/msg01106.html.

162 Tim May, "DigiCash can use whatever currencies are valued," originally sent to the Cypherpunks mailing list, May 4, 1994, accessed via: https://cypherpunks.venona.com/date/1994/05/msg00243.html.

163 Tim May, "Re: Hettinga's e$yllogism," originally sent to the Cypherpunks mailing list, June 28, 1997, accessed via: https://cypherpunks.venona.com/date/1997/06/msg01637.html.

164 Tim May, "'Stopping Crime' Necessarily Means Invasiveness," originally sent to the Cypherpunks mailing list, October 17, 1996, accessed via: http://cypherpunks.venona.com/date/1996/10/msg01269.html.

165 Tim May, "Untraceable Payments, Extortion, and Other Bad Things," originally sent to the Cypherpunks mailing list, December 21, 1996, accessed via: https://cypherpunks.venona.com/date/1996/12/msg01468.html.

166 Tim May, "'Stopping Crime'."

167 Douglas Barnes, "Re: cypherpunks digicash bank?," originally sent to the Cypherpunks mailing list, October 8, 1995, accessed via: https://cypherpunks.venona.com/date/1995/10/msg00731.html.

168 Tim May, "Software Patents are Freezing Evolution of Products," originally sent to the Cypherpunks mailing list, October 7, 1995, accessed via: https://cypherpunks.venona.com/date/1995/10/msg00685.html.

169 Eduard de Jong, "Electronic Money: From Cryptography and Smart Cards to Bitcoin and Beyond," *Fraunhofer SmartCard Workshop 2017* (2017).

170 Laurie Law, Susan Sabett, and Jerry Solinas, "How To Make a Mint: The Cryptography of Anonymous Electronic Cash," National Security Agency Office of Information Security Research and Technology, Cryptology Division, June 18, 1996, https://groups.csail.mit.edu/mac/classes/6.805/articles/money/nsamint/nsamint.htm.

171 Hadon Nash, "Digital Gold," originally sent to the Cypherpunks mailing list, August 24, 1993, accessed via: https://cypherpunks.venona.com/date/1993/08/msg00698.html.

172 Hal Finney, "Digital Gold, a bearer instrument?," originally sent to the Cypherpunks mailing list, August 26, 1993, accessed via: https://cypherpunks.venona.com/date/1993/08/msg00788.html.

173 Black Unicorn, "DigiCash Announcement," originally sent to the Cypherpunks mailing list, May 10, 1994, accessed via: https://cypherpunks.venona.com/date/1994/05/msg00616.html.

174 Pr0duct Cypher, "Magic Money Digicash System," originally sent to the Cypherpunks mailing list, February 4, 1994, accessed via: https://cypherpunks.venona.com/date/1994/02/msg00247.html.

175 Perry E. Metzger, "Re: Virtual Cash," originally sent to the Cypherpunks mailing list, May 3, 1994, accessed via: https://cypherpunks.venona.com/date/1994/05/msg00131.html.

176 Robert Hettinga, "Re: digital cc transactions, digital checks vs real digital cash," originally sent to the Cypherpunks mailing list, May 3, 1997, accessed via: https://cypherpunks.venona.com/date/1997/05/msg00147.html

177 Robert Hettinga, "Re: Bypassing the Digicash Patents," originally sent to the Cypherpunks mailing list, April 29, 1997, accessed via: https://cypherpunks.venona.com/date/1997/04/msg00811.html.

178 Tim May, "Re: alternative b-money creation," originally sent to the Cypherpunks mailing list, December 11, 1998, accessed via: https://cypherpunks.venona.com/date/1998/12/msg00455.html.

179 Tim May, "What backs up digital money?," originally sent to the Cypherpunks mailing list, March 27, 1996, accessed via: https://cypherpunks.venona.com/date/1996/03/msg01576.html.

180 Adam Back, "Re: Bypassing the Digicash Patents," originally sent to the Cypherpunks mailing list, April 30, 1997, accessed via: https://cypherpunks.venona.com/date/1997/04/msg00822.html.

181 Adam Back, "digital cc transactions, digital checks vs real digital cash," originally sent to the Cypherpunks mailing list, May 2, 1997, accessed via: https://cypherpunks.venona.com/date/1997/05/msg00104.html.

182 Adam Back, "Re: Bypassing."

183 Leslie Lamport, Robert Shostak, and Marshall Pease, "The Byzantine Generals Problem," *ACM Transactions on Programming Languages and Systems* (July 1982): 382–401.

184 Adam Back, "Re: 'why privacy' revisited," originally sent to the Cypherpunks mailing list, March 22, 1997, available via: https://cypherpunks.venona.com/date/1997/03/msg00586.html.

185 Adam Back, "The Bitcoin Game #59: Dr. Adam Back," interview by Rob Mitchell, *The Bitcoin Game*, YouTube, October 25, 2018, https://youtu.be/xxYsRjanphA?si=XVdLXPWGUk6oVPXg&t=647 10:47–11:19.

186 Adam Back, "Re: cypherpunks digicash bank?," originally sent to the Cypherpunks mailing list, October 8, 1995, accessed via: https://cypherpunks.venona.com/date/1995/10/msg00734.html.

187 Adam Back, "cypherpunks digicash bank?," originally sent to the Cypherpunks mailing list, October 7, 1995, accessed via: https://cypherpunks.venona.com/date/1995/10/msg00690.html.

188 Barnes, "cypherpunks digicash."

189 Adam Back, "distributed virtual bank," originally sent to the Cypherpunks mailing list, August 27, 1997, accessed via: https://cypherpunks.venona.com/date/1997/08/msg01289.html.

190 Tim May, "Re: More on digital postage," originally sent to the Cypherpunks mailing list, February 15, 1997, accessed via: https://cypherpunks.venona.com/date/1997/02/msg02295.html.

191 Adam Back, "Re: bulk postage fine (was Re: non-censorous spam control)," originally sent to the Cypherpunks mailing list, August 3, 1997 accessed via: https://cypherpunks.venona.com/date/1997/08/msg00070.html.

192 Adam Back, "no government regulation of the net (was Re: bulk postage fine)," originally sent to the Cypherpunks mailing list, August

3, 1997, accessed via: https://cypherpunks.venona.com/date/1997/08/msg00087.html.

193 Cynthia Dwork and Moni Naor, "Pricing via Processing or Combatting Junk Mail," *Advances in Cryptology—Crypto '92* (1992): 139–147.

194 Adam Back, "[ANNOUNCE] hash cash postage implementation," originally sent to the Cypherpunks mailing list, March 28, 1997, accessed via: https://cypherpunks.venona.com/date/1997/03/msg00774.html.

195 Adam Back, "Re: Remailer problem solution?" March 23, 1997, accessed via: https://cypherpunks.venona.com/date/1997/03/msg00631.html.

196 Back, "Re: Bypassing."

197 Back, "Re: Bypassing."

198 Nick Szabo, "Why Cryptocurrency? Governments Abuse Their Power—Nick Szabo Interview Part 1," interview by Zulu Republic, *Zulu Republic*, YouTube, October 25, 2018, https://youtu.be/LZw4LNL-YUgc?si=_FilNeaFnWxp cdvv9U.

199 Nick Szabo (@NickSzabo4), "Some of the most important books I've read," *X*, January 31, 2016, https://twitter.com/NickSzabo4/status/693682157525401601.

200 Nick Szabo, "Re: Crypto + Economics + AI = Digital Money Economies," originally sent to the Cypherpunks mailing list, September 19, 1995, accessed via: https://cypherpunks.venona.com/date/1995/09/msg01303.html.

201 Nick Szabo, "Smart Contracts: Building Blocks for Digital Free Markets," *Extropy* 16 (1st Quarter of 1996): 50–64.

202 Szabo, "Smart Contracts," 51.

203 Nick Szabo, "Re: Crypto + Economics + AI = Digital Money Economies," originally sent to the Cypherpunks mailing list, September 19, 1995, accessed via: https://cypherpunks.venona.com/date/1995/09/msg01303.html.

204 Nick Szabo, email to author, July 10, 2018.

205 Nick Szabo, "Trusted Third Parties are Security Holes," Satoshi Nakamoto Institute (2001), https://nakamotoinstitute.org/trusted-third-parties/.

206   Nick Szabo, "Nick Szabo on Cypherpunks, Money and Bit-coin," interview by Peter McCormack, *What Bitcoin Did*, November 1, 2019, https://www.whatbitcoindid.com/podcast/nick-szabo-on-cypherpunks-money-and-bitcoin.

207   Nick Szabo, "Bit Gold," Unenumerated, December 27, 2008, https://unenumerated.blogspot.com/2005/12/bit-gold.html.

208   Richard Dawkins, *The Selfish Gene* (Oxford: Oxford University Press, 2016), 244.

209   Nick Szabo, "Shelling Out: The Origins of Money," Satoshi Nakamoto Institute (2002), https://nakamotoinstitute.org/shelling-out/.

210   It is worth noting however that this number—named after primatol-ogist Robin Dunbar—has (more recently) been criticized, and isn't, in the scientific community today, held with the specificity that it sug-gests. While there is a limit on the number of stable social relationships people can maintain, the actual number isn't necessarily (around) 150 for everyone. See for instance Patrick Lindenfors, Andreas Wartel, and Johan Lind, "'Dunbar's Number' Deconstructed," *Biology Letters*, May 5, 2021: https://royalsocietypublishing.org/doi/10.1098/rsbl.2021.0158

211   Strictly speaking a "public goods game" is the more precise game the-ory analogy.

212   Szabo, "Bit Gold."

213   In Szabo's original proposal, Bit Gold would actually use a "secure benchmark function," which is slightly different from a hash function, but similar enough that referring to the product as a "hash" and the act of producing it as "hashing" is accurate enough for the purpose of understanding Bit Gold's mechanics (and probably easier to follow).

214   Nick Szabo, "Secure Property Titles with Owner Authority," Satoshi Nakamoto Institute (1998), https://nakamotoinstitute.org/secure-property-titles/.

215   Nick Szabo, "Nick Szabo—The Quiet Master of Cryptocurrency | Co-Hosted by Naval Ravikant" interview by Tim Ferriss, *The Tim Fer-riss Show*, YouTube, August 12, 2017, https://youtu.be/3FA3UjA0igY

216   Szabo, "Secure Property Titles."

217   Nick Szabo, "Bit Gold: Towards Trust-Independent Digital Money" (1999), accessed via https://web.archive.org/web/20140406003811/http://szabo.best.vwh.net/bitgold.html.

218 Nick Szabo, "Bit Gold Markets," Unenumerated, December 27, 2008, https://unenumerated.blogspot.com/2008/04/bit-gold-markets.html.

219 Szabo, "Bit Gold Markets."

220 Szabo, "Bit Gold."

221 Wei Dai, "Work on Security Instead of Friendliness?" *GreaterWrong*, July 21, 2012, https://www.greaterwrong.com/posts/m8FjhuELdg7iv6boW/work-on-security-instead-of-friendliness.

222 Wei Dai, "Law vs Technology," originally sent to the Cypherpunks mailing list, February 10, 1995, accessed via: https://cypherpunks.venona.com/date/1995/02/msg00508.html.

223 Wei Dai, "PipeNet 1.1 and b-money," originally sent to the Cypherpunks mailing list, November 26, 1998, accessed via: https://cypherpunks.venona.com/date/1998/11/msg00941.html.

224 Wei Dai, untitled b-money description, 1998, accessed via https://web.archive.org/web/20090415130807/https://www.weidai.com/bmoney.txt.

225 Dai, untitled b-money description.

226 Wei Dai, "Re: alternative b-money creation," originally sent to the Cypherpunks mailing list, December 11, 1998, accessed via: https://cypherpunks.venona.com/date/1998/12/msg00448.html.

227 Wei Dai, comment in the discussion thread "AALWA: Ask any Less-Wronger anything," *LessWrong*, 2014, https://www.lesswrong.com/posts/YdfpDyRpNyypivgdu/aalwa-ask-any-lesswronger-anything.

228 Dai, comment.

229 Eric Hughes, "Kid Gloves or Megaphones," originally sent to the Cypherpunks mailing list, March 14, 1996, accessed via: https://cypherpunks.venona.com/date/1996/03/msg00932.html.

230 Hughes, "Kid Gloves."

231 Austin Hill, draft document from 2005 shared with author, March 30, 2022.

232 Ori Brafman and Rod A. Beckstrom, *The Starfish and the Spider: The Unstoppable Power of Leaderless Organizations* (New York: Portfolio, 2006), 22–27.

233 Damien Cave, "The Mojo solution," *Salon*, October 9, 2000, https://www.salon.com/2000/10/09/mojo_nation/.

234 As a mildly interesting detail, most Mojo transactions were actually only recorded between two peers at first, each building up credit or debit with the other peer, to only settle the debt using an actual Mojo token when a certain threshold was met.

235 Cave, "The Mojo solution."

236 Daniel A. Nagy, comments in response to "The Mojo Nation Story— Part 2," *Financial Cryptography*, October 12, 2005, https://www. financialcryptography.com/mt/archives/000572.html

237 Bryce Wilcox-O'Hearn, "Experiences Deploying A Large-Scale Emergent Network," *Peer-to-Peer Systems* (2002): 104–110.

238 Wilcox-O'Hearn, "Large-Scale Emergent Network."

239 Liang Wang, "BitTorrent Mainline DHT Measurement," MLDHT, 2013, accessed via: https://www.cl.cam.ac.uk/~lw525/MLDHT/.

240 BitTorrent, "BitTorrent and µTorrent Software Surpass 150 Million User Milestone; Announce New Consumer Electronics Partnerships," BitTorrent.com, January 9, 2012, accessed via https://web.archive.org/ web/20140326102305/http://www.bittorrent.com/intl/es/company/ about/ces_2012_150m_users.

241 Hendrik Schulze and Klaus Mochalski, "Internet Study 2008/2009," ipoque (2009).

242 Tim May, "My Departure, Moderation, and 'Ownership of the List,'" originally sent to the Cypherpunks mailing list, February 2, 1997, accessed via: https://cypherpunks.venona.com/date/1997/02/msg02898. html

243 Mark Frauenfelder, "Homeless Cypherpunks Turn to Usenet," *Wired*, February 17, 1997, https://www.wired.com/1997/02/ homeless-cypherpunks-turn-to-usenet/.

244 Declan McCullagh, "Digging Those Digicash Blues," *Wired*, June 14, 2001, https://www.wired.com/2001/06/digging-those-digicash-blues/.

245 Nicole Weinstock, "Member Profile: Hal Finney," *Cryonics* 40, issue 2 (2nd Quarter 2019): 9.

246 Hal Finney, "Re: Physical to digital cash, and back again," originally sent to the Cypherpunks mailing list, August 19, 1993, accessed via: https://cypherpunks.venona.com/date/1993/08/msg00581.html.

247 Hal Finney, "Why remailers…," originally sent to the Cypherpunks mailing list, November 15, 1992, accessed via: https://cypherpunks. venona.com/date/1992/11/msg00108.html.

248 Hal Finney, "Re: Voluntary Governments?" originally sent to the Cypherpunks mailing list, August 4, 1994, accessed via: https://cypher-punks.venona.com/date/1994/08/msg00239.html.

249 Hal Finney, "POLI: Politics vs Technology," originally sent to the Cypherpunks mailing list, January 2, 1994, accessed via: https://cypher-punks.venona.com/date/1994/01/msg00014.html.

250 Hal Finney, "Re: Re: re: re: digital cash," originally sent to the Cypher-punks mailing list, March 16, 1994, accessed via: https://cypherpunks. venona.com/date/1994/03/msg00694.html.

251 Finney, "Re: Re: re: re: digital cash."

252 Hal Finney, "Reusable Proofs of Work," RPOW website index page, accessed via: https://web.archive.org/web/20090217090451/http://rpow. net/index.html.

253 Hal Finney, "RPOW Theory," RPOW website theory page, accessed via https://web.archive.org/web/20040815154951/http://rpow.net/theory. html.

254 Hal Finney, "RPOW FAQs," RPOW website FAQ page, accessed via https://web.archive.org/web/20090217090439/http://rpow.net/faqs. html#inflation.

255 Gregory Maxwell, IRC message to author, August 13, 2020.

256 Andrea Wong, "The Untold Story Behind Saudi Ara-bia's 41-Year U.S. Debt Secret," *Bloomberg*, May 31, 2016, https://www.bloomberg.com/news/features/2016-05-30/ the-untold-story-behind-saudi-arabia-s-41-year-u-s-debt-secret#xj4y7vzkg.

257 Energy Exploration & Exploitation, "World Oil Reserves 1948–2001: Annual Statistics and Analysis," *Energy Exploration & Exploita-tion*, vol. 19, no. 2 & 3 (2001), https://journals.sagepub.com/doi/ pdf/10.1260/0144598011492561

258 Alex Gladstein, "Uncovering The Hidden Costs of the Petrodollar," *Bitcoin Magazine*, April 28, 2021, https://bitcoinmagazine.com/culture/ the-hidden-costs-of-the-petrodollar

259 Wapshott, *Keynes Hayek,* 258–59.

260 Wapshott, *Keynes Hayek,* 261.

261 Wapshott, *Keynes Hayek*, 211–214.

262 Milton Friedman and Anna Schwartz, *A Monetary History of the United States* (Princeton, NJ: Princeton University Press, 1963).

263 The Economist, "Why don't rising house prices count towards inflation?" *The Economist*, July 29, 2021, https://www.economist.com/the-economist-explains/2021/07/29/why-dont-rising-house-prices-count-towards-inflation.

264 US Department of the Treasury, "Troubled Asset Relief Program (TARP)," available via: https://home.treasury.gov/data/troubled-asset-relief-program; Federico Mor, Bank Rescues of 2007-09: Outcomes and Cost, House of Commons Research Briefing, October 8, 2018, available via: https://commonslibrary.parliament.uk/research-briefings/sn05748/

265 Rupal Patel and Jack Meaning, *Can't We Just Print More Money? Economics in Ten Simple Questions*, The Bank of England (London: Cornerstone Press, 2022), 238.

266 New Keynesians integrated more of the neoclassical (and therefore Hayekian) ideas on free markets, but also assumed more potential market failures, in particular due to an inability of some prices to adjust to new circumstances quickly, justifying government intervention. This most notably includes the price of labor (wages) due to psychological factors.

267 Satoshi Nakamoto and Wei Dai, "Wei Dai/Satoshi Nakamoto 2009 Bitcoin emails," gwern.net, last modified September 14, 2017, https://gwern.net/doc/bitcoin/2008-nakamoto.

268 Nakamoto and Dai, "Wei Dai/Satoshi Nakamoto 2009 Bitcoin emails."

269 Satoshi Nakamoto, "Bitcoin P2P e-cash paper." Originally sent to the Cryptography mailing list. October 31, 2008. Accessed via: https://www.metzdowd.com/pipermail/cryptography/2008-October/014810.html.

270 Satoshi Nakamoto, "Bitcoin: A Peer-to-Peer Electronic Cash System" (2008), available via: https://bitcoin.org/bitcoin.pdf

271 James A. Donald, "Bitcoin P2P e-cash paper," originally sent to the Cryptography mailing list, November 2, 2008, accessed via: https://www.metzdowd.com/pipermail/cryptography/2008-November/014814.html.

272   Satoshi Nakamoto, "Bitcoin P2P e-cash paper," originally sent to the Cryptography mailing list, November 2, 2008, accessed via: https://www.metzdowd.com/pipermail/cryptography/2008-November/014815.html.

273   James A. Donald, "Bitcoin P2P e-cash paper," originally sent to the Cryptography mailing list, November 3, 2008 accessed via: https://www.metzdowd.com/pipermail/cryptography/2008-November/014819.html.

274   Satoshi Nakamoto, "Bitcoin P2P e-cash paper," originally sent to the Cryptography mailing list, November 6, 2008, accessed via: https://www.metzdowd.com/pipermail/cryptography/2008-November/014823.html.

275   Ray Dillinger, "Bitcoin P2P e-cash paper," originally sent to the Cryptography mailing list, November 6, 2008, Accessed via: https://www.metzdowd.com/pipermail/cryptography/2008-November/014822.html.

276   Ray Dillinger, "Bitcoin P2P e-cash paper," originally sent to the Cryptography mailing list, November 14, 2008, Accessed via: https://www.metzdowd.com/pipermail/cryptography/2008-November/014857.html.

277   James A. Donald, "Bitcoin P2P e-cash paper," originally sent to the Cryptography mailing list, November 9, 2008, accessed via: https://www.metzdowd.com/pipermail/cryptography/2008-November/014837.html.

278   Ray Dillinger, "Bitcoin P2P e-cash paper," originally sent to the Cryptography mailing list, November 15, 2008, accessed via: https://www.metzdowd.com/pipermail/cryptography/2008-November/014859.html.

279   James A. Donald, "Bitcoin P2P e-cash paper," originally sent to the Cryptography mailing list, November 9, 2008, accessed via: https://www.metzdowd.com/pipermail/cryptography/2008-November/014841.html.

280   John Levine, "Bitcoin P2P e-cash paper," originally sent to the Cryptography mailing list, November 3, 2008, accessed via: https://www.metzdowd.com/pipermail/cryptography/2008-November/014817.html.

281   Hal Finney, "Bitcoin P2P e-cash paper," originally sent to the Cryptography mailing list, November 7, 2008, accessed via: https://www.metzdowd.com/pipermail/cryptography/2008-November/014827.html.

282   Hal Finney, "Bitcoin P2P e-cash paper," originally sent to the Cryptography mailing list, November 7, 2008, accessed via: https://www.metzdowd.com/pipermail/cryptography/2008-November/014827.html.

283 Hal Finney, "Bitcoin P2P e-cash paper," originally sent to the Cryptography mailing list, November 13, 2008, accessed via: https://www.metzdowd.com/pipermail/cryptography/2008-November/014848.html.

284 Satoshi Nakamoto, "Bitcoin P2P e-cash paper," originally sent to the Cryptography mailing list, November 14, 2008, accessed via: https://www.metzdowd.com/pipermail/cryptography/2008-November/014853.html.

285 Satoshi Nakamoto, "Bitcoin P2P e-cash paper," originally sent to the Cryptography mailing list, November 8, 2008, accessed via: https://www.metzdowd.com/pipermail/cryptography/2008-November/014832.html.

286 Perry E. Metzger, "ADMIN: end of bitcoin discussion for now," originally sent to the Cryptography mailing list, November 17, 2008, accessed via: https://www.metzdowd.com/pipermail/cryptography/2008-November/014867.html.

287 Friedrich A. Hayek, "F. A. Hayek on Monetary Policy, the Gold Standard, Deficits, Inflation, and John Maynard Keynes," interview by James U. Blanchard III, re-uploaded by Libertarianism.org on April 19, 2015, https://youtu.be/EYhEDxFwFRU.

288 Hayek, interview.

289 Satoshi Nakamoto, "Bitcoin v0.1 released," originally sent to the Cryptography mailing list, January 8, 2009, Accessed via: https://www.mail-archive.com/cryptography@metzdowd.com/msg10142.html.

290 Michael J. Casey, "Bitcoin Foundation's Andresen on Working With Satoshi Nakamoto," *The Wall Street Journal*, March 6, 2014, https://www.wsj.com/articles/BL-MBB-17626.

291 Since Bitcoin was ultimately released on January 8, this would have left the system's creator with a maximum of six days to comfortably generate coins in absence of any competition—but early block timestamps indicate that he didn't do this either.

292 It's worth noting though that each bitcoin can be divided up to eight decimal points, so in a way there are 2.1 quadrillion currency units. The smallest unit, 0.00000001 bitcoin, is today usually referred to as a "satoshi," or "sat" for short.

293 Hal Finney, "Bitcoin v0.1 released," originally sent to the Cryptography mailing list, January 10, 2009, accessed via: https://www.metzdowd.com/pipermail/cryptography/2009-January/015004.html

294 Satoshi Nakamoto, "Bitcoin v0.1 released," originally sent to the Cryptography mailing list, January 16, 2009, accessed via: https://www.metzdowd.com/pipermail/cryptography/2009-January/015014.html.

295 Satoshi Nakamoto, "Bitcoin v0.1 released," originally sent to the Cryptography mailing list, January 16, 2009, accessed via: https://www.metzdowd.com/pipermail/cryptography/2009-January/015014.html.

296 This most famously included the 1-megabyte block size limit, preventing the block chain from growing so fast that most regular users wouldn't be able to run a Bitcoin node on their home computer.

297 The currently best-known example of such a payment layer is called the Lightning Network.

Printed in Great Britain
by Amazon